Pressure
groups today

Rob Baggott

Manchester University Press
Manchester and New York

distributed exclusively in the USA and Canada by St. Martin's Press

Copyright © Rob Baggott 1995

Published by Manchester University Press
Oxford Road, Manchester M13 9NR, UK
and Room 400, 175 Fifth Avenue, New York, NY 10010, USA

Distributed exclusively in the USA and Canada
by St Martin's Press, Inc., 175 Fifth Avenue, New York, NY 10010, USA

British Library Cataloguing-in-Publication Data
A catalogue record for this book is available from the British Library

Library of Congress Cataloging-in-Publication Data
Baggott, Rob.
    Pressure groups today / Rob Baggott.
        p.   cm. — (Politics today)
    Includes bibliographical references and index.
    ISBN 0–7190–3578–3 (alk. paper). — ISBN 0–7190–3579–1 (pbk. : alk.
paper)
    1. Pressure groups—Great Britain.   I. Title.   II. Series:
Politics today (Manchester, England)
JN329.P7B34   1995
322.4'3'0941—dc20   95–22399
                                                                     CIP

ISBN 0 7190 3578 3 hardback
        0 7190 3579 1 paperback

First published in 1995

99 98 97 96 95   10 9 8 7 6 5 4 3 2 1

Typeset in Great Britain
by Northern Phototypesetting Co Ltd, Bolton

Printed in Great Britain
by Bell & Bain Ltd, Glasgow

Pressure groups today

Politics today
Series editor: Bill Jones

Of related interest

Contents

Exhibits

To Debbie

Preface and acknowledgements

This book attempts to satisfy those who wish to know more about pressure groups in Britain today, and is particularly aimed at 'A'-level students and undergraduates. My objective has been to produce a book which is fairly easy to understand and which at the same time represents a coherent analysis of pressure groups in contemporary Britain. Chapter 1 sets the scene by examining the various attempts to define the term 'pressure group'. Chapter 2 looks at the different approaches to the study of pressure groups, and the problems and pitfalls encountered. Chapter 3 evaluates the role of pressure groups in a modern democracy. Chapter 4 takes a look inside pressure groups, at their internal organisation and resources. The remaining chapters explore the relationship between pressure groups and the political system. Chapters 5 and 6 consider the interface between pressure groups and central government, while Chapter 7 examines the links between pressure groups and Parliament. The various ways in which groups interact with the public and the media are explored in Chapter 8. Chapter 9 examines the relationship between groups and other decision-makers, focusing upon local government and the European Community.

There are a number of people who have played a crucial role in this project and who deserve mention. These include Bill Jones, the series editor, who first suggested (over a pint of bitter at the Rampant Lion in Manchester, as I recall) that I consider writing the book. I am grateful, too, to Richard Purslow of Manchester University Press, my publisher, who has been very patient and understanding. I would also like to thank Graham Thomas, another MUP author, for his invaluable comments on earlier drafts of the manuscript.

The book has involved a considerable amount of research and I am grateful for the financial support of the Leicester Business School (which enabled me to undertake a survey of groups, which I refer to throughout the book). I must also acknowledge several of my colleagues in the Department of Public Policy and Managerial Studies (PPMS) who have given me the benefit of their expertise at various stages of the project. They include Merrill Clarke, Clive Gray, Professor John Greenwood, Victoria McGregor-Riley, Lynton Robins, Tony Stott and Melvin Wingfield. I am indebted to the Resource Centre team (Sue Dewing, Julie Conroy and the now-retired Dorothy Root) for their technical assistance, to Carole Shaw and her colleagues in Central Services for producing the final manuscript, to Roy Freer of Computing Services, and Elizabeth O'Neill of Scraptoft Campus Library. I would like to thank Bob Waterton and Ted Cassidy, for their help with the Saffron Boot House Action Group case study in Chapter 9, and Arthur Chimes, the chairman of the group, for his co-operation. I would also like to acknowledge the help of two students on the BA Public Administration degree course at De Montfort University, John Conroy and Rachel Harratt, whose projects first drew my attention to two campaigns mentioned in the book, namely Surfers Against Sewage and the English Collective of Prostitutes. Thanks also to Professor Peter Hennessy, who pointed me in the right direction regarding links between the civil service and pressure groups. I am grateful to Professor Coyne, Head of the Leicester Business School, Professor David Wilson, Head of PPMS, and Professor Albert Weale of the University of Essex, for the encouragement they have given over the years.

But, above all, I would like to thank my wife Debbie, and our children, Mark, Danny and Melissa for their love, support and tolerance.

Rob Baggott
De Montfort University, Leicester
July 1995

1

What is a pressure group?

Defining pressure groups

Simple questions are often the most difficult to answer. There is, as we shall see, a lot of disagreement over the meaning of the term *pressure group*. Perhaps we should not be surprised at the failure to generate an undisputed definition. After all, there are thousands of organisations which could be regarded as pressure groups. The *Directory of British Associations* (1994), for example, lists around 7,000 bodies, many of which are engaged in lobbying in some form or other. But these are the tip of the iceberg. One can think of many other organisations which act as pressure groups in certain circumstances, such as businesses, schools, hospitals, voluntary organisations and community groups.

Pressure groups are not only numerous, but extremely diverse. Some are small, relatively unknown, and are formed on the basis of highly specific functions, interests and activities. Their involvement in politics tends to be sporadic and low-profile. Obscure examples include the Zip Fastener Manufacturers' Association, the Ladies' Sidesaddle Association and All Mod Cons (a group which campaigns for better quality public lavatory provision). In contrast, others, such as the Trades Union Congress (TUC), the Confederation of British Industry (CBI), the British Medical Association (BMA) and the National Farmers' Union (NFU), are huge organisations employing hundreds of staff. These groups are heavily involved in politics and have a high public profile. Some are 'household names', and are often referred to simply by their initials without fear of confusion.

There are also important variations in the way in which pressure groups interact with the political system. Some operate mainly in national politics, while others are focused at a local level. Increasingly, pressure groups also try to influence decisions in Europe, while some operate at a global level. Furthermore, the tactics of pressure groups and their relationships with political institutions vary. Some pressure groups enjoy close links with ministers and civil servants, while others target the legislature, or concentrate on influencing public opinion.

In short, the term 'pressure group' covers an enormous diversity in scale, organisation, objectives and behaviour, which makes it difficult to derive a simple definition, acceptable to all. However, in spite of this, there have been many attempts to define the term (see Exhibit 1.1). These range from narrow definitions which seek to make a clear distinction between pressure groups and other political organisations to a more general approach which places less emphasis on such distinctions. Let us first consider the narrow approaches. These are based on attempts to distinguish pressure groups from other key political organisations, namely political parties and government agencies.

Exhibit 1.1   **Definitions of a pressure group**

'those units, organised or not, of the democratic process which have a set purpose or set of purposes, but which are nonetheless neither political parties nor formal agencies of government'. (Alderman, 1984, p.21)

'A pressure group is an organisation which seeks to influence the details of a comparatively small range of public policies and which is not a faction of a recognised political party'. (Baggott, 1988, p.26)

'In general, pressure groups are social aggregates with some level of cohesion and shared aims which attempt to influence the political decision-making process.' (Ball and Millard, 1986, pp.33–4) 'any group attempting to bring about political change whether through government activity or not, and which is not a political party in the sense of being represented at that particular time in the legislative body'. (Castles, 1967, p.1)

'the sum of organisations in so far as they are occupied at any point in time in trying to influence the policy of public bodies in their own chosen direction; though (unlike political parties) never themselves prepared to undertake the direct government of the country'. (Finer, 1966, p.3)

'A pressure group is an organisation which seeks as one of its functions to influence the formulation and implementation of public policy, public policy representing a set of authoritative decisions taken by the executive, the legislature, and the judiciary, and by local government and the European Community.' (Grant, 1989a, p.9)

'the field of organised groups possessing both formal structure and real common interests, in so far as they influence the decisions of public bodies'. (W. J. M. Mackenzie, 1955)

'organisations whose members act together to influence public policy in order to promote their common interest'. (Pross, 1986, p.9)

'an organised group which has as one of its purposes the exercise of influence ... on political institutions, for the purpose of securing favourable decisions or preventing unfavourable ones'. (Roberts, 1971, p.173)

Pressure groups and parties

What distinguishes pressure groups from political parties? It is often said that pressure groups, unlike parties, do not seek to govern. What does this actually mean? The usual interpretation is that pressure groups do not put forward candidates for parliamentary elections in a serious attempt to win seats and form a government. Although this is broadly true, one should be aware that occasionally pressure groups do get involved in electoral politics. Some seek to influence the selection of candidates within the parties in an attempt to ensure, for example, that they are 'pro-Europe', 'unilateralist', 'anti-abortion', 'pro-hunting' and so on. At election time some groups campaign on behalf of candidates supporting their aims. Others monitor the views of election candidates and circulate this information to members and in some cases to the wider public. There have been cases where pressure groups have put up their own candidates at elections. Though comparatively rare, this remains an option particularly at by-elections, where the media focus upon the individual candidate is more intense, and in marginal constituencies, where the loss of a few hundred votes from the main parties could affect the overall result. Finally, pressure groups often seek to build close links both with prospective candidates and sitting MPs in an effort to create a significant bloc in Parliament. The trade unions, for example, seek to achieve this through the sponsorship of candidates, while many industrial lobbies attempt to build bridges with MPs who have relevant constituency and financial interests (see Chapter 7).

Nevertheless, the involvement of British pressure groups in electoral politics is low. There are a number of reasons for this. First of all, the power of the party organisations is such that most pressure groups find it difficult to influence the choice of candidates. The exception is the trade unions which have exerted influence over candidate selection in the Labour Party, though even this role has been challenged in recent years. Secondly, in Britain the electorate still vote mainly for parties rather than for individual parliamentary candidates. Hence the impact of a campaign on behalf of a particular candidate is likely to be marginal. It should also be noted that there are legal restrictions (in the form of the Representation of the People Acts) on such campaigns. Finally, election candidates standing for pressure groups rarely attract many votes, and are extremely unlikely to win parliamentary elections, though, as noted earlier, in marginal constituencies they may affect the outcome.

Pressure groups therefore have little incentive to become

involved in electoral politics in the UK. This is not necessarily the case in other political systems, however. In the USA, for example, the existence of primary elections, the use of referendums, the weakness of national parties, the volatility of the electorate, and the dependence of the candidates on political donations, all combine to make electoral politics a far more fruitful area for pressure groups than in the UK. Furthermore, in countries with electoral systems based on the principle of proportional representation pressure groups tend to become more closely involved in electoral politics. This is because they often have more opportunity to influence the outcome of elections, even to the extent of having their own candidates elected. Indeed in some of these countries some political parties are little more than special interest groups representing a small section of the population (such as those living in a particular region or engaged in a particular occupation).

Some pressure groups in the UK do have close relationships with political parties and it is often difficult to distinguish these interests (for example, the trade unions and the Labour Party). In such cases it is possible to speak of a movement, where political activity is undertaken through both party organisations and pressure groups as well as other, looser, forms of collective action, such as protest marches, boycotts and mass demonstrations. The labour movement, incorporating the Labour Party and the trade unions, is one example. Others include the green movement – consisting of the Green Party and pressure groups such as Greenpeace and Friends of the Earth. The women's movement, animal welfare movement and the peace movement also transcend party and pressure-group politics.

The distinction between parties and pressure groups is further complicated by the fact that pressure groups can be found within parties. Parties can cover an enormous range of views. Where there is a relatively small number of parties, as in the UK, this range is extremely broad. This encourages the growth of pressure groups within parties, as a means of representing the diverse views of members.

The intra-party groups, or factions as they are more commonly known, are commonplace within the British political parties, and have been present since the nineteenth century at least (Brand, 1989). For example, in the Labour Party one finds the left-wing Campaign group of MPs, the soft-left Tribune group and the right-wing Solidarity group. The Conservative Party, on the other hand, contains the No Turning Back group and the 92 group, platforms for right-wing opinion, while the Tory Reform group and One Nation group of MPs organises moderate Conservative opinion. Such factions are broad in the sense that they form and articulate opinion on a wide range of issues. Other party factions focus on specific issues, such as the Charter Movement, which campaigns for greater democracy and openness in the Conservative Party. Often, opposing party factions form within the parties. In the Labour Party for example, support for electoral reform is organised by the Campaign for Electoral Reform, while the Campaign for Electoral Success opposes such a move.

Another way of distinguishing between pressure groups and parties is on the basis of their policy focus. Put simply, British political parties are generally concerned with the application of broad principles to a wide range of policy areas, whereas pressure groups are mainly concerned with the details of a much smaller range of policy areas. Such a distinction is attractive, but there are always exceptions to the rule. Some pressure groups have a broad focus. For example, the Confederation of British Industry (CBI) and the Trades Union Congress (TUC) are both concerned with issues ranging from education and training, health and welfare matters, energy and environmental policy through to questions of industrial relations, taxation and economic policy.

Although it is difficult to maintain a clear distinction between parties and pressure groups in principle, in the vast majority of cases one can easily distinguish between the two. Political parties are highly specialised political organisations, geared to winning representation in Parliament (or other assemblies) with a view to forming a government with a broad programme. Pressure groups may be involved in party and electoral politics to some extent, and may even be active within particular parties. Yet even where this occurs they retain their own institutional identity, distinct from that of the political parties with which they are associated.

Pressure groups and government bodies

As we have seen, it is not always easy to draw a line between parties and pressure groups. But what about the distinction between pressure groups and government organisations? There seems to be a world of difference between, say, a Whitehall department, such as the Department of Health for example, and a pressure group, such as the BMA. The Department of Health is publicly funded, its personnel are civil servants, and it exercises statutory powers granted by Parliament. The BMA is a private organisation, funded by its members' subscriptions.

This provides a clear example of the difference between the two kinds of institution. But there are grey areas. Some private organisations are highly dependent on public funding. Action on Smoking and Health (ASH), for example, receives approximately 80 per cent of its income from the Department of Health. This is not an isolated example. The National Association for Mental Health (MIND) receives around 25 per cent of its income from the same department. Indeed the Department of Health is a major contributor to the finances of voluntary associations. The Department gives around £15 million each year to over 250 organisations, many of which are actively engaged in trying to influence public policy.

Government funding for private organisations blurs the distinction between government agencies on the one hand and pressure groups on the other. This is particularly so when government uses grants as a carrot to encourage groups to behave in a particular way. For example, in 1980, MIND had to apologise for its earlier criticism of central government for mishandling allegations of brutality in secure psychiatric hospitals (Whiteley and Winyard, 1987, p.30).

This distinction is further clouded where pressure groups actually perform functions on behalf of government. The groups often advise government on policy (see Chapter 5), while others help to implement it. The National Farmers' Union, for example, advises and assists the Ministry of Agriculture, Fisheries and Food.

Notably, some groups, such as the NSPCC and the RSPCA, for example, have statutory powers.

At the margin the distinction between groups and government is also muddied by the existence of non-departmental public bodies, commonly known as quangos. In 1992 there were 1,412 non-departmental public bodies in Britain, spending around £14 billion and employing 114,000 staff. They are created for a variety of reasons: to implement policies, to advise government, to co-ordinate action in a particular area of policy, and they are usually publicly funded. The membership of such bodies is often drawn from outside government, including in some cases representatives of pressure groups. They are also at arms-length from government, despite their official status, tend to be focused on specific issues, and are often in regular contact with pressure groups in their field. In some situations non-departmental public bodies act very much like pressure groups themselves, campaigning for or against policies. An example is the Commission for Racial Equality, which was established under the Race Relations Act 1976 to work towards the elimination of racial discrimination and the promotion of equal opportunity. In practice, the Commission acts as a pressure group, campaigning against racism and raising issues of racial equality. A further example is the National Consumer Council. This body was established by government in 1975 to promote consumer interests. It has campaigned on a range of issues in recent years, such as shopping hours, food safety and the quality of public utilities. It also behaves as a pressure group, lobbying government departments and Parliament and promoting issues through the media. Nevertheless, it is in fact a government agency, funded by the Department of Trade and Industry, which appoints its chairperson and members.

Alternative approaches

Attempts to define the term 'pressure group' are laudable. They represent an effort to mark out the field of study, to focus clearly upon these institutions, rather than upon political parties, or government departments and agencies. However, some authors, while recognising the need for definition, dislike the term 'pressure group'. They feel that the term creates a (false) perception of government being pressurised by outside bodies into pursuing certain policies (Finer, 1966, p.3). This image is criticised for giving an inaccurate impression of the overall style of pressure-group politics. It is well known that compromise and negotiation are important elements in the relationship between government and pressure groups. In most cases pressure groups seek to persuade government rather than to pressure them into submission. It is also argued that the term 'pressure group' is misleading because it focuses too much attention on the government as the target of lobbying, and plays down the equally important impact which government has upon groups.

Some authors prefer to use the term *group* (for example, Jordan and Richardson, 1987a, though they do use the term 'pressure group' in the title of their book). Finer prefers the *lobby* (see Exhibit 1.1), while others use the term *interest group* (Marsh, 1983; Norton, 1984; Wilson, 1990). 'Interest group' does not have the same aggressive connotations as 'pressure group'. It also conveys the idea that groups are representing the different interests in society. Hence we speak of the farmers' interest being represented by the National Farmers' Union, or the doctors' interest being represented by the British Medical Association. Unfortunately the term 'interest group' is also reserved by some authors for a particular type of pressure group – one which defends and promotes the self-interests of a section of society (see p.14 below). The term 'interest group' is therefore ambiguous as it could refer to pressure groups in general or a specific type of group.

Some authors, recognising a similarity in the aims and tactics of pressure groups and other political institutions, prefer to place all such activity under the umbrella of *pressure politics*. In this very broad sense almost any form of organisation that clarifies its objectives in relation to policy, and uses its political resources in an attempt to shape public policy is, in effect, a pressure group. From this perspective what matters is not the constitution of a particular organisation, nor its place within the political system, but rather its role in relation to the policy-making process. In short, pressure-group politics is a *process* rather than a set of distinct institutions. This is the approach taken by some theorists such as Bentley (1967). According to Bentley, groups – and the balance of power between them – determine public policy. As he himself put it 'the balance of the group pressures is the existing state of society' (pp.258–9). For Bentley, government itself is a process of group interaction. This accepts that government institutions operate as pressure groups, a point developed by Latham (1965), who saw little difference in the behaviour of government agencies and non-governmental groups, except that the former had the privilege of official status.

Jordan and Richardson (1987a) also adopt a broader concept of pressure group in their analysis. As they make clear 'the emphasis of our variant of group theory is more about pressure between bodies rather than about formal groups. Group theorists are writing about how decisions are made; group theory is about the role of groups in decision-making, not merely theories about groups' (pp.15–16). Writers in this tradition view attempts to formulate a single, restrictive definition of pressure groups as rather futile and misguided: futile, because no definition can encapsulate the diversity of the pressure group world, and because a clear line cannot be drawn between pressure groups and parties on the one hand and pressure groups and government on the other; misguided, because a narrow definition of pressure groups, which excludes institutions such as government departments and political parties, narrows the range of study and thereby impedes our understanding of the policy-making process.

The broader concept of a pressure group is in many ways attractive. It explicitly recognises the fusion between the world of pressure groups and the corridors of Whitehall, and between pressure groups and the party political scene. On a practical level, the adoption of a broader concept of pressure group saves the trouble of having to distinguish between political institutions. Instead, the focus is upon the role of groups in the policy process and their relative strengths – irrespective of whether they be government organisations, private or voluntary associations, businesses or political parties.

There are problems, however, with the broad concept of pressure group, and these must be set against the insights provided by this approach. Virtually everything that moves in the political arena becomes in effect a pressure group. If, in the extreme, everything is a pressure group, then the term itself becomes rather meaningless. Furthermore, the broad concept of pressure group can widen the scope of analysis to such an extent that the focus shifts too far away from the behaviour of private organisations and towards relationships between political organisations in general. Yet the politics of private organisations is an essential aspect of pressure-group politics, and one which should not be neglected. Furthermore, in blurring the distinction between different political organisations the broad concept of groups may be seen as too general. In other words the differences between the aims, tactics and behaviour of parties, government agencies and private organisations are more significant than their similarities.

Conclusions

The broader interpretations of the term 'pressure group' and the narrower definitions are both valuable. Indeed, the two approaches complement each other and help us to determine the scope of our study. The narrower definitions focus our attention upon the role of organisations which lie beyond government and party politics – such as charities, business organisations, voluntary associations, professional bodies and trade unions – while the broader interpretations remind us that in practice these organisations are often highly integrated with other political institutions within the policy process, and that we should not neglect the relationships between groups or those which exist between groups and other political organisations.

2

Analysing pressure groups

The modern approach to the study of pressure groups in Britain dates from the second half of the 1950s (see for example Beer, 1956; Mackenzie, 1955, 1958; Stewart, 1958). Although they had been an important feature of the British political system for well over a century, playing an important role in promoting laws on issues such as slavery, free trade and public health (Hamer, 1977; Hollis, 1974), little was known about the role of pressure groups in the modern political system. The call for 'more light' on the 'anonymous empire' of pressure groups (Finer, 1958) ended this neglect and signalled a wave of interest that has not abated since. Over the years a variety of approaches have been used in the study of pressure groups. In this chapter we shall explore the main ones.

Classifying pressure groups

One of the main problems facing the student of pressure groups has already been encountered in the previous chapter: their number and diversity. Some have tried to deal with this by devising various categories. Such categories are only useful if they improve our understanding of pressure-group politics (Ball and Millard, 1986). Classification certainly has the potential to generate important concepts and hypotheses regarding the behaviour of pressure groups and their relationships with other political institutions. Sadly, this ideal has not always been pursued and many classifications have neither theoretical or practical value. Further-more, as Jordan and Richardson (1987a) have pointed out, the lit-erature of classification is non-cumulative. Each study has tended to develop its own categories of pressure group without reference to those devised previously. In many cases the method of classification adopted by different authors has been rather simi-lar. But because authors have used different labels even to iden-tify the same phenomena, confusion has reigned supreme.

Interest groups and cause groups

Despite the confusion over labels, the key distinction made by most authors is that between groups which represent the interests of a particular social or economic *group*, and those which promote a common *cause*. Stewart (1958) adopts the term 'sectional group' for the former and 'cause group' for the latter. Others have used different labels for essentially the same distinction. Finer (1966), for example, uses the term 'interest group' for the former and 'promotional group' for the latter. Castles (1967) and Kimber and Richardson (1974) depart from the existing typologies by employ-ing the term 'attitude group' instead of 'promotional' or 'cause' group. To avoid unnecessary confusion, the terms 'interest group' and 'cause group' will be used here (see Exhibit 2.1). Essentially, the basis of all these classifications is much the same. Most authors assume that the groups are different in two main respects: their membership and their aims. Interest groups have 'closed' or 'defined' memberships. Only those exhibiting certain social or economic characteristics are eligible to join. Hence (putting aside honorary memberships, which do not usually carry full member-ship rights) the membership of the BMA is open only to doctors, the Society of Motor Manufacturers and Traders only to busi-nesses in this particular trade. The aims of interest groups reflect the narrow background of their membership, and are therefore mainly concerned with the protection and advancement of the self-interests of members.

The membership of cause groups is not as clearly defined. Members are not necessarily drawn from a narrow socio-eco-nomic group. They join on the basis of a shared attitude rather

Exhibit 2.1 **Classifying pressure groups**	
Types of group	
Interest groups	Cause groups
Membership *restricted* to those with a shared background, or performing a common socio-economic function	Membership *open* to those who support the cause, or who share common values
Primarily exists to protect *members' self-interests* as defined by the group	Primarily exists to further the *interests of others* (or the *public interest*) as defined by the group
Examples Confederation of British Industry British Medical Association National Farmers' Union	*Examples* Action on Smoking and Health Child Poverty Action Group RSPCA
Also known as sectional groups	*Also known as* attitude groups promotional groups

than a common social background. Cause groups do not exist primarily for the self-interest of their members; their aims are generally more outward-looking, and indeed seek to benefit society as a whole, or a specific section of society, such as children (as in the case of the NSPCC), or the elderly (Age Concern) or even other species (the RSPCA). Cause groups can therefore be distinguished from sectional groups in that they are 'organisations for' a cause rather than 'organisations of' a specific interest. This distinction has been developed in studies of the disability lobby (Oliver, 1990) and the poverty lobby (Whiteley and Winyard, 1987).

The cause/interest group dichotomy has often been used as an analytical framework for studying the behaviour of pressure groups. Indeed, at one time it was believed that the typology was useful in explaining patterns of pressure-group activity. It was suggested that the two types of group behaved in significantly different ways, interest groups focusing their lobbying activities on ministers and civil servants in the executive branch of government, while cause groups were more heavily engaged in lobbying Parliament and seeking to influence public opinion. It was also believed that interest groups were more influential than cause groups because their tactics, organisation, political contacts and resources were superior. Yet the dichotomy does not create an unambiguous link between pressure-group characteristics, such as a membership and aims, and pressure-group behaviour such as lobbying strategies. Nor can it link characteristics with effectiveness. There is no systematic evidence to suggest that cause groups will use different tactics or will be less influential over policy when compared with interest groups.

Other problems with the cause/interest dichotomy

The cause/interest group dichotomy is flawed in a number of other ways. It is often impossible in practice to distinguish self-interest from the pursuit of causes. Interest, groups sometimes pursue causes to the benefit of others. Indeed, there are cases where an interest group's activity appears to contradict the narrow self-interests of its membership: the British Dental Association's (BDA) support for water fluoridation is one example. It is particularly difficult to distinguish selfish and altruistic motives in professional groups, which are classified as interest groups, but which also have ethical codes based on a notion of the public interest.

Interest groups often pursue causes: teachers' unions campaign for better quality education, doctors' organisations campaign for policies which tackle underlying causes of ill-health such as drink-

ing and smoking. In some cases interest groups establish separate
organisations for the purpose of promoting a particular cause. For
example, in 1971 the Royal College of Physicians created the
pressure group Action on Smoking and Health (ASH) to campaign against smoking, while in 1984 some of the larger retailers
supporting a reform of shopping hours on Sundays formed a
cause group called Open Shop to press for a change in the law.
Other interest groups help to maintain cause groups with financial donations or other means of support such as the provision of
offices rent-free. For example, the pro-smoking pressure group
FOREST (Freedom Organisation for the Right to Enjoy Smoking Tobacco) receives donations from the tobacco industry
(Taylor, 1984).

Furthermore, self-interested motives can be found in cause
groups, even those which are not backed by sectional groups.
After all, cause groups provide material and non-material benefits
to their staff and senior members, including jobs, salaries and
status. One suspects that this could lead to strategies based more
on personal goals and self-interests than altruism. Other trends
such as the greater employment of professional staff, and the
increasing use of pressure groups as a stepping-stone to a political career (see p.63 below) adds to this suspicion.

In addition there are some groups which do not fit easily into
the cause/interest group dichotomy. What about amenity groups,
for example, which consist of people with a particular interest in
some sport or leisure activity? These are self-interested organisations but their memberships are usually open to anyone wishing
to join. Similarly consumer groups and NIMBY ('Not in My
Back Yard', see pp.198–9) groups are difficult to classify. These
organisations too, are mainly self-interested but have relatively
open memberships.

Although the dichotomy is far from perfect, it has proved to
be very durable. Most pressure-group studies accept shortcomings of this classification, with a caveat about 'hybrid groups' to
cover cases which do not fit into either category easily. The belief
that a two–category classification could comprehensively account
for the sheer diversity of the pressure-group universe was, at best,

optimistic. Even so an alternative – a more complex method of classification – is regarded as having little to recommend it (Potter, 1961). It is the simplicity of the cause/interest group dichotomy which is attractive. Others have sought to preserve the advantages of a simple classification by inventing new typologies.

Alternative typologies

Efforts to develop new typologies reflect a desire to make them more relevant to the study of public policy-making, by focusing on different systems of interaction between groups and the policy process. For example, Cawson (1982) distinguishes between *corporate* groups – defined by their location in the social and economic division of labour – and *competitive* groups which emerge from the voluntary interaction of people with shared preferences. Business groups, professional associations and trade unions are examples of the former; consumer, client and philanthropic groups, examples of the latter. Moran (1985) follows Cawson's approach, but uses a different terminology. He prefers the term *functional* group instead of corporate group; and *preference* group instead of competitive group. But the distinction is essentially the same, with the former representing the main economic functions in society and the latter representing shared attitudes.

In Cawson's model the influence of competitive groups depends on their organisational strength, numbers, resources and publicity, while the influence of corporate groups reflects the function of the group in question, how important this function is to the state, and the extent to which the group is embedded in decision-making. The two kinds of groups are therefore operating in a different political context. According to Cawson this means that they cannot really be compared. 'To compare the power of the Child Poverty Action Group with that of a trade union', he argues, 'is to decline to compare like with like' (Cawson, 1982, p.43). It is not that competitive groups are necessarily weaker than corporate groups, but rather that the interaction between corporate groups and the state dictates the boundaries within which competitive groups can exert influence.

Other typologies seeking to distinguish pressure groups on the basis of their interaction with the policy process include those devised by Benewick (1973) and Grant (1989a). Benewick argues that pressure groups can be divided into three 'worlds'. The first of these includes those whose access to decision-makers is continuous, who have resources which are impressive and which are seen as legitimate by government. Groups occupying the second world can obtain access to decision-makers, but contact is less frequent. The third world groups are not perceived as legitimate and do not generally have access to decision-makers. These groups tend to operate against the current balance of power, and militancy is their major resource.

Benewick therefore distinguishes between groups that are regarded as legitimate by decision-makers and those which are not. The implication is that the former will exert more influence within the political system. However, Benewick does not rule out the possibility that groups in the 'third world' may in certain circumstances be politically important.

Grant (1989a) identifies two main types of group: insider and outsider groups. The difference between them is that insider groups are viewed as legitimate by government and are consulted on a regular basis, while outsider groups either do not wish to become involved in a consultative relationship or cannot secure recognition. Within these categories, Grant makes further distinctions. Insiders can be 'high profile' or 'low profile' depending on the extent to which they cultivate media support as a means of reinforcing their contact with government. Insider groups can also be 'prisoner groups', dependent on government for assistance or support.

Outsider groups can also be divided into three categories. Potential insider groups, a status which can be achieved by pursuing a strategy which is more acceptable in the eyes of government. Outsider groups by necessity – groups which are politically less skilful and knowledgeable than potential insiders. Finally, there are ideological outsider groups, who do not wish to become insiders because of the radical nature of their aims.

Grant's classification, rather like Benewick's, cuts across the cause/interest dichotomy. Not all interest groups will be insiders; not all cause groups will be outsiders. There is much to support this approach. For example, Ryan's (1978) study of the penal lobby revealed how a cause group, the Howard League for Penal Reform, was treated as an insider group by the government. On the other hand, Grant cites the National Union of Ratepayer Associations as an example of an interest group lacking insider status.

Grant's classification is perhaps more useful than most other typologies because it is so flexible. Unlike the sectional and cause group categories, the insider and outsider typology is based on status, which may be acquired or lost as circumstances change. An outsider group can become an insider; and vice versa. This focuses attention on the factors which make some groups acceptable and others not, from the point of view of government.

The implication of Grant's distinction is that insider status is linked to effectiveness. The assumption appears to be that most groups will seek insider status. There is considerable evidence to support this, as we shall see in Chapter 5. However, 'acceptability' and 'insider status' bring responsibilities which may threaten the autonomy of groups and their freedom to pursue certain strategies. It may even be a means of imposing decisions through an artificially constructed consensus (Nettl, 1965). Moreover, it is possible for outsider groups to play an important role in the determination of public policy by mobilising public sentiment, as shown by the Anti-Poll Tax Federation, for example.

One should also note that insider groups often undertake a combination of both insider and outsider tactics. While this does not invalidate the insider/outsider model, it does reveal its limitations. For example, the Brewers' Society campaign against the government's planned reforms of the industry in 1989 involved media campaigns to shape public opinion, a parliamentary campaign in both Houses, direct lobbying of government departments and even pressure through Conservative constituency parties (Exhibit 7.1). Moreover, it has been shown that insider groups, despite their status, are actually more frequently in touch with Parliament than outsider groups (Baggott, 1992; Judge, 1990).

May and Nugent (1982) have modified Grant's typology to take account of groups which oscillate over time between insider and outsider strategies. They call such groups 'thresholder groups', and note that trade unions, for example, fall into this category. Changes in the political environment, such as a change of government, often produce changes in status and strategies, as we shall see later in the book. In addition, one should note that status and strategy are likely to vary, not only over time, but from issue to issue. The BMA, for example, may be regarded as an insider group on medical issues, but an outsider group on broader health and safety issues, such as the controversy over boxing.

Whiteley and Winyard (1987) observe that one of the problems with Grant's categories (and this applies to Benewick's typology too), is that it confuses strategy and status. Hence a group may have insider status, but may pursue a broader political strategy that does not rely solely on contacts with Whitehall. Whiteley and Winyard attempt to separate out the different strategies and status of groups, as well as their other characteristics by using a four-dimensional system of classification (see Exhibit 2.2). They made a distinction between focused groups – those which concentrated mainly on Whitehall – and open groups – those which pursued a strategy which placed emphasis on other political contacts, such as the media and Parliament, but which did not necessarily ignore relationships with central government. But this distinction is separate from judgements about the status of a group, which is either 'acceptable' (i.e. accepted by government as legitimate) or 'not acceptable'.

Exhibit 2.2   **Classifying the poverty lobby**

Whiteley and Winyard's study (1987) of the poverty lobby led them to classify groups in four dimensions. These were as follows:

1 *Strategy*
   Groups were classified as either F = Focused (on Whitehall), or O = Open (adopted a broad range of strategies).

2 *Support*

Groups classified as either P = Promotional (speaking on behalf of a client group) or R = Representational (directly representing members of a client group).

3 *Status*

Groups classified as A = Accepted (by policy-makers) or N = Not accepted.

4 *Aims*

Groups classified as L = Lobbying (primary purpose to lobby policy makers) or S = Service provision (main purpose to deliver services to a client group).

The most common profiles found in the poverty lobby were the OPAL (Open–Promotional–Accepted–Lobbying) and the FRAS (Focused–Representational–Accepted–Service provider) profiles. Whiteley and Winyard found that the OPAL profile was found more commonly among groups created in the 1960s and 1970s, and that this profile was generally found among the more effective groups.

Source: Whiteley and Winyard 'Pressure for the Poor' (1987)

The typologies developed in recent years have been far more useful as a framework to analyse the behaviour of pressure groups, particularly with regard to their role in the policy process. In the next section we examine the relationship between pressure groups and policy process further, in the context of other theoretical frameworks.

Pressure groups and the policy process

There are many ways in which one can try to comprehend the policy process and the role of pressure groups in relation to it. First of all the policy process can be seen as a series of *stages*. Secondly, it can be perceived as a number of *arenas*. Third, it can be viewed as a collection of *networks*. Let us now explore these images of the policy process.

The stages of the policy process
For analytical purposes it is possible to divide policy-making into a number of stages or phases (see Exhibit 2.3). Pressure groups have the potential to influence policy at these stages (see Hogwood, 1987, p.12). Pressure groups can influence the *political agenda* by generating public support for their aims, or by directly persuading the government to consider taking action (Benyon, 1985). Alternatively, pressure groups may exert influence by dissuading the government from taking action, or may prevent issues from reaching the political agenda.

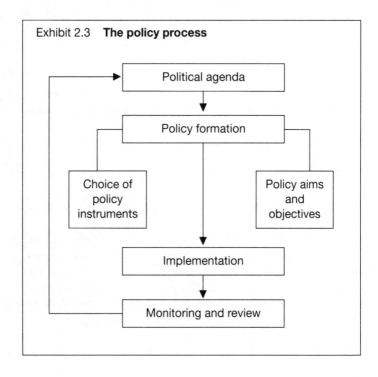

Exhibit 2.3   **The policy process**

At the *policy formation stage,* groups may seek to influence the broad aims of government policy. More often though they will concentrate upon the details of policy, such as the choice of policy instruments – legislation, regulation, taxation or public expenditure, and so on. Pressure groups may be involved in the *implementation of policy,* shaping policies as they are put into practice. Significant changes can occur at this stage and pressure groups can be extremely influential here (Marsh and Rhodes, 1992b). They may also promote further policy changes by monitoring the operation of the new policies and highlighting any problems arising from them.

Dividing the policy process into stages not only makes it more comprehensible, but also enables us to appreciate the opportunities to influence policy. Moreover, this approach may help us to develop and test theories about the role of groups at different stages in the policy process. For example, it is often suggested that the most influential groups are those which shape government policy at an early stage in its development.

Pressure points and political arenas
Another way of looking at the policy process is to focus on structures of decision-making. Decisions affecting pressure groups can be made at various places within the political system. These are known as *political arenas* (Jordan and Richardson, 1987b) or *pressure points* (Baggott, 1994). The main pressure points are shown in Exhibit 2.4 and include local, national and international decision-making institutions as well as organisations which mobilise and focus opinion, such as political parties, the media, and other private organisations, including other pressure groups.

This approach is valuable because it helps us to appreciate that policy process is a multi-layered system and that pressure groups have a variety of targets which they can seek to influence. Of course, in political systems like Britain, where decision-making is relatively centralised and where some decision-making bodies are fairly weak, the diversity of targets may be more apparent than real. Yet even in Britain pressure groups have been influential in certain circumstances by lobbying apparently less powerful insti-

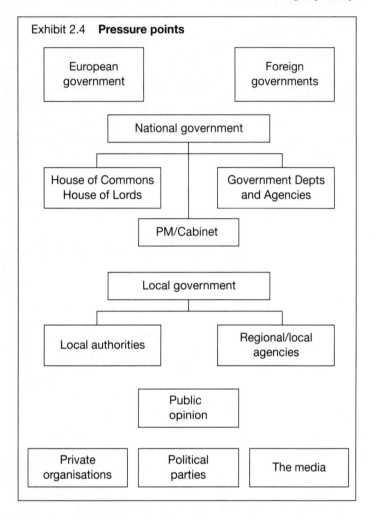

Exhibit 2.4   **Pressure points**

tutions, such as the House of Lords (see Chapter 7). Moreover, the increasing influence of Europe has provided a useful option in recent years for pressure groups which have lost favour with the British government, such as the trade unions for example (see Chapter 8).

Policy networks

The concept of *policy network* has attracted a great deal of attention in the field of policy studies in recent years (Marsh and Rhodes, 1992a; Richardson and Jordan, 1979; Smith 1993). There are several different types of policy networks, but the two main categories are *policy communities* and *issue networks* (see Exhibit 2.5). Policy networks describe the different kinds of relationship between pressure groups and government. They can also be used to analyse the policy process and the role of pressure groups in relation to the policy process.

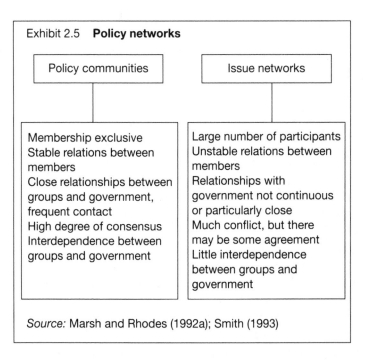

Exhibit 2.5 **Policy networks**

Policy communities	Issue networks
Membership exclusive Stable relations between members Close relationships between groups and government, frequent contact High degree of consensus Interdependence between groups and government	Large number of participants Unstable relations between members Relationships with government not continuous or particularly close Much conflict, but there may be some agreement Little interdependence between groups and government

Source: Marsh and Rhodes (1992a); Smith (1993)

The concept of policy networks helps us to appreciate that the relationship between groups and government varies considerably, and that these different relationships have implications for the way in which policy is made. Policy communities, for example, have a much more restricted membership, and policy is developed in a much more consensual manner than is the case in an issue network. Secondly, the concept is based on a belief that the impact of pressure groups upon policy does not depend solely on their resources and strategies, but upon the structure of decision-making and on the interests of the government itself. Hence government agencies are not merely focal points for pressure, they actively seek to shape policy preferences and the political environment within which pressure groups operate. Finally, the concept of policy network takes account of the complexity of the modern state, and in particular the fact that different parts of the state apparatus (i.e. government departments and agencies) are often in conflict with each other. This approach helps us to understand that policies often emerge as a result of conflict between different government agencies, each supported by an alliance of pressure groups.

In recent years the policy networks approach has been used in several policy studies (see Marsh and Rhodes, 1992a), including food policy (Smith, 1991), the privatisation of the water industry (Richardson, Maloney and Rudig, 1992) and the Technical and Vocational Education Initiative (TVEI) (Moon and Richardson, 1984). Nevertheless, the policy networks approach can be criticised on several grounds. First, there is little explanation of how policy networks emerge. In particular, it is assumed rather than demonstrated that a mutual dependence between groups and government leads to the formation of policy communities. Secondly, the approach is rather static and is geared to explaining how new policies can be blocked or diluted rather than how new policies emerge. Thirdly, this approach has difficulty in explaining how and why policy networks themselves change. Finally, while the focus upon the relationship between government and groups is clearly important, there is a tendency to disregard other political arenas and the broader political environment within which groups operate, both of which can shape the behaviour of pressure groups and their ability to influence policy.

Problems and pitfalls

Moving from theoretical to empirical issues, the remainder of this chapter seeks to highlight the problems and pitfalls faced by those who study the behaviour of pressure groups.

Generalisation

The main method of investigation used by those studying pressure groups has been the case study. Many of the earlier pressure group studies were case studies of particular groups or campaigns. For example Eckstein's (1960) study of the British Medical Association (BMA), Self and Storing's (1962) analysis of the National Farmers' Union (NFU) and H. H. Wilson's (1961) account of the introduction of commercial television.

There is nothing inherently wrong with the use of case studies. But while many of the early studies were very useful, shedding light on a hitherto neglected area of study, there were problems in making generalisations on the basis of their findings. To their credit, researchers were often at pains to point out the shortcomings of the case study approach. Eckstein (1960, p.15), for example, warned that 'case studies never prove anything; their purpose is to illustrate generalisations which are established otherwise, or to direct attention towards such generalisations'.

Sadly, such warnings were not heeded by those who followed. Case studies mushroomed, but in a haphazard way, unrelated to any common framework of analysis. Each additional case study added little to the understanding of the role of pressure groups in the political system. These shortcomings were not, however, confined to the study of pressure groups in Britain. Schattschneider (1960), writing in an American context, criticised the study of pressure groups, and in particular the tendency of researchers to deal only with successful pressure campaigns.

The situation has improved in recent years, however. The development of new frameworks of analysis, such as policy networks for example, has enabled us to make more sense of case study material. In addition studies now tend to focus upon broad policy areas rather than specific decisions or particular pressure groups. This approach is displayed, for example, in the studies by Whiteley and Winyard (1987) of the poverty lobby, Lowe and Goyder (1983) of the environmental lobby, and Ryan (1978, 1983) of the penal lobby. This approach is extremely useful because it sets pressure-group politics in context while permitting in-depth exploration of inter-group and group–government relationships across a range of issues, and over a period of time.

Yet generalisation remains a problem. Aspects of pressure group politics may be specific to certain sectors of policy-making or to certain kinds of group. This makes it very difficult to generalise about trends observed in a particular policy area. Of course one can overcome this to some extend by a broad survey of groups. This has been tried, with some success (Baggott, 1992; Rush, 1990a). Such surveys have confirmed trends for which there was previously only anecdotal evidence. But given the diversity of groups and the lack of a comprehensive database, the representation of samples is always open to question.

Comparative studies (Ball and Millard, 1986; Smith 1993; G. K. Wilson, 1990) can make a useful contribution to the analysis of pressure groups by exploring their role, conduct and influence in different political systems. This can give a greater insight into general trends in pressure-group politics. Comparative studies can also raise important questions about the influence of similar groups in different political systems. For example, why does the tobacco industry appear to be more influential in the UK than in Norway (Baggott, 1987)? Yet there are difficulties in adopting a comparative approach to pressure group studies. As Eckstein (1960) noted, pressure groups adapt themselves to the political system they inhabit – and in particular to the distribution of effective power in that system. Many aspects of pressure group behaviour may well be determined by differences between political systems rather differences between groups.

Profile
A second problem one encounters when studying pressure groups is that some have a higher profile than others. Some proclaim their aims and activities quite openly, while others prefer to

pursue a hidden or covert strategy and may conceal their objectives and motives. Moreover, irrespective of the group's overall strategy, certain pressure group activities are difficult to detect and evaluate: for example, informal meetings with officials and ministers. This problem is reinforced by the secrecy of the British political system. Indeed, insider status (see above) is generally regarded as being dependent in part at least on the extent to which government can trust groups to maintain confidentiality.

The influence of groups which pursue covert strategies, and the usefulness or otherwise of low profile contacts with government is difficult to evaluate. As a result their success (or failure) is often not fully taken into account, producing a rather distorted picture of group activity and influence. The problem of hidden activities and motives is a general problem for political study. Concrete evidence regarding the role of pressure groups in the policy process may come to light many years after the issue in question has been decided, if at all. The publication of memoirs and official documents can sometimes enable one to obtain a clearer picture of the patterns of influence and power. For example, there have been a number of publications recently which have re-examined the policy-making process which led to the creation of the National Health Service (NHS) after the Second World War in the light of official documents not available to previous studies (Honigsbaum, 1990; Webster, 1988). The passage of time, if it yields such evidence, can offer a partial solution to this problem.

Finally, it should be noted that pressure groups are essentially 'private' bodies. They are not obliged to divulge information about their activities, except where (as in the case of charities, for example) they are specifically required to do so by law. Their internal deliberations – and many of their other activities – can therefore be kept secret.

Separability
A further problem is separability, and there are two aspects to it. First of all it is difficult to separate the impact of a single pressure group when it is acting with others. For example, the gov-

ernment's defeat in the House of Commons on the second reading of the Shops Bill in 1986 was brought about by a coalition of
three main groups: shopworkers, the churches and businesses
who opposed the plan (see Exhibit 4.4). But which group (if any)
exerted a critical influence? One could explore such coalitions by
breaking them up into their constituent parts and then evaluating
each group's effectiveness in other policy areas – to see how different alliances affect its influence. But such an analysis would
probably tell us little, since coalitions are often synergic – their
combined impact is greater than the sum of the constituent parts.
It is also often difficult to separate the relative influence of pressure groups and other political institutions such as government
departments, Parliament, parties and the media. It is particularly
difficult where the relationship between pressure groups and
these institutions is very close. Furthermore, one must be careful
not to credit a group with influence when it has benefited from
other events and developments. The Campaign for Nuclear Disarmament (CND), for example, can be credited with mobilising
opinion on the issue of nuclear weapons, but it would be foolish
to attribute to it the changes in nuclear policy in the late 1980s
which resulted largely from changes in East–West relations.

Time dimension
The judgement about whether or not a pressure group has been
influential often depends on the time-scale concerned. There are
many cases of groups being unsuccessful in the short term, yet
securing (or helping to secure) important policy changes in the
long run. The classic example is the pro-abortion lobby, and the
Abortion Law Reform Association (ALRA), in particular, which
campaigned for many years before securing the passage of the
1967 Termination of Pregnancy Act (Hindell and Simms, 1971;
Marsh and Chambers, 1981). This case also illustrates that the
pendulum can also swing back, as exemplified by the resurgence
of the anti-abortion lobby in the years since this Act was passed.
  Moreover, an examination of the long-term beneficiaries (or
losers) from a particular policy decision does not tell us the full
story either. Indeed pressure groups sometimes oppose a partic-

ular policy, believing it to be against its interests, yet find in the long run that they have benefited from the policy. For example, in the early years of this century the BMA opposed the introduction of a state health insurance scheme, yet it was introduced in spite of their protests. Although the BMA refused to co-operate, large numbers of general practitioners (GPs) voted with their feet and joined the new scheme. In the longer term their judgement proved wise. Most independent observers agree that the new scheme benefited most doctors not only financially, but also improved their social status and their political influence in the long term (Brand, 1965).

Conclusions

This chapter has provided an insight into the main approaches to the study of pressure-group politics. A number of conceptual frameworks exist, and these have been evaluated in terms of their ability to help us to understand the behaviour of pressure groups and their role in the political system. It is clear that there is no ideal framework, though some of the older typologies seem less useful than modern approaches which focus more clearly on the role of groups within the policy process. Furthermore, the chapter has shown that students of pressure-group politics face difficulties, particularly with respect to generalisation and the measurement of pressure-group influence. Yet, as we have seen, these problems are not insurmountable, and it is therefore possible to develop and test propositions about pressure-group behaviour and influence in a meaningful way.

3

Pressure groups and democracy

In this chapter we shall explore the role of pressure groups in a democracy by looking at a number of basic political perspectives. These are: pluralism, neo-pluralism, corporatism, the New Right and Marxism. Each perspective operates on two levels, embodying both an analysis of the nature and extent of pressure-group participation in the political system, and a judgement about the consequences of this involvement.

At the outset, two important points need to be considered. First, each perspective goes beyond an analysis of the British political system. Indeed, some have been strongly influenced by academics from other countries. The most prominent pluralist and neo-pluralist writers are from the USA, and the New Right perspective, too, has strong American connections, while corporatism, in contrast, has strong Central European links. Even so, the ideas put forward by such writers can be applied to all democratic states, though their arguments may be more applicable to some democracies than to others. Secondly, each perspective is rather broad. One can find quite serious disagreements between writers sharing the same perspective. Our purpose here, however, is to outline the main features of each perspective, not the detailed arguments between their adherents, and this necessarily involves some simplification.

Pluralism

There is no single, definitive statement of pluralism, (Jordan, 1990; Smith 1990). Nevertheless, one can identify a number of principles central to pluralist thinking (Brown, 1989; Dunleavy and O'Leary, 1987). These are, first, that power should be dispersed throughout society, rather than narrowly concentrated. Second, that government should be based on the consent of the public. Third, that government should share power with the people's chosen representatives. Fourth, that public participation in decision-making should be encouraged. Fifth, that diversity in society should be at least tolerated, if not encouraged. Pluralists believe that these widely accepted principles are, in general, upheld in modern democracies.

Pluralist studies of the political process in democratic states have tended to focus on the role of pressure groups (see, for example, Truman, 1951). They conclude that pressure groups are at the heart of the policy process in representative democracies, and that one cannot comprehend this process without a clear understanding of their role. Some pluralist writers, such as Bentley (1967), believe that political activity can only be understood in terms of the balance of group pressures, although most would not go as far as this (see Exhibit 3.1).

Exhibit 3.1 **The pluralist view of pressure groups**

1 Pressure groups are key political institutions which strongly influence policy-making in modern democracies.

2 Pressure groups uphold the main pluralist principles by representing the whole range of views and interests in society, by providing an important channel of communication between government and the governed, by encouraging participation and by acting as a check on the powerful.

3   There are checks and balances which prevent any single
    group from becoming too powerful.

4   There are no barriers to the formation of groups.

5   Political resources are not equally distributed among
    groups, but no single group has the lion's share of all
    political resources.

6   Access to the political system is fairly open, with pressure
    groups being able to put their case forward with little dif-
    ficulty.

7   Pressure groups are democratic organisations. The lead-
    ers of these organisations are responsive to the demands
    of the rank-and-file members.

Pluralists also believe that pressure groups are instrumental in
upholding their central principles. They are regarded as important channels of representation. Pluralists argue that while election results reflect numerical support for broad programmes
adopted by the major parties, the activities of pressure groups can
reflect more accurately the intensity of feeling across a much narrower range of issues. Moreover, they feel that pressure groups
are more persistent than electoral preferences expressed through
the ballot box. While elections are infrequent, and politicians are
able to provide short-term responses to satisfy voters, pressure
groups are not so easily satisfied. They have a considerable degree
of permanence and can represent views on a continuous basis.
Their permanence also enables them to adopt a longer-term view.
Pluralists therefore view pressure groups as providing a valuable
complement to the electoral process, providing a clear and continuous representation of society's preferences on specific issues
(see D. Wilson, 1984).

Pressure groups are also a means through which the public can
participate in politics. In representative democracies there are few
real opportunities to participate directly in the political process.
Pressure groups offer an accessible route for those wishing to

influence political decisions. Moreover, by participating in groups, it is believed that people may become more willing to participate in the political process more generally. There is evidence that groups play an important role both in encouraging people to participate in a range of political activities and providing resources to enable them to get involved (Parry, Moyser and Day, 1992).

Pluralists believe that by representing a broad range of interests and preferences in society, and by mobilising public opinion, pressure groups can check the concentration of political power. They may do this by generating opposition to government policies formulated without regard to the views of the general public or to the interests of a significant minority likely to be affected. Alternatively, if pressure groups are recognised by government, they may exert influence through consultation before policy is finally decided, a procedure clearly in line with the principle of government by consent.

As well as providing a check on excessive government power, pressure groups are believed to counterbalance each other, the net effect being that no single group will exercise too much influence over government. One can find several examples where groups do this, neutralising to an extent each other's campaigns. For example, Action on Smoking and Health (ASH) presses for greater restrictions on smoking while the Freedom Organisation for the Right to Enjoy Smoking Tobacco (FOREST) campaigns for smokers' rights.

Pluralists identify mechanisms which they believe prevent any single group from becoming all-powerful, even where opposing groups do not exist. They believe that if one group goes too far in asserting its demands, it will begin to affect other interests which will then organise opposition to it. They also claim that decision-makers bear in mind the potential response of interests in society which are not formally organised, such as taxpayers for example. Pluralists also point out that groups often have overlapping memberships, since people may participate in any number of groups. They argue that, as a consequence, if one group threatens to become too dominant or extreme in its view it could lose support from members who have additional interests. They might leave the group, thereby weakening it, or exercise political influence within the group to change its aims and policies.

Pressure groups clearly have the potential to promote pluralist principles. But pluralists themselves recognise that a benign role cannot be taken for granted. Indeed, they accept that the contribution of pressure groups to a truly democratic society will only be realised if certain conditions are satisfied.

First, there should be a large number of groups in society, and there should be no significant barriers to the formation of groups. As will become clear later in this chapter, others have levelled a great deal of criticism on this point, arguing that in practice there are considerable barriers to the formation of particular groups.

Second, all groups should have access to political resources. This does not mean, as some critics of the pluralist standpoint believe, that groups should have equal resources. Rather it implies that any inequalities which do exist are non-cumulative. Hence groups that are relatively well-endowed with some resources (say, wealth or economic power) will not have a large share of other resources (for example, public support). Dahl (1961) calls such a distribution 'dispersed inequality'.

A third condition is that access to the decision-making process is fairly open. Again this does not mean that every group has an equal influence or even the same access to decision-makers. Rather it implies that the political system enables all groups having an interest in a particular issue to put their case.

Finally, pluralists argue that pressure groups themselves should be responsive to the wishes of their members and supporters. Although they do not deny that pressure groups may be run by élites, such as full-time officials and part-time office holders (see Chapter 4), the aims and objectives of groups must be in line with the interests and preferences of the rank-and-file and there should be mechanisms for achieving this.

Pluralists believe generally that these conditions are fulfilled in democratic states. Moreover, their perspective is often employed to argue for a greater role for pressure groups, or for more participation (see D. Wilson, 1984). Others are critical of the pluralist standpoint, both as a description of the decision-making process and as a prescription of how decisions should be made. Indeed, some pluralists have themselves reformulated their position in recent years to take account of the political realities of the late twentieth century. In addition, the pluralist position has been challenged by other perspectives, such as corporatism and the New Right, which are explored later in this chapter.

Neo-pluralism

Over the last couple of decades there has been a definite shift in thinking among pluralist writers such as Dahl (1982) and Lindblom (1977). This reinterpretation of the pluralist perspective is known as neo-pluralism (see Exhibit 3.2).

Exhibit 3.2   **The neo-pluralist view of pressure groups**

1   Government agencies are actively involved in pressure-group politics. They are not simply the focus of pressure-group lobbying but seek to persuade pressure groups to support their aims and policies.

2   Government is fragmented and there is no single concentration of power. Government agencies, allied with particular pressure groups which share their views, are often in conflict with each other.

3   Some groups dominate policy-making and the political agenda. Business interests are particularly influential. Other groups possessing specific professional or technical expertise can also exert a dominant influence in particular policy areas.

4   Pressure groups and the other institutions of representative democracy are flawed. The influence of a particular pressure group over policy is not necessarily related to the degree of public support for it.

5   Some movement towards the achievement of pluralist
    principles may be achieved by reform of the policy-
    making process and of political institutions.

The neo-pluralist perspective departs from the original standpoint in several ways (Dunleavy and O'Leary, 1987). First of all,
it takes a different view of the relationship between groups and
government. Secondly, it embodies a more explicit recognition
that certain groups in society are much more powerful than
others. Third, it is generally more pessimistic about the extent to
which the fundamental principles of pluralism, outlined earlier,
are being upheld in democracies.

Neo-pluralists see the relationship between government and
groups as a means through which government can manage group
activity in its own interests. So, government is not simply a ref-
eree arbitrating between opposing pressure groups, but is an
active participant in pressure-group politics, mobilising support
for and discouraging opposition to its preferred policy options.
Neo-pluralists appreciate that government has the resources to
shape the behaviour of groups. For example, it may confer special status on certain groups, giving them privileged access to the
decision-making process, or it may provide particular groups with
resources enabling them to lobby more effectively. Such intervention has a number of consequences. On the one hand some
groups will gain. Those having privileged access to the decision-
making process may be able to win significant concessions by bargaining and negotiating directly with government. Meanwhile,
groups excluded from this process are likely to be disadvantaged.
As a result, existing inequalities between groups may be reinforced, a point we shall return to in a moment.

The intervention of government in pressure-group politics also
has implications for the independent role of groups. Neo-pluralists recognise that if groups are manipulated by government they
are likely to become less responsive to rank-and-file membership
and grassroots opinion.

Although neo-pluralists appreciate the possibility of a powerful state, which manipulates groups rather than responds to pressure from below, they also identify factors which may inhibit this. They observe that government is often internally divided, with different government agencies pursuing their own policies. This is known as 'departmental pluralism' (Richardson and Jordan, 1979). Moreover, they believe that policies are determined in a range of policy networks (see pp.25–6 above), which are scarcely co-ordinated, let alone controlled by the state.

Neo-pluralists do not, however, share the traditional pluralist view that political influence in democracies is fairly widely distributed and that, therefore, no single group in society is dominant. They believe that certain groups have a systematic advantage over others, stemming from their superior resources, and their key position in modern capitalist society. Business groups are identified as dominant interests by a number of neo-pluralist writers. Lindblom (1977) argues that business organisations are not simply powerful pressure groups, well-organised, favourably endowed with economic resources and possessing exclusive political contacts. Rather, business has a privileged position in view of its economic and political role in market democracies. Government appreciates that business is the provider of economic resources on which its own existence depends. It recognises the political impact of business decisions, such as investment plans for example. Government therefore takes into account the business viewpoint when making decisions, often without having to consult business organisations directly. In addition, business interests are able to exert a powerful influence on the political agenda by shaping public preferences, inhibiting the promotion of issues which are damaging to business interests.

Other neo-pluralists, such as Dahl (1982) and Galbraith (1974), have also argued that the power of business is formidable in capitalist societies. Dahl, for example, notes the wider political impact of business decisions and that 'many important decisions on public matters are neither on the public agenda nor decided by a democratic process' (Dahl, 1982, p.202). Galbraith outlines the various ways in which large business corporations and government are interdependent, and demonstrates their common interests in promoting a stable, technologically advanced economy. According to Galbraith, government identifies with the goals of business, while at the same time business corporations actively seek to shape wider social attitudes. The net effect is that public policy will tend to reflect business values. Moreover, Galbraith argues that business values are, in turn, determined by those with specialist expertise employed by the business corporations. These experts, collectively known as the technostructure, therefore not only have a key role in shaping the goals of business organisations, but also exert a powerful influence over social attitudes and public policy.

Business organisations are not alone in possessing technical knowledge and expertise. Indeed, neo-pluralists recognise that some non-business groups may have considerable power in view of their technical expertise (Lindblom, 1977, p.176). Professions such as law and medicine, for example, have enjoyed considerable freedom within their sphere of competence, while their professional associations have exerted a great deal of influence over policy in the past. However, neo-pluralists tend to argue that the professions have a much more limited range of influence than business organisations. Moreover, as we shall see later in this chapter, the power of professional groups, particularly those representing the public sector professions, has been challenged in recent years.

In summary, neo-pluralism is a more pessimistic perspective than the traditional pluralist standpoint. Although neo-pluralists accept the basic principles of traditional pluralism (indeed, many are former pluralists who have revised their ideas), they doubt that these are being upheld in practice. Compared with the pluralist standpoint, neo-pluralists are less optimistic about the democratic contribution of pressure groups. In particular they are less likely to accept that the balance of power between pressure groups mirrors the strength of support for them in society. They are also less likely to see pressure groups as autonomous, independent of government manipulation, and accept that the inequalities between groups are systematic and often damaging to democracy.

Even so, few neo-pluralists have lost faith entirely in modern democracy. This is reflected by their support for improvements in decision-making to move democracies some way towards satisfying pluralist principles. They suggest a number of constitutional changes to enhance participation and disperse power, including decentralisation of decision-making, freedom of information and more open forms of decision-making. Some have argued for even more radical steps, such as economic democracy, to counter the power of business, enabling workers to participate more fully in decisions affecting them (see Dahl, 1982). Such reforms clearly have implications for the role of pressure groups, their relationship with political institutions and their potential influence over policy. In the final chapter we shall return to consider the potential impact of some of these reforms in the British context.

Corporatism

There is much confusion and disagreement over the meaning of corporatism (Williamson, 1989), but, as with pluralism, there are a number of common themes amongst those adopting this perspective (see Cawson, 1982, 1985; Pahl and Winkler, 1974; Schmitter and Lehmbruch, 1979).

Corporatists emphasise the role of government in shaping systems of representation. Thus the process through which pressure groups put their views to government does not emerge by default but is devised by the state with clear objectives in mind (see Exhibit 3.3). The system of representation draws pressure groups into a close and stable relationship with government. The emphasis is on mutual co-operation; groups bargain and negotiate with government agencies while broadly agreeing on policy objectives. Groups are not compelled to enter into such a relationship with government. They do so voluntarily because they believe that high-level political contacts are valuable and enable them to exert influence over policy.

In return for access to key decision-makers, groups co-operate with government. They may provide information and advice, help formulate policy or assist with the implementation and monitoring of policies. Pressure groups may have to convince their own members and supporters of the benefits of government policy and may even have to discipline and regulate members in order to achieve the objectives set out by government.

Exhibit 3.3 **The corporatist perspective**

1   The interaction of pressure groups with the political system is strongly influenced by government.

2   Pressure groups exert influence mainly through close and stable relationships with key decision-makers in government agencies.

3   In return for access to decision-makers, pressure groups co-operate with government to a high degree, even to the extent of disciplining and regulating their own members.

4   There is only one group representing each specific function or interest in society. Each group therefore has a monopoly of representation and there is no competition between pressure groups for members.

5   Pressure groups are dominated by their leaders. The rank-and-file influence over decision-making is indirect and limited by the need to maintain a close, stable relationship with government.

6   Pressure groups may undertake government functions or be closely associated with special purpose 'quasi-governmental agencies' that perform these functions.

In the ideal corporatist scenario there is only one recognised pressure group for each specific function or interest in society: for example, one group representing miners, one for teachers, one for firms manufacturing chemicals, one for banks, and so on. Groups therefore have a monopoly of representation within their area and there is no competition between rival groups for members. Broad interests such as labour and business are represented by peak organisations to which more specialised groups will be affiliated. For example, individual trade unions representing workers in specific industries will be affiliated to a broad organisation covering the entire trade union movement.

Corporatist writers view pressure groups not only as a means of representation but also as a means of regulation, ensuring, for example, that members comply with policies agreed by their leaders and the government. Leaders of groups therefore cannot be automatically responsive to the views of rank-and-file members. This is not to say that the members' views can be disregarded. Indeed, strong feelings at the grassroots level will give group leaders considerable bargaining power in their dealings with government and significant concessions may be won as a result. But pressure-group leaders also know that ultimately they must cooperate with government if they are to retain their privileged position in the policy process. They will therefore seek to suppress demands from the rank-and-file which jeopardise a close, stable relationship with government.

Finally, a further feature of corporatism is the delegation of certain government functions to groups. Groups may be given a specific task to perform, such as regulating activities with which they are closely associated. Alternatively, the government may create quasi-government agencies to perform such functions and allow groups to be represented on these bodies.

Corporatists appreciate that the kind of decision-making process they describe is an ideal type, and that their model is more relevant to some countries than others. Countries such as Austria, the Netherlands, Norway and Sweden show strong features of corporatism. The adoption of corporatist decision-making appears to be related to the nature of democracy in these countries (Lijphart and Crepaz, 1991). Consensus democracies – those which have features such as proportional representation, coalition governments and federal decision-making structures – are more likely to have corporatist features. In addition, countries which have been governed predominantly by parties of the 'centre-left' are also more likely to exhibit corporatism.

The UK has never been seriously regarded as a corporatist state. However, it has in the past adopted a fairly weak form of corporatism, particularly in the area of economic policy-making (Grant, 1985). This approach, known as 'tripartism', brought together government, business and trade unions to discuss economic and industrial policies from the 1960s onwards. In addition to tripartism there have been other close relationships between groups and government which could be described as mildly corporatist. For example, the relationships between the BMA and the Department of Health, the NFU and the Ministry of Agriculture and the defence equipment manufacturers and the Ministry of Defence. These 'bipartite' relationships exhibit many of the features described by the corporatists and have had a great deal of impact on policy-making in these specific areas. In addition, there has been a growth in quasi-governmental institutions during the post-war period (Barker, 1982; Birkinshaw et al., 1990). At their peak during the late 1970s, there were over 2,000 of these bodies.

Few corporatists believe that the arrangements they describe represent an unambiguously good way of making decisions, but some have identified a number of reasons why corporatist forms of decision-making may be viewed in a positive light (see Grant, 1985). They believe that corporatism can produce stability and reduce conflict. As neither government nor pressure groups wish to undermine their close and stable relationship there is a strong pressure to maintain consensus and to search for mutually acceptable policy solutions. By creating stable conditions corporatist arrangements can facilitate planning of key economic and social functions, without the government assuming direct control. Such arrangements may be used to improve efficiency and effectiveness in specific areas. Grant's study (1985) of the Milk Marketing Board illustrates how corporatist-style decision-making stabilised the market for this important commodity. Another feature of corporatism, self-regulation, can also yield benefits, particularly where organised groups seek to incorporate wider social values when governing the conduct of their own members (Streeck and Schmitter, 1985). Finally, it is maintained that corporatism can help produce solutions to the complex problems faced by modern societies. Highly specialised areas of policy-making are in effect delegated to experts (in pressure groups, in government or in quasi-government agencies) who have the knowledge and competence to formulate an appropriate response.

However, even those who appreciate the value of this perspective identify a number of problems with corporatism in practice (Birkinshaw et al., 1990). Corporatist arrangements tend to lack accountability and public supervision is often inadequate. The public and their representatives may be excluded from decisions which affect their welfare. Indeed, they may be unaware that such decisions are even being made. Some corporatists, such as Cawson (1982), for example, are explicit about the threat of authoritarianism which could develop from corporatist decision-making processes, and warn of the dangers of delegating power to unelected and largely unaccountable bodies. Other criticisms come from the New Right which sees corporatist arrangements as impeding the ability of democratically elected governments to function properly. Corporatist institutions are seen as an outgrowth of a sprawling state bureaucracy which chokes the market and impedes, rather than enhances, economic efficiency.

Finally, corporatism has been criticised on theoretical grounds. Some believe that it fails to explain adequately the relationship between government and groups (Bull, 1992; Cox, 1988). In particular, critics argue that corporatists do not explain adequately why groups wish to surrender their independence by becoming closely associated with government. It is also argued that corporatists fail to explain why corporatist-style decision-making emerges in certain policy areas and not others.

In summary, the corporatist perspective identifies a number of important features of the policy process, in particular the close and stable relationship between some pressure groups and government, and the delegation of important decisions to private organisations and quasi-government bodies. Corporatists have encouraged further investigations into these relationships and institutions, which, in turn, have increased our knowledge about the modern state. However, corporatists are not alone in identifying such features. As we have seen, neo-pluralists also focus on privileged access and the role of technical experts in the policy process. The corporatist perspective is also fairly limited in that it cannot adequately explain developments in areas where corporatism is weak or non-existent. It is also unable to comment with any certainty about how and why corporatist styles of decision-making have developed. Finally, at least in the British context, corporatism suffers from a rather bad image in view of its association with ineffective economic policies of the 1960s and 1970s. It is also believed to be in decline in other countries (Bull, 1992). However, as we shall see in later chapters, some corporatist institutions and decision-making processes have survived the assault of hostile governments.

The New Right

As Gamble (1988) correctly points out, the New Right is not a unified movement or a coherent doctrine. It is, in fact, an amalgam of ideas drawn from different political traditions. However, in spite of this, the principles of the New Right have been highly influential over the last two decades, particularly in Britain.

The New Right is essentially a fusion of authoritarian conservative principles and free-market liberalism (Gamble, 1988; Green 1987; D. S. King 1987). Authoritarian conservatives favour strong government, social order and discipline, clear standards of public morality, and have a strong commitment to the nation-state and to national sovereignty. On the other hand, free-market liberals call for a reduced role for the state, particularly in economic matters, a greater role for market forces, and more freedom for the individual.

There are obvious tensions between these two sets of principles. In particular, the hierarchical and disciplined conservative society contrasts starkly with the open, free and competitive liberal ideal. Such tensions have been resolved to some extent in practice by the adoption of a dual strategy. For example, Gamble notes that the Thatcher government took the view that the state should be strong, while the economy should be free. In practice, however, it is not easy to separate state and economy, and the internal conflict between New Right principles has often been evident. Although most writers believe that in such situations liberalism has triumphed over conservatism, there are many cases where the opposite has been the case. Indeed, according to Brittan (1988), both the Reagan and Thatcher governments exhibited strong conservative authoritarian tendencies, such as a desire to return to 'traditional' values and a hawkish attitude to defence and foreign affairs.

Despite these tensions within the New Right, there appears to be a fairly consistent view of pressure groups (Exhibit 3.4). Both authoritarian conservatives and free-market liberals take a rather hostile view of pressure groups and their relationship with the state. They see democratically elected government as the legitimate source of authority, and view pressure groups as self-interested organisations undermining this (Pirie, 1988). They argue that relatively small groups with narrow self-interests are able to shape decisions in their favour, against the interests of the wider community.

Exhibit 3.4 **The New Right perspective**

1 Pressure groups are self-interested organisations.

2 Pressure groups are not representative of the public interest and seek to distort the views of the public.

3 Important sections of society (consumers, taxpayers) are not adequately represented by the pressure-group system. Other interests (professions, industries seeking special subsidies from the state, labour) are too well-organised and exert too much influence.

4 Pressure groups prevent democratically elected governments from taking a clear and unbiased view of the public interest.

5 The close, stable relationships which exist between pres-

sure groups and government weaken government and
undermine its authority.

6 Pressure groups are able to block vital economic and
   political changes which are essential for the long-term
   future of the economy and for the survival of a free
   society.

The New Right view pressure groups as economic units, deliv-
ering specific material benefits to their members. People who join
pressure groups do so for rational economic, and largely selfish,
reasons. Prospective members weigh up the benefits of membership against the costs, and if the balance is favourable they will
join. By adopting an economic explanation of the link between
individual preferences and group membership, the New Right
denies that pressure groups are legitimate representative institutions. It points out that certain sections of society are under-represented by pressure groups while others are over-represented,
and argues that these differences occur not because one section of
society has a strong case or a more legitimate interest than
another, but because the balance of costs and benefits favours the
formation of some groups while impeding the formation of others.

Olson's (1965) analysis of collective action provides the basis
for this viewpoint. He argues that one cannot take the formation
of groups for granted because those with a common interest may
not necessarily form a group if the personal costs of doing so are
higher than the possible benefits. He notes that many of the
benefits of pressure group activity are 'non-excludable', that is,
non-members can benefit from pressure group lobbying without
having to join a group, pay a subscription or become actively
involved in campaigning. For example, if a teachers' union successfully lobbies for improved pay and conditions of work, the
benefits of its campaign will accrue to members and non-members alike.

According to Olson some groups get around this problem by
offering special benefits, called 'selective incentives', which can

only be enjoyed by members. For example, the benefits of the Automobile Association's roadside breakdown service, unlike the organisation's lobbying activities, yields benefits only to members. Olson also notes that groups can use other means, such as intimidation or discrimination, to force people into becoming members.

In Olson's view, the existence of groups, and their size and effectiveness as lobbying organisations, depends more on their ability to offer exclusive benefits to potential members (or alternatively their ability to intimidate them into joining) than upon the underlying support for the group in society. Some interests will therefore be well-organised, such as professional associations, trade unions and producer groups, because they offer clear incentives to join. Other important interests, such as consumers and taxpayers, which cannot offer such incentives, will not emerge, or will be smaller and weaker than their potential membership and underlying support would imply.

Olson's analysis directly contradicts the standard pluralist view discussed earlier. It will be recalled that pluralists place great faith in the freedom of groups to form. They believe generally that the balance of pressure between groups reflects the strength of the underlying interests in society. Not surprisingly they have reacted with some hostility to Olson's thesis.

There are three main criticisms of Olson's approach. First, there is evidence that groups do form in spite of economic disincentives. Consumer groups (such as the Consumers' Association and the Campaign for Real Ale) have been created, as have groups representing taxpayers (for example, campaigns against specific taxes such as the Anti-Poll Tax Federation, and the campaign against the imposition of VAT on fuel). Secondly, doubt has been cast on the role of selective incentives as an inducement to join groups. Indeed, researchers have found that members of pressure groups often value political representation as highly, if not more highly, than other services provided for members only (Grant and Marsh, 1977; P. R. Jones, 1981). In addition, it appears that members may still join even when relative costs exceed perceived benefits (R. King, 1985).

Olson's thesis has also been criticised for failing to take into account subjective views of the benefits of membership. Individuals may be prepared to join groups if they perceive them as being a viable and effective vehicle for representing interests which they share with others (Dunleavy, 1988). Moreover, the participation of individuals within groups may generate considerable benefits in addition to material advantages resulting from effective lobbying. The membership of groups often has an expressive function. For example, people tend to join the peace movement or environmental groups because these organisations express their values rather than secure material benefits for them (Cotgrove, 1982; Parkin, 1968). Furthermore, individuals may derive a range of intangible benefits from activity within the groups. They may get satisfaction from being part of a specific community of like-minded people. They may develop friendships and contacts, or may build self-esteem as a result of participating in the organisation.

The main problem with Olson's thesis is that it is based on a rather narrow view of individual motivation. As the peace and environment movements illustrate, people can be motivated by non-material benefits and are prepared to stand up and be counted. Olson's thesis cannot cope with such behaviour, because it fails to recognise that participation in pressure groups often has a subjective value to their members.

Olson's thesis is a main pillar of the New Right's attack on pressure groups, but it is not the only one. Their perspective is also based on the belief that pressure groups' participation in decision-making is damaging both to the authority of government and to the long-term welfare of the country. It is argued that government in the post-war period took on too many responsibilities, and became overloaded. As a result, it became unable to manage any single task effectively, giving rise to political problems. At the same time, too much government intervention resulted in the economy becoming stagnated, so creating further political problems (Birch, 1984).

Pressure groups, and in particular the trade unions, were blamed for this trend (Brittan, 1975). Trade unions were criticised as self-interested organisations whose sole concern was to generate higher material benefits for their members. They were held responsible for poor national economic performance, in particular the high inflation and economic stagnation of the 1970s. At the same time, it was argued that rising public expectations, expressed by pressure groups and through the ballot box, prompted further government intervention. This is turn led to higher public expenditure, identified as a factor in the growth of inflation and economic stagnation.

The New Right analysis goes beyond accusing groups of wrecking the economy. Its adherents believe that by intervening in economic and social affairs, the government had come to rely too much on pressure groups. For example, a policy on incomes required the co-operation of the trade unions and employers. Welfare policies required the co-operation of doctors and nurses. Government was also too dependent on groups for advice and often heavily influenced by producer, professional and trade union views. In short, the dependence of government on pressure groups weakened its authority and prevented it from governing effectively in the public interest. The political crises of the 1970s in Britain, in particular the fall of the Heath government in 1974 and the 'winter of discontent' in 1978/9 are held up as examples of the excesses of pressure-group power, and in particular trade union power. These crises are also seen by the New Right as an indictment of corporatist decision-making.

Pressure groups are perceived not only as part of the problem; they are seen as a major obstacle to potential solutions. The entrenchment of pressure groups within the governing process is held responsible for restricting efforts to solve Britain's economic and political problems. Policies such as abolishing restrictive labour practices, dramatically cutting public expenditure, deregulating labour markets, rolling back the welfare state and so on were regarded by politicians as impossible, not simply because they were unpopular with the public but because powerful pressure groups opposed them. Indeed, Olson (1982) has suggested that stable democratic societies like Britain are more likely to stagnate economically because they encourage the formation of special interest groups which are effective in preventing the search for economic solutions.

The difficulties facing Britain as a result of the entrenchment of groups within the political system has been noted by others writing from a neo-pluralist standpoint (Beer, 1982; Birch, 1984). The phenomenon of government overload and loss of political authority has also been pursued by some neo-Marxists (see below). Nevertheless, it is the New Right analysis which has had the most impact, following the election of governments in a number of countries, including Britain, which were prepared to adopt to some extent its prescription for change.

The Thatcher government

It has been pointed out that the Thatcher government was not as ideologically motivated in practice as some claim (Kavanagh, 1990; Young, 1991). Indeed, Margaret Thatcher herself is regarded above all as a pragmatist and a practical politician, rather than an ideologist. This was apparent from the way in which the Thatcherite programme evolved rather than followed a pre-ordained course. However, the Thatcher government differed from its post-war predecessors in the way it adhered to a partic- ular vision which drew heavily on New Right principles. It was, in relative terms, an ideological government (Gilmour, 1993).

The policies which emerged – public expenditure restraint, pri- vatisation, reforming the welfare state and so on – brought the Thatcher government into open conflict with a range of pressure groups, many of which had previously enjoyed close relationships with government in the past. At the same time, the Thatcher regime adopted a style of government which in many respects reflected the overt hostility towards pressure groups embodied in the New Right perspective.

The rhetoric of the Thatcher government was certainly anti- group, with the trade unions attracting particular contempt (Tebbit, 1988). Others which had been party to the 'corporatist' era, such as the Confederation of British Industry (CBI), were also snubbed by ministers. But beyond the criticism of particular groups, ministers appeared critical of the role of pressure groups in general. Moreover, their comments were not confined to hard-line Thatcherites. In a speech in 1986 Douglas Hurd publicly criticised pressure groups for strangling the political process, preventing politicians from making decisions in the public interest (*Daily Telegraph*, 20 September 1986).

This modern conservative view of pressure groups departs quite sharply from the more traditional Tory view of democracy as expressed, for example, by Lord Gilmour (1983) and Lord Pym (1984), who emphasised the importance of government by consent, which means involving people and their representatives in the policy process and reaching agreement wherever possible. The Tory view of democracy recognises the importance of pressure groups both as a vehicle of representation and as a buffer between the government and the governed. From this standpoint, pressure groups are regarded as legitimate organisations within the political system whose views should be taken into account in the governing process.

Some believe that the departure of Margaret Thatcher in 1990 has signalled a movement back towards this more traditional Tory view of democracy in recent years. Indeed, her immediate successor, John Major, was perceived to have departed from the Thatcherite style of government and appeared more willing to recognise the legitimacy of pressure groups. However, in later chapters we shall be able to judge more carefully the impact of recent conservative governments upon pressure-group politics, and any differences between the Thatcher and post-Thatcher period.

The Marxist perspective

Finally, one should not ignore the Marxist perspective. Marxists tend not to focus on pressure groups as such, being primarily concerned with analysing underlying social processes such as capital accumulation and conflict between social classes based on division between capital and labour. Furthermore, most regard the institution of democracy in capitalist societies as a sham, obscuring the true nature of power in society, though some are less dismissive of pressure-group activity than others.

Marxists are aware of pressure groups representing capitalist interests, but do not regard them as the most important channel through which political power is exercised. It is the capitalists' control of the means of production and their social and economic power which is seen as paramount. Yet pressure groups are not unimportant as a means of business representation. For example, others have noted that, in the financial sector, formal representative structures – including the formation of pressure groups – have become more rather then less important in recent years (Moran 1981).

Marxists are cynical about the ability of other pressure groups to challenge capitalist interests. There is considerable doubt, for example, about the ability of trade unions to perform this role (Clarke and Clements, 1977). Nevertheless, some recognise that trade unions can be a useful vehicle for channelling political demands and bringing about social changes. According to Miliband (1992, p.98), 'trade unions for all the limitations and constraints on their power, are pressure groups which governments have to reckon with'. He also identifies other groups that can have an impact, including the women's movement, immigrant groups and the peace movement. Miliband does differ from most Marxists in that he accepts that pluralist-style pressure politics can take place even within the constraints of a capitalist system. Others, however, recognising that the two major classes are divided on a number of important issues, have conceded that separate groups acting in their own specific interests are significant (Habermas, 1976; O'Connor, 1973; Poulantzas, 1975)

Moreover, there has been a great deal of debate in recent years concerning the role of pressure groups and broader social movements. Some believe that the activities of those groups which have grown dramatically in recent years – such as the environmental lobby – represent part of a new paradigm of politics which has the potential to release forces enabling the transformation of capitalist society (Habermas, 1981; Laclau and Mouffe, 1987; Offe, 1985).

Mainstream Marxists tend to emphasise structural power, rather than institutional or pressure-group power. They argue that capitalism has survived because it gave concessions to working-class groups, such as the establishment of the welfare state. At the same time the capitalists have been able to maintain an 'ideological hegemony' (Gramsci, 1971): they have set the parameters of political debate through their ability to shape social values. Pressure groups representing working-class interests are therefore operating in a political environment dominated by capitalist interests.

Offe (1984), O'Connor (1973) and Habermas (1976) have developed theories of crisis which describe scenarios similar to those envisaged by the New Right, discussed earlier. According to the Marxist approach, the state cannot indefinitely go on giving concessions to the working class while supporting capitalist interests and values. The result is conflict within the state itself, as its authority is increasingly challenged by sectional groups.

Although the Marxist approach does not focus strongly on pressure groups, it is nevertheless useful in helping us to understand the political environment within which groups operate. Like the New Right perspective, it also sheds light on the underlying tensions which can disrupt relations between groups, and their relationship with government. Like the neo-pluralist approach, it reminds of the underlying power of business in market democracies and warns that by focusing purely on business representative bodies one may fail to appreciate fully the nature of this power.

Conclusions

The broad perspectives discussed in this chapter are useful in helping us to place the role of pressure groups in a broader context. With the exception of Marxism, each perspective shares a belief that pressure groups are highly significant institutions in modern democracies. They differ, however, in their assessment of groups' involvement with the political system, and of the distribution of power both between different groups and between groups and government. Each perspective also makes a particular judge-ment about the contribution of each group to a democratic system of government. As we have seen, pluralists and some corporatists take a rather favourable view of the role of groups, while corpo-ratists and neo-pluralists adopt a less sanguine position, with the New Right having an explicitly hostile stance.

This discussion sheds light on the wider debate about the role of pressure groups in democratic states, and in Britain in partic-ular. Each perspective also provides support for those who par-ticipate in this debate, whether they are opponents or supporters of pressure-group politics. Political actors draw on these perspec-tives when justifying, or denying, a role for groups. Ultimately, these perspectives have an impact on the governing process itself. On the one hand, they may be used to justify changes to politi-cal structures, affecting the way in which pressure groups func-tion. Or they may inform attitudes towards groups, among decision-makers or the public, thereby having an impact upon the political environment within which pressure groups operate.

4

Organisation, co-operation and resources

One should not underestimate the importance of the organisational structure of a pressure group, the nature of its decision-
making processes, the way it relates to other groups and the
resources at its disposal. All of these can have a significant impact
on its strategies and tactics, its credibility in the eyes of policy-
makers and, ultimately, its influence over policy. Moreover, as the
previous chapter indicated, there is much disagreement over the
role of pressure groups in a democracy. By exploring the internal
features of groups, in particular their decision-making processes,
we may be able to judge more accurately their contribution to the
democratic process.

The chapter is divided into three sections. First, we concentrate on the organisational features of pressure groups. Second,
we explore the relationships between pressure groups that form
coalitions or lobbies. Finally, in this chapter we examine the different kinds of resources which pressure groups have at their
disposal.

Organisation

If a pressure group is to make the most of its resources and exert
maximum influence over policy it must be well-organised. In particular, it needs good leadership and an effective decision-making
process. In addition, a pressure group must also be able to satisfy
to some extent the expectations of its members. Failure to do this

may lead to a loss of support, undermining the group and possibly advantaging its rivals.

Leadership

Good leadership is essential if a pressure group is to make maximum use of its resources. Those who lead pressure groups require a number of skills and traits. They must be effective negotiators; they must be willing to work with other pressure groups towards common goals when necessary; they must have charisma and a persuasive personality when dealing with the media and with politicians.

Leadership involves dealing with important internal matters as well as external agencies. Sound financial management and efficient administration are important considerations; as with any other organisation, the books have to balance. But the main task of the leadership is political management. Pressure groups often contain a wide range of views and it is the task of the leadership not simply to respond to these views when there is agreement among members but to manage conflict when there is disagreement.

There are many sources of conflict within pressure groups, but the main ones are economic, geographic and ideological. Economic conflicts arise either from the different market conditions faced by members or because they undertake different economic or occupational roles. Taking the National Farmers' Union (NFU) as an example, we find significant differences of opinion between arable farmers and those who farm livestock. In addition, farmers running large concerns often see things differently to small operators. Such differences have led to conflict within the NFU (Charlesworth et al., 1990; Self and Storing, 1962). Similarly, the British Medical Association's (BMA) membership is divided on economic and occupational lines. The most important division is that between the general practitioners (GPs) and the hospital consultants (Honigsbaum, 1979). There have also been significant conflicts between junior and senior doctors.

A second source of conflict is produced by geographical factors. These are sometimes underpinned by economic and occupational differences. Welsh farmers, for example, have developed a different perspective on agricultural issues, partly because of Welsh nationalism and partly because they face different economic conditions from those in England. In 1955 tensions between Welsh farmers and their fellow members in the NFU led to the formation of a breakaway Welsh Farmers' Union. Another example of such a split was that between the Nottinghamshire miners and the National Union of Mineworkers during the strikes of 1926 and 1984/5. Nottinghamshire miners have proved to be less militant than those in other areas, for a variety of reasons. An undoubtedly important factor has been that the Nottinghamshire coalfields are among the richest in the country. As a result, miners working in this area have tended to have a different perspective from those working in poorer and declining coalfields (Adeney and Lloyd, 1987).

A third source of conflict within pressure groups arises from ideological factors. Even where there are shared interests, conflict can arise over specific aims and tactics. For example, throughout its history the Royal Society for the Prevention of Cruelty to Animals (RSPCA) has been divided on the issue of hunting, particularly that of fox hunting. There is also considerable disagreement between RSPCA members on how best to campaign on animal welfare issues: the conservatives preferring quiet deliberation with MPs and government departments, the radicals favouring media campaigns and direct action (Garner 1991; Thomas 1983).

Similar conflicts have arisen in other cause groups, such as anti-abortion and nuclear disarmament groups (Byrne, 1988; Marsh and Chambers, 1981). They are also found in groups representing economic or occupational interests. Grant and Marsh (1977), in their study of the CBI, identified conflict between the progressive and traditionalist elements in British business. This ideological division operated alongside other economic differences – such as those between large and small businesses.

Disputes, whether they are based on economic, geographical or ideological differences, are common. They are found particularly in mass membership groups, although some large groups are relatively free of conflict. The Automobile Association (AA), for example, has a huge membership, but little internal conflict. This is partly due to the passivity of the members (the vast majority do not participate in decision-making) and the absence of any obvious source of division between them.

Conflict within pressure groups could be seen as a sign of a healthy democracy. But from the point of view of the leaders of the group it can be damaging. If a dispute enters the public arena, it can undermine the lobbying efforts of the group. Ministers, civil servants, MPs and the media may begin to doubt its credibility and, in particular, its ability to speak on behalf of members. Ultimately the group could fragment, leading to the creation of splinter groups, as happened in the case of the NFU and the Welsh farmers, and also the BMA which, during the 1970s, faced a loss of members to two rival groups, one representing hospital specialists and another representing junior doctors.

The fragmentation of groups tends to weaken their case. Take the teachers' unions for example. Government has for the most part been able to divide and rule over a weak teaching profession, except on the rare occasion (as with the boycott of testing in 1993 – see Chapter 6) when these organisations have been able to unite. In order to avoid damaging splits, the leadership must therefore be able to manage conflict. They may resolve such conflict by using personal appeal. If this fails they can resort to various internal procedures to minimise open dissent. This happened in the case of the National Trust when faced with a damaging dispute over deer hunting (see Exhibit 4.1).

Exhibit 4.1   **The National Trust and the hunting debate**

Pressure groups sometimes find that they themselves are a focus for pressure-group activity. The National Trust, for example, in recent years has been an important battleground between the pro- and anti-hunting lobby. Those who believe that the National Trust should actively oppose hunting have secured key positions within the organisation in an attempt to introduce a hunting ban on its land. An unknown number of individual members who support this campaign are members of anti-hunting groups such as the League Against Cruel Sports. Similarly, opponents of this campaign within the National Trust have been associated with pro-hunting groups such as the British Field Sports Society.

The anti-hunting groups appeared to have gained the upper hand when in 1990 National Trust members passed a motion at the Annual General Meeting (AGM) to ban deer hunting on land in Exmoor and the Quantocks. If implemented the ban would have effectively ended hunting in these areas. The National Trust's executive body, the Council, attempted to defer the decision by setting up a special working party to explore the issue in greater depth. The working party subsequently favoured the continuation of hunting on National Trust land. The Council approved the report's conclusions and overruled the decision of the 1990 AGM. Yet this is unlikely to be the end of the matter. Anti-hunting activists within the National Trust will continue with their efforts to shape the organisation's policy on this issue.

Many groups are well aware of the potential damage of internal discord and take this into account in their decision-making processes. The BMA, for example, recognises the potential for conflict between members drawn from different specialisms (or crafts, as they are known). It therefore delegates considerable powers to special sub-committees representing each of the main crafts: general practitioners, consultants, public health doctors and junior doctors (see Exhibit 4.2). Conflicts which do arise between these different interests are resolved through the Executive Committee of the BMA Council, a sort of clearing-house for inter-craft disputes.

Permanent staff and professionalisation
Pressure groups employ permanent staff, though most authors

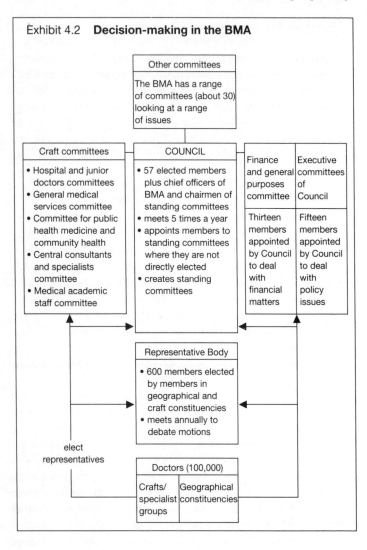

Exhibit 4.2   **Decision-making in the BMA**

Other committees

The BMA has a range of committees (about 30) looking at a range of issues

Craft committees

- Hospital and junior doctors committees
- General medical services committee
- Committee for public health medicine and community health
- Central consultants and specialists committee
- Medical academic staff committee

COUNCIL

- 57 elected members plus chief officers of BMA and chairmen of standing committees
- meets 5 times a year
- appoints members to standing committees where they are not directly elected
- creates standing committees

Finance and general purposes committee

Thirteen members appointed by Council to deal with financial matters

Executive committees of Council

Fifteen members appointed by Council to deal with policy issues

Representative Body

- 600 members elected by members in geographical and craft constituencies
- meets annually to debate motions

elect representatives

Doctors (100,000)

Crafts/ specialist groups | Geographical constituencies

agree that staffing levels are fairly low. In Lowe and Goyder's (1983) study of the environmental lobby, around a fifth of the groups studied had no permanent staff at all, and over half employed fewer than five people. A further survey, of over a hundred pressure groups chosen at random, found that half the groups had fewer than twenty staff (Baggott, 1992).

Even relatively large-scale campaigning groups, such as CND for example, do not employ large numbers of people. CND has only forty full-time staff; Friends of the Earth employs ninety-five people, though only a quarter of these are directly involved in campaigning. Other groups, particularly those providing services to members in addition to lobbying, do employ considerable numbers of people. The NFU employs over 800 staff nationwide, the BMA over 400. The National Society for the Prevention of Cruelty to Children (NSPCC) (1,300 staff) and the Royal Society for the Protection of Birds (RSPB) (over 500 staff) are also large employers, though many of their employees are part-time.

The numbers of pressure-group staff involved directly in policy work may still be small, but they are increasingly professional. Many pressure groups, particularly those with large memberships, employ permanent staff to help formulate policy and to lobby. These people often have experience in management or public relations, or have worked previously for other pressure groups. Indeed, one can detect certain career patterns. Former senior armed services personnel appear to be an important source of senior staff for charities and trade associations. For example, the director of the Engineering Industries Association formerly held the rank of colonel in the British Army, while the chief executive of the RSPCA was a former rear-admiral in the British Navy. Other pressure groups draw their senior staff from the trade union movement. For example, Sheila McKechnie, the director of the Consumers' Association, and David Gee, director of Friends of the Earth, were both formerly employed by trade unions.

One also finds considerable movement between groups. Sheila McKechnie was at the helm of Shelter before joining the Consumers' Association. Tom Burke, the director of the Green Alliance, was with Friends of the Earth. Don Steele, of the Family Heart Association, was formerly the director of Action on

Alcohol Abuse. Des Wilson, the former director of Shelter has been involved at a senior level in a number of pressure groups, including the Child Poverty Action Group, the Campaign for Lead Free Air (CLEAR) and the National Council for Civil Liberties (now known as Liberty).

For some, the ultimate career path is Parliament. Quite a few MPs have prior experience of pressure-group politics. Most are Labour MPs, including Frank Field (Child Poverty Action Group), Harriet Harman (Liberty) and Joan Ruddock (CND). Pressure groups also provide a career move for former MPs. For example, after losing his seat in the 1992 general election, Roger King joined the Society of Motor Manufacturers and Traders (SMMT), while former MP Alf Dubs became the director of the British Refugee Council following his defeat in 1987. Pressure groups also employ ex-ministers and former civil servants, a practice we shall explore further in later chapters.

Full-time officials exert most influence in groups where members cannot elect their own representatives to positions of authority. Many cause groups, as we shall see, do not have representative mechanisms. Indeed, some do not have members as such, but supporters who, not being officially part of the organisation, do not have any right to participate in decision-making.

Even where ultimate authority does lie with elected leaders, permanent staff can make an important contribution to policy-making. According to Lowe and Goyder (1983) although officials made major decisions in only one-fifth of the environmental groups they studied, they had a much larger role in the initiation of policy. In almost 40 per cent of groups, officials were identified as the major source of policy initiatives. Studies of the NFU, CND and the CBI also suggest that staff have a significant role in policy-making in the presence of democratic mechanisms. In the NFU, for example, electoral mechanisms give ultimate power to members' representatives, but they are influenced by permanent officials (Holbeche, 1986). Similarly, Byrne (1988) found that in CND although the important decisions are made by a network of elected representatives, officials are quite influential. Grant and Marsh (1977), in their study of the CBI, discovered that staff could be influential, but did not have the capacity to dominate elected members.

Specialisation and expertise

Pressure groups which have a wide range of interests, those which deal with highly complex issues, or which have a large and diverse membership, tend to devolve decision-making to special committees within the organisation. Some committees focus on strategic issues, while others monitor specific functions such as finance or fundraising, or examine particular issues of concern. Some committees are advisory, while others undertake an executive function. The number of committees can vary considerably. The CBI, for example, has almost forty, the BMA has around thirty, while the RSPCA, in contrast, has only nine committees, and CND has eight. In some organisations, committees have considerable autonomy, as in the case of the BMA, mentioned earlier. In others their freedom is more constrained. In the RSPCA, for example, committees can only make recommendations to the Council, a body elected by the membership.

Committee systems can enhance the decision-making process. They are often the only practical way of making decisions. But there is a concern that committees undermine democracy and accountability in pressure groups. For, apart from those which are directly elected, committees are insulated to some extent from members' views and opinions. Indeed, in some cases, they are used by the leadership to suppress demands from the rank-and-file members.

Democracy and accountability

The ability of leaders to withstand pressure from their own members is limited mainly by the existence of democratic mechanisms, such as elections. However, as we have already noted, some groups do not have members as such and therefore have no need for these mechanisms. In such cases, the members of the ruling body are either self-appointed, nominated by a board of trustees or by other organisations. Help the Aged, for example, a charity which campaigns on behalf of the elderly, does not have a membership. Most decisions are taken by a small committee of senior permanent staff, supervised by a Board of Trustees. There is some local participation in the form of local fundraising committees, though participants do not have formal voting rights within the organisation. Help the Aged also has a list of its regular supporters, which includes many large companies, but these organisations also lack voting rights.

In groups with small memberships it is possible to allow individual members to participate directly in decision-making. Yet, in practice, small groups tend to delegate decision-making to an executive committee, while perhaps consulting the wider membership. Take, for example, the Campaign Against Drinking and Driving (CADD), which has around 500 members. Here policy-making is in the hands of a board of directors, which is appointed not elected. However, the board actively encourages members to raise policy issues and submit ideas for them to discuss. Moreover, all major initiatives, whether raised by the board or by individual members, are subject to a vote by the entire membership.

Groups with large memberships usually practise a form of representative democracy. In most cases there are at least two main decision-making bodies containing representatives of the membership. The first body (usually called the council or governing body), tends to be the larger, and its function is essentially to approve decisions proposed by the second, smaller body (usually called the executive committee), which oversees the implementation of policy and the management of the organisation. This is not a description of any particular group, but of a model which pressure groups adapt in various ways to suit their own particular requirements. There is considerable variation in the constitution of council/governing body and executive committee, and in their relative powers. Moreover, in the larger groups executive powers are often further delegated to a system of specialised standing committees, as we mentioned earlier.

In large-membership groups, members serving on the main policy-making committees are usually elected. In some cases, election systems can be quite elaborate. Take the BMA for example (see Exhibit 4.2). The 600-member Representative Body, the 'parliament' of the BMA, is elected through two types of constituency. Half are elected in geographical divisions. The rest are elected by the members of each craft or specialism (general practitioners, junior hospital doctors, senior hospital doctors and so on). The Representative Body formally decides policy, but it is too large and meets too infrequently (once a year) to manage the BMA's affairs directly. The management function is undertaken by the Council (which meets five times a year) and by other specialist committees. The majority of the Council are elected by the membership in various geographical and craft categories. Direct elections are also held for the membership of specialist standing committees, though some committee members are also ex-officio and some are appointed by the Council or the Representative Body.

Not all large-membership groups have such highly developed representative systems. Many groups, such as CND for example, simply have an annual conference or annual general meeting (AGM) where resolutions can be passed by delegates. Many groups also elect senior officers and executive committee members at their AGM. However, AGM attendances are usually quite low. In order to safeguard against the domination of a small group of members, some pressure groups – including the RSPB, RSPCA and MIND, for example – now hold postal ballots (see Exhibit 4.3).

Some pressure groups appoint delegates to their decision-making bodies. This is common practice among federal groups such as Age Concern, the TUC and the CBI, where the membership is composed to some extent of other organisations. In the case of Age Concern, member organisations (which include the TUC, the BMA and Help the Aged) are allowed to nominate delegates to the main decision-making bodies.

The appointment of delegates is not, however, confined to federal groups. Pressure groups which have local branches often allow the nomination of branch delegates to national decision-making bodies: examples include CND and NSPCC. This is seen as a cheaper alternative to holding elections. Delegation may be seen as undemocratic, but this is not always the case. Indeed,

delegates can be effective in protecting the interests of important
sections of a group's membership. Moreover, locally-nominated
delegates are often more in touch with the feelings of grassroots
membership than nationally-elected representatives.

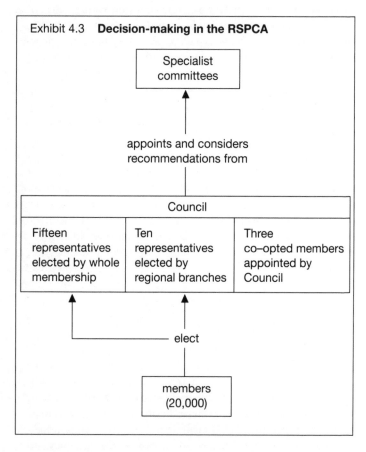

Exhibit 4.3   **Decision-making in the RSPCA**

Specialist
committees

appoints and considers
recommendations from

Council

Fifteen representatives elected by whole membership	Ten representatives elected by regional branches	Three co-opted members appointed by Council

elect

members
(20,000)

It should also be noted that elections do not guarantee democracy or accountability. Indeed, in some groups participation in
elections is restricted to a special class of member. In the Royal
Automobile Club (RAC), for example, the vote is confined to full

members, all male, who constitute only 0.3 per cent of the total membership (Fogarty, 1990). Only 2 per cent of the Consumers' Association membership can vote in elections, and although it is fairly easy for an ordinary member to acquire voting rights (a small registration fee has to be paid), few choose to do so.

Even when there are no formal restrictions on voting, participation is often low. For example, only 0.5 per cent of RSPB members take part in elections to the governing body (Fogarty, 1990) while BMA Council elections rarely achieve a turn-out over 40 per cent, and can be as low as 20 per cent. Ballots on specific issues, however, often attract a larger turn-out, particularly where the issue is contentious. For example, in 1989 a ballot of the BMA's general practitioner members on changes to their contracts achieved a turn-out of 82 per cent.

Apart from elections there are other ways in which members can exert influence. The fear of losing members, for example, can reduce the freedom of movement of leaders. One recalls that the at times aggressive attitude of the CBI towards the first Thatcher government led to a number of resignations amongst its members which produced a more cautious approach from the leadership.

Resignation from a group (or 'exit' in the terminology of Hirschman, 1970) can be a useful device for registering dissatisfaction with the performance of any organisation. However, it should be noted that when members leave an organisation their preferences can no longer be registered (through elections and so on), unless of course they seek to rejoin in future. Furthermore, their absence may lead to the group being dominated by those that remain. As a result the group may move even further out of step with those who have left, making it less likely that they will rejoin. The threat of resignation is perhaps more influential in shaping the group's policies. Empirical evidence also suggests that 'exit' is less important than is commonly believed. For example, Lowe and Goyder's (1983) survey of environmental groups suggested that membership turnover was not a significant factor in the relationship between the rank-and-file and the leadership.

According to Hirschman, another way in which an organisation can be influenced is through 'voice'. The member's voice may be transmitted through ballots on particular issues and through elected representatives or delegates. However, there are other ways in which individual members may raise issues within the group. Direct communication with the leadership is possible even in the larger groups. Some groups (including CND, for example) undertake membership surveys every so often to gauge the opinion of members concerning aims, strategy and tactics. Furthermore, groups which have a strong regional and local organisation (such as the NFU, for example) find that the views of the membership are often channelled upwards through these structures. Meanwhile, among environmental groups direct contact with members by letter and telephone and views transmitted by local branches were shown to be more important channels of communications than elections (Lowe and Goyder, 1983).

It is difficult to generalise about the effectiveness of various channels of communication since their importance often varies according to circumstances. Moreover, they tend to work together rather than in isolation. For example, direct communication with the leadership is less likely to be effective in organisations where the members have no opportunity to elect representatives or appoint delegates.

The importance of the various channels of communication varies between groups. Some have highly developed electoral systems, and one would expect these to play a greater role in these organisations. Membership turnover is also more important in some groups than in others. Where a group derives a large part of its income from membership subscriptions, the leadership may have to be more responsive to rank-and-file views compared with groups which derive their income mainly from other sources – investments, public donations and legacies, government agencies and so on. However, dependence on other sources of income can create further constraints, such as a fear of offending those who provide external funding.

It is therefore difficult to generalise about the nature of pressure-group democracy since the quality is so uneven. In most groups participation in decision-making by members is fairly limited. It could be argued that this undermines the quality of democracy in pressure groups, leading to the creation of self-perpetuating élites. On the other hand, low levels of participation may reflect that the membership is broadly happy with the policies, leadership and management of the organisation. Perhaps the most important thing is not that individuals participate regularly, but that members are able to influence the leadership when they are dissatisfied. In other words they have the potential to communicate their views and influence the policy of the organisation.

An ideal model of organisation?
It should now be clear that pressure groups adopt a variety of organisational structures. Yet there are essentially two basic models. These are the highly centralised organisation, controlled by an élite; and the representative organisation with highly developed channels of communication and accountability.

Which of these is likely to be the more effective? There seems to be some support for the view that the more bureaucratic and centralised a group, the more effective it will be (Gamson, 1975). Lowe and Goyder (1983) have observed that groups run by a small élite are more flexible tactically in dealing with organs of government. In this context, Mike Daube, the former director of the pressure group Action on Smoking and Health (ASH), has argued that 'the most effective pressure groups tend to be those which can be run by a small, highly professional core' (quoted in M. Davies, 1985, p.3). Furthermore, Whiteley and Winyard (1987), in the context of the poverty lobby, note that, in general, 'promotional' lobbying groups tended to be more successful than the more democratic 'representative' groups.

The advantages of a small, centralised élite group are not available to all. Indeed, this model is highly inappropriate to large membership interest groups like trade unions and professional associations. Certainly, a group needs to be flexible and to be able to present a coherent viewpoint. Over-elaborate democratic arrangements may inhibit this. But groups should seek to harness members' support rather than deny them influence. One should not forget that group members are a basic resource for many groups, not only because of the income raised from subscriptions, but also in view of their potential contribution to campaigning at the grassroots level. Furthermore, a group which is representative is likely to have considerable legitimacy from the point of view of those in government (see p.98).

Relations between pressure groups

Pressure groups often form broad coalitions in an attempt to influence public policy. In such a situation the relationship between the groups involved is at least as important as the internal organisation of each group in determining the effectiveness of the coalition.

Coalitions are often formed in an effort to present a united front. In reality the coalition may be divided on specific matters. As division is generally a source of weakness it makes sense to heal or conceal these differences. The establishment of a common front makes it more difficult for the government, the public and opponents to perceive differences and exploit weaknesses. Coalitions also provide the means to co-ordinate the activities of groups. Co-ordination is essential to avoid the duplication of lobbying efforts. A third reason behind the formation of coalitions lies in the advantages which can be reaped from pooling group resources. Groups have different strengths; some possess certain sanctions, others have economic resources. By pooling resources, the coalition may be able to achieve more collectively than any group acting alone.

In the case of the poverty lobby, Whiteley and Winyard (1987) noted that out of the forty-two groups, thirty-eight had undertaken joint action. Even groups exhibiting a high degree of rivalry can agree to submerge their differences on some issues. The AA and the RAC, for example, liaise closely on matters concerning road safety. Some issues produce strange bedfellows indeed. The coalition which successfully opposed the government's Sunday trading legislation in 1986 consisted of shopworkers, the churches and some business organisations (see Exhibit 4.4).

Exhibit 4.4 **The Shops Bill of 1986**

On 15 April 1986, the House of Commons rejected the government's Shops Bill, which sought to deregulate Sunday trading in England and Wales. The Conservative government had a comfortable majority of over 140, yet it was unable to prevent the defeat of the Bill at the second reading stage by fourteen votes.

The opponents of the Bill had limited resources. They comprised the shopworkers' union (USDAW), the churches and other Christian organisations, such as the Evangelical Alliance and the Lord's Day Observance Society. In addition, some businesses supported the campaign, notably the Co-operative Societies and many small businesses. Together they formed the Keep Sunday Special campaign. None of the groups in isolation was particularly well-resourced, but together they were to prove a powerful coalition.

The supporters of reform, on the other hand, included large commercial retailers such as Woolworths, W. H. Smith, Harris Queensway, Mothercare, Habitat and Asda. Some consumer organisations, such as the National Consumer Council, supported deregulation. Those in favour of deregulation also formed a coalition group called Open Shop. But they were unable to harness their substantial individual resources and political contacts as effectively as the Keep Sunday Special campaign. In the early stages of the campaign the supporters of the Shops Bill were slow in putting their case to MPs and the public, believing that they had already won the argument by securing the government's support for their proposals. Given the government's large majority in Parliament the deregulation lobby believed that victory was assured.

The public was largely in favour of relaxing the controls on Sunday trading. Opinion polls showed that around two-thirds supported deregulation. However, public opposition, though smaller in numerical terms, was intense. The government received 40,000 letters opposing the Bill and only 800 supporting it. Retailers in favour of deregulation sought to redress the balance by handing in large petitions signed by their customers.

The Keep Sunday Special campaign successfully exploited potential divisions among Tory MPs. The arguments put forward by the churches and small businesses had considerable impact, persuading seventy-two Conservative MPs to vote against the party whip. At the same time lobbying by USDAW and the Co-operative movement influenced Labour MPs against the Bill.

This impressive victory was always going to be fairly short term, given the balance of public opinion and the political and economic resources of those in favour of Sunday trading. But the government had at least learned that any future attempts at reform would have to be introduced far more cautiously. Total deregulation was unlikely, particularly in view of the reduction of the government's majority in 1992. When, in the following year, the government introduced another Bill to deregulate Sunday trading, it offered MPs a menu of options: unrestricted opening; restricted opening (where only certain shops would be able to open on Sundays); and partial deregulation (limiting large stores to six hours' trading, while allowing smaller shops unrestricted trading). Parliament eventually voted for the third option, which became law in 1994.

Source: Bown (1990); Regan (1988)

Coalitions operate on a number of levels. At a very basic level groups may decide to keep one another informed of their actions. A greater degree of co-operation is signalled by a joint report on an issue of common interest. Groups may also collaborate by sending a joint delegation to Parliament or to see ministers and civil servants. More advanced forms of co-operation involve the formation of joint organisations. The RSPCA and the RSPB, for example, have in recent years established a joint committee to consider the problems raised by the growing international trade in rare birds.

Where there are a number of groups having an interest in a particular issue, they may decide to form an umbrella organisation. For example, Wildlife Link exists to co-ordinate the activities of groups concerned with wildlife and the environment, while the Maternity Alliance is a coalition of groups seeking to defend the rights of mothers and pregnant women in relation to health services, social services and the social security system. Some umbrella organisations are temporary, established to fight against a particular piece of legislation. One example is the Flexible Hours Action Group (FLAG), which campaigned successfully to extend drinking hours in public houses, and which brought together organisations representing the brewers, pub landlords, the tourist industry and drinkers. Another, the Campaign for Quality Television, was established to oppose aspects of the Conservative government's broadcasting legislation. In this context one should not forget the role of federal groups, mentioned previously. These are in a unique position to co-ordinate action by member organisations. They have well-established decision-making machinery to manage potential conflicts and formulate a common front.

Although groups usually realise that they are more effective as part of a coalition than acting alone, it would be wrong to assume that whenever groups have a common aim, they will always undertake joint action. For instance, there are often cases where personality clashes between group leaders inhibit co-operation. Dame Elizabeth Ackroyd of the Patients' Association commented on this in the context of voluntary associations in the health field, observing that people who successfully start pressure groups are by their very nature strong personalities who find it difficult to get on with rivals (R. Evans, 1983). Personality clashes do not set insurmountable obstacles to co-operation between groups, but they can exacerbate other sources of dispute, such as those rooted in ideological and economic conflict.

Economic conflicts are of two main types. On the one hand,

co-operation is inhibited where there is conflict between groups on the basis of market relationships. Employers and unions, for example, have a common interest in lobbying for government subsidies. But such co-operation is undermined where industrial relations have been poor. There seems to be a similar reluctance to co-operate where there has been bitter rivalry between groups representing different stages of the production process, such as manufacturing and retailing.

The second type of economic conflict between groups reflects the competition within the pressure group world itself. Pressure groups compete with each other in many different fields. They compete for members and their subscriptions, for media and public support, for donations and other forms of income, for government recognition and financial support. In a competitive environment even groups which are supposed to be on the same side can be in conflict. Almost all pressure groups operate in a competitive environment. Take charities, for example, where the analogy of a competitive market has been employed (Jones and Cullis, 1990). The application of concepts such as market and competition to charities may initially appear odd. Yet, as Latham (1965, p.28) has noted 'the philanthropic organisation devoted to good works often regards other agencies in the same field with a venomous eye'. Charities themselves recognise the competition they face. For example, to quote from the RSPCA's *Annual Report* of 1989 (p.2) 'the Society is now one of dozens of charities seeking support by progressively more sophisticated and persuasive means. The RSPCA must compete to survive.'

Another source of conflict is ideological. This includes disagreement between groups on tactics as well as aims. The animal welfare lobby, for example, is divided between those who prefer legitimate strategies and those which pursue violence and direct action (Garner, 1991). The penal lobby is also divided by 'very real differences over strategies and tactics' (Ryan, 1983 p.177), while the disability lobby is divided, both in terms of aims and tactics, between organisations of disabled people and those which speak out on their behalf (Oliver, 1990).

So groups do not always co-operate even when it seems they

would gain as a result. The advantages of joint action are sometimes not valued as highly as the costs, which include a loss of
independence. Yet benefits of co-operation are tempting. As
many case histories have shown (including the defeat of the 1986
Shops Bill, for example) a well-organised coalition can pay off.
This is why it is a key task of leadership to build bridges and seek
co-operative relationships with other like-minded organisations
on issues of common concern.

Resources

So far we have explored the ways in which resources can be maximised through effective organisation. But what resources do
pressure groups actually possess? There are four main types:
financial resources, sanctions, social resources and political contacts.

Financial resources

Beyond a basic level of activity, pressure groups require financial
resources to mount their campaigns. There are certain fixed costs
which have to be paid, including the wages of permanent staff and
the costs of office space and equipment. On top of this the business of lobbying can be very expensive. Only the wealthiest pressure groups can afford to wine and dine MPs, hire lobbyists or to
mount high-profile media campaigns (although these are not necessarily the best tactics). Even those groups which adopt less
expensive tactics find that lobbying does not come cheap. Fairly
basic activities, such as the production and dissemination of pam-
phlets or the organisation of a protest rally, are not without cost.

Raising financial resources is not a problem for some groups.
Large businesses can finance lobbying out of their profits. Industries such as banking and finance, food, alcoholic drink, tobacco,
defence equipment, oil, the motor trade and pharmaceuticals
spend a vast amount of money on political campaigns aimed at
persuading the government either to adopt policies which
enhance their profitability, or not to adopt policies which might
damage it. Exhibit 4.5 illustrates how in recent years the motor

trade has lobbied successfully against moves to introduce greater competition into the UK car market.

Trade associations and trade unions have a ready source of finance in the form of subscriptions from their members. Consumer groups, too, are also funded by subscriptions, including the Consumers' Association and the motorists' organisations, the AA and the RAC. Some of the larger cause groups, such as the National Trust, the RSPCA and the RSPB also generate substantial income from their members and from the general public.

Exhibit 4.5   **The Monopolies Commission and the motor trade**

In 1992 the Monopolies and Mergers Commission (MMC) produced its report on the UK motor car market. The MMC had discovered that car prices in the UK were considerably higher than in other European countries. It recommended a number of changes to improve competition, but stopped short of abolishing the exclusive franchise system – where dealers are prevented by manufacturers from selling rival makes of car. The report also failed to compel manufacturers to cut the list price of cars sold in Britain. Both steps had been urged by the main consumer organisations, who expressed their disappointment with the MMC report.

The report represented a considerable move away from the MMC's original position. It had earlier proposed twenty measures to combat high car prices, many of which provoked a furious reaction from the motor trade. Car manufacturers such as Ford, Vauxhall and Rover, and the main motor trade organisations, the Society of Motor Manufacturers and Traders and the Motor Retail Industry Federation, lobbied strongly and this resulted in the number of proposals being reduced to five. Even these had been diluted.

Several factors played a key part in this outcome. First, the motor trade was able to argue successfully that the changes would result in lower profits and job losses. At a time of economic recession, these arguments carried a great deal of weight. Second, the motor trade had excellent political contacts, not only with Parliament, but with government departments, particularly the Department of Trade and Industry, thus putting pressure on the MMC. In addition the motor trade was able to put its case directly. It was reported that the motor trade met with the MMC on thirty-one occasions, while consumer organisations were invited only five times.

Sanctions

Pressure groups and their members often find themselves in a position where the government is dependent on their co-operation. In these circumstances groups often find that they are able to win concessions by threatening sanctions which might in some way damage the government.

Pressure groups can enhance their potential for influence if they or their members exert some control over economic resources or important economic indicators. Hence organisations representing business and industrial interests tend to get a sympathetic hearing because their members are major investors, important sources of national prosperity, and generate employment, tax revenues and export earnings. Not all industrial interests are equally powerful, however (Grant, 1993). For example, the financial sector is generally regarded as having more clout than the manufacturing sector. When such interests conflict it is possible to see which is the stronger. It was often claimed that, in the 1980s, the financial sector appeared to have much more influence over economic policy than the manufacturing industry. This was reflected in government policies on interest rates during this period, which remained too high from the point of view of manufacturers, while enabling the financial sector to make huge profits on lending.

Other groups have also exercised economic leverage. During the post-war period, until the 1980s, the trade unions were a major economic player. In the era of full employment they exerted much influence over labour markets, wages and productivity, In particular, the use of the strike weapon in industrial disputes had an impact on the economy as a whole. At the same time, the government also depended upon the unions to help implement key economic policies, such as incomes policies for example. By the 1970s the trade unions were a major political force in Britain, and were able to defeat measures – such as industrial relations legislation – to which they were opposed. The power of trade unions to disrupt production through industrial action was restricted by legislation introduced by the Thatcher government, but it was also undermined by other factors affecting the labour market, such as the growth of mass unemployment and the increasing use of non-unionised labour in the new service-based growth industries. These factors seriously diluted the political influence of the unions (see also Chapter 6).

Consumers can also exert economic leverage. Attempts have been made in the past to persuade consumers to boycott goods and services in an effort to influence policies. Perhaps the best example was the campaign waged by the anti-apartheid movement over the years to persuade consumers not to buy South African products. It is difficult, however, to evaluate the success of such campaigns because a variety of factors is likely to influence the sales of goods and services over a period of time.

Another type of sanction is where a group refuses to co-operate with a particular aspect of government policy: for example, the teachers' unions' boycott of assessment tests in the summer of 1993 (see Chapter 6) which forced the government to undertake a review. The non-payment campaign promoted by the Anti-Poll Tax Federation represents a further example of an effective sanction. This campaign added to the costs of the tax and was one of a number of factors behind its subsequent abolition.

Sanctions are an important resource. But they are often regarded as rather crude weapons. Government does not like to be openly threatened and it is generally accepted that such threats jeopardise the kind of close and harmonious relationship between group and government which most observers believe is the most effective way of influencing policy in the long term. Nevertheless, it is true that those which do not enjoy such a relationship with government have little to lose and much to gain by such a strategy.

Social resources
Many pressure groups have social resources. These are advantages gained from the mobilisation of support from the public as a whole, or from significant sections of it. Some groups are able to mobilise support because of the status and prestige of their members. For example, professional bodies and associations, such as the royal colleges of medicine and the BMA, can build on public respect for the profession. Others may possess social resources by being clearly representative of a particular section of society: around three-quarters of doctors are members of the BMA, while a similar proportion of farmers are members of the NFU.

The overall size of a group's membership is also a resource. Some groups have very large memberships, such as the AA (seven million members), the National Trust (over two million members) and the Consumers' Association (over one million members). Three trade unions, the Transport and General Workers Union (TGWU), the Amalgamated Engineering and Electrical Union (AEEU) and the public sector union UNISON, have over a million members each. While the overall size of a pressure group's membership is important, it is crucial that it can be mobilised when the need arises. Some of the mass membership groups have a large proportion of passive members who are difficult to mobilise. The intensity of feeling among the group's membership is perhaps on balance the key factor. A numerically small but intense group can often exert more influence than a larger, less committed one. As the Shops Bill case illustrated, it is possible to block or delay decisions, even when a majority of the public is in favour of change. Small, intense groups are often active at a local level, attempting to prevent developments which they believe affect their community in an adverse way. The rise of so-calledNot In My Back Yard (NIMBY) groups is explored in more detail in Chapter 9.

Finally, some pressure groups mobilise a much broader and deeper kind of support from the wider community. Professional groups, such as doctors and nurses, can generate public support not simply because of their status, but on the basis of respect. Other groups may win support because the plight of their members has attracted the sympathy of the public. The protests against British Coal's pit closure programme during the winter of 1992/3 provides a good example of this (see Exhibit 6.3). Cause groups which represent a particular client group, such as Shelter (the housing and homelessness organisation), the Child Poverty Action Group and Age Concern, are often able to attract public support by demonstrating the conditions faced by the homeless, the poor and the elderly respectively. For some groups, however, this task is not easy. If the client group is one which does not readily attract public sympathy (criminals, for example) the group will face an uphill struggle. Also, in many cases groups face an adversary competing for the sympathy of the public, which makes it more difficult to mobilise public support. For example, the pro-abortion lobby's efforts are negated to some extent by the pro-life campaigners. The battle for public support and the social leverage this brings is obviously easier in the absence of a group campaigning for the opposite viewpoint.

Political contacts
The political contacts which pressure groups have with other groups, opinion formers and policy-makers can also be regarded as a resource. It is particularly important that groups possess the right kind of contacts to influence policy when the need arises. For example, it is no use having excellent contacts with Whitehall if a decision is to be resolved by a free vote in Parliament. In the chapters which follow we shall be looking in depth at the type of political contacts possessed by groups and the way in which they use these resources to influence policy.

Conclusions

It is clear that pressure groups vary considerably both in organisation and in terms of the resources at their disposal. There are many different types of resource which a group may possess. Some are well-endowed: large businesses, for example, can draw on financial resources. Professional associations and large mass membership groups have both financial and social resources. Such groups are often in a position to inflict sanctions when necessary. In contrast, many other groups are less well endowed, although groups representing the poor and vulnerable are still able to raise public awareness and can win sympathy and support. Though great inequalities are evident, few groups are entirely without resources.

There is also a wide variation in the organisation of pressure group activity; the sharpest contrast being between the large mass member democratic group and the small élitist campaigning body. As we saw earlier, each has its particular advantages and disadvantages. We also found that democracy is rather patchy in the pressure group world: sophisticated election systems coexist with what could be described as personal dictatorships. However, existence of other channels of communication and opportunities for joining, leaving and forming groups create additional pressures for leaderships to be accountable and to accommodate the views of members and supporters.

Good organisation is essential if groups are to maximise their available resources. But it is not enough on its own. Pressure groups also require a coherent political strategy, effective tactics and, above all, a political environment which is conducive to their activities. These aspects will be addressed in the chapters that follow.

5

Pressure groups and the executive

The executive is identified by most observers as the key pressure point in the British political system (see Grant, 1989a; Jordan and Richardson, 1987a; Miller, 1990). The resounding message is that the most influential groups are those which have good contacts with the executive arm of government, and in particular with central government departments. The concentration of executive power in the British system of government in recent years has, if anything, enhanced the importance of such contacts. Surveys have indicated that pressure groups themselves recognise the importance of the executive. The Study of Parliament Group found that ministers and civil servants were ranked more highly than other agents (such as MPs, the media and parties) in terms of their influence over policy (Rush, 1990a). A further survey (Baggott, 1992) generated similar findings.

The executive

What, precisely, is the executive? Essentially it comprises four sets of institutions: the *core executive*; *government departments*; *government agencies*; and other *public bodies*.

The core executive relates to the offices and institutions at the heart of government, and includes the Cabinet, the system of Cabinet committees and the support services provided by the Cabinet secretariat. It also includes the prime minister and his or her advisory and support services, such as the Policy Unit, the prime minister's Private Office, Press Office and Political Office.

In the second category – government departments – most attention is focused on the nineteen departments headed by ministers. These departments, such as the Treasury, the Department of Health and the Ministry of Defence, have a much higher profile in relation to policy-making than the other, non-ministerial departments, which undertake mainly operational or regulatory functions.

Government agencies are the third category. Most of these have been created in the wake of the 'Next Steps' reform programme, adopted by the Conservative government in 1987, the aim of which is to hive off operational matters from government departments, leaving them free to make policy. The new agencies operate in a policy and resources framework set by departments and are responsible for managing their own operations on a day-to-day basis. In 1993 'Next Steps' agencies employed two-thirds of the Civil Service, and this proportion is expected to rise further by the end of the decade.

Finally, there are the non-departmental public bodies (NDPBs), which vary considerably in size and function. They include public corporations (such as the BBC), regulatory bodies (like the Health and Safety Commission), executive bodies (for example, the Sea Fish Authority), promotional bodies (such as the National Consumer Council), advisory bodies (for example, the Advisory Committee on the Misuse of Drugs – see Exhibit 5.1) and even quasi-judicial bodies (such as the Monopolies and Mergers Commission). Some non-departmental bodies are involved in more than one of these kinds of activity, such as the Commission for Racial Equality which is an advisory body that also seeks to promote equality of opportunity and good race relations between the racial groups, and which has a regulatory role in relation to the investigation of complaints about racial discrimination.

Why is it important to distinguish between various institutions within the executive? First of all, some have more influence over policy than others. Secondly, some are more accessible to outside groups. It is difficult to generalise here because the accessibility of executive institutions varies according to the nature of the issue, as well as over time. Nevertheless, one can identify a sort of policy hierarchy, where decisions are made at various levels in the executive. Groups that have access to the higher levels are able in general to exert a more powerful influence than those which are mainly in contact with the more peripheral bodies. The core executive and government departments are regarded as less accessible and yet have more influence over policy when compared with executive agencies and non-departmental bodies.

Indeed, non-departmental bodies have been seen by some as 'buffers', designed to absorb pressure from outside interests (Miller, 1990). In the case of the environmental lobby, Lowe and Goyder (1983) found that groups had easier access to, and gained more support from, the environmental agencies compared with government departments. The environmental lobby did not lack contact with government, but rather lacked higher level access to organs of central government which exerted more influence over policy. The creation of these bodies was seen as a way in which government could channel pressure towards sympathetic but peripheral agencies, allowing ministers and civil servants freedom to manoeuvre. It is sometimes assumed that the new 'Next Steps' agencies, too, have relatively little impact over policy, although it is perhaps too early to assess their influence. Indeed, as Davies and Williams (1991 p.33) surmise, agencies in highly specialised areas may well play a substantial, if largely unattributable, role in policy-making in the future.

Certain institutions within the executive exert a great deal of influence over issues which fall within their defined responsibilities. Groups must be aware of the distribution of responsibilities in government and should build contacts with the relevant institutions (Gray and Jenkins, 1985; Richardson and Jordan, 1979). Furthermore, policies are often the result of interaction between different departments which have overlapping responsibilities. In some cases the interaction is co-operative. For example, co-operation between the Home Office and the Ministry of Transport in the 1960s led to the introduction of the breathalyser to combat drinking and driving. However, there is often conflict between departments, such as that between the Department of Health and the Ministry of Agriculture, Fisheries and Food in recent years on food policy issues (Smith, 1991).

The executive is not monolithic, but a collection of institutions each with different patterns of influence and accessibility, often possessing contrasting ideas on policy. Recent reforms such as 'Next Steps' have, if anything, fragmented the executive even further. It is not enough that a pressure group has access to parts of the executive. In order to be influential it must have access to those institutions within the executive which exercise a critical influence over the policy issues which affect it.

Group–executive relationships

Several aspects of the relationship between pressure groups and the executive must be considered. These are: the formal machinery of policy advice and consultation; personal contacts and informal relationships; inside knowledge of the 'corridors of power'; and the stability of relationships between groups and the executive.

Advice and consultation

Government bodies may take advice from outside organisations. This advice is often of a technical nature. Pressure groups have a great deal of expertise, and can complement that available 'in-house'. But advice usually has a political dimension too. The choice of advisers is often politically sensitive. Furthermore, this choice can have an important bearing on the formulation of policy.

The way in which government seeks the views of outside organisations, known as the consultation process, has three main purposes, according to Jordan and Richardson (1987a): first, to inform those outside government of its intentions; second, to discover the nature of the problem in a particular policy area; third, to ascertain how to respond to such problems, once identified.

In some cases the government has a statutory obligation to consult, as in the case of the 1947 Agriculture Act, section 2(3) of

which states that when holding reviews on the condition of the
agricultural industry 'the ministers shall consult with such bodies
of persons as appear to them to represent the interests of pro-
ducers in the agricultural industry'. There is little comprehensive
evidence on the extent of such statutory consultation, although
Jordan and Richardson (1987a) discovered that one-third of the
sixty Acts of Parliament which related to the Department of
Trade and Industry stated that consultation had to take place
when new regulations were being introduced. The same authors
note that, in addition to statutory consultation, departments frequently consult groups even when it is not mandatory to do so.

The consultative process is difficult to define simply. It takes
the form of a complex web of relationships between groups and
the government. Some of these relationships are formal, others
less so. We shall begin by looking at the formal machinery of consultation.

Formal consultation
There are a variety of ways in which government formally consults outside interests. One approach, which is less common
today, is the establishment of a Royal Commission or a departmental committee of inquiry. These have been established in the
past to explore a particular policy issue or problem. They are able
to canvass a wide range of opinion (the Royal Commission on the
NHS in 1979 attracted submissions from over 1,200 organisations
and 800 individuals) and make recommendations, which are then
considered by the government (who are at liberty to reject them).
Royal Commissions and departmental committees are usually dis-
solved following the submission of their report. Some, however,
are permanent and continue to advise government on policy for a
number of years. An example is the Royal Commission on Environmental Pollution which has continued to advise government
since its creation in 1973.

Royal Commissions and departmental committees of inquiry
have, in the past, performed a useful role in collecting evidence
from a wide range of sources, providing a possible basis for the
future development of policy. But they have also provided politi-

cians with a useful means of postponing controversial decisions. It was said of Harold Wilson, for example, that he bought the years with Royal Commissions (Whitehead, 1985, p.54). It has also been argued that their reports were influenced by the deliberate selection of members and chairmen who were likely to eschew radical changes (see Hennessy, 1986). Royal Commissions and departmental committees of inquiry were, however, instruments of consensus, which had the potential to build a cross-party agreement about a particular problem on the basis of the evidence submitted. As we shall see in the next chapter, this approach did not fit well with the Thatcher government's approach, which was based on the politics of conviction rather than consensus.

Government does not have to establish a Royal Commission or departmental committee in order to receive advice. It can set up advisory committees or working parties which have a much lower profile. According to Jordan and Richardson (1987a, p.185) these are commonly established where issues are technical and complex, and where the government itself lacks expertise. In the late 1980s, for example, the Home Office established a working party to look at the implication of population changes upon police recruitment. This committee included civil servants from the Home Office plus representatives from the main police associations and organisations (Association of Chief Police Officers, Police Superintendents Association, Police Federation and the Metropolitan Police) and the local authority organisations (Association of County Councils and the Association of Metropolitan Authorities).

Government includes a wide range of groups on its committees. According to one survey, over half the groups which responded were represented on advisory committees, while another survey (Lowe and Goyder, 1983) of environmental groups, found that 40 per cent had representation. It should be noted that some groups are represented on many committees: the CBI, for example, has representatives on over a hundred of these bodies (Grant and Marsh, 1977).

Many advisory committees are not strictly representative, however. Some committee members are chosen on the basis of their expertise, rather than their ability to represent interests. Even so, the dividing line between independent expertise and representative capacity is often blurred. Frequently experts have some connection with organised interests. It has been revealed, for example, that more than half of the members of the government's Committee on the Safety of Medicines have connections with the pharmaceutical industry (*Independent*, 15 December 1988, p.6). Moreover, government often appoints individuals after consulting outside organisations. The membership of the Advisory Committee on the Misuse of Drugs, for example, is determined following consultation with organisations having an interest in this issue (see Exhibit 5.1).

Exhibit 5.1   **The Advisory Committee on the Misuse of Drugs**

The Advisory Committee on the Misuse of Drugs was established under the Misuse of Drugs Act of 1971 to keep under review the nature and extent of the drug problem in the UK and to give advice to ministers on how the problem should be tackled. The Advisory Committee is appointed by the Home Secretary following consultations with organisations having an interest in the drugs problem. The twenty-three members currently include a drugs counsellor, a magistrate, a youth worker, a nurse, a headmistress, a probation officer, a chief constable, a director of social services, a health authority manager, a health education officer, a representative from the Citizens' Advice Bureau, a representative of the British pharmaceutical industry and a number of scientists, academics and doctors.

Green Papers and consultative documents

Prior to introducing legislation, government departments may circulate details of their proposals to those who have an interest in the matter. Every year government departments together produce between 200 and 300 consultative documents. Most have a restricted circulation and are not well-publicised. Indeed, departments maintain lists of organisations who routinely receive documents relating to particular issues (Jordan and Richardson, 1987a, p.158). For example, for the purposes of implementing Part III of the Food and Environment Protection Act 1985, the Ministry of Agriculture, Fisheries and Food sent out a consultative document inviting comments to 130 organisations, including the National Farmers' Union, the British Bee Keepers' Association, and the Salmon Net Fishing Association of Scotland.

Some consultative documents are more widely publicised and invite comments from a much broader range of organisations. These are usually given the status of Green Papers and published by Her Majesty's Stationery Office (HMSO). It was in the 1960s that the Labour government began a practice of issuing Green Papers prior to introducing legislation. The first of these, entitled 'The Development Areas: A Proposal for Regional Employment Premium' (1967), was a novelty because it was the first time an official government document made it clear that it did not represent declared policy (Silkin, 1973). This practice was continued by both Labour and Conservative governments during the 1970s. The Thatcher government, in spite of its reputation as a conviction government, continued to issue Green Papers and other consultative documents, though as we shall see in the next chapter it was heavily criticised for not consulting fully on important policy issues and for ignoring the views of groups who believed they had a contribution to make.

Green Papers are issued mainly in two contrasting circumstances. First, where there is a wide divergence of views so that government wishes to dissociate itself from controversy (as in the Green Papers on British Summer Time (1989) and Divorce (1993). Second, in those cases where the government wishes to demonstrate public backing for its policy objectives (as in the Green Papers on trade union reform throughout the 1980s). Indeed, the latter were Green Papers in name only, since the government already had a clear policy on this issue.

Views on Green Papers and other consultative documents are sought within a confined time period. This period varies, but usually lasts about two months. Pressure groups communicate their views to government by sending a written submission or memorandum, and may be invited to put their case directly to ministers or civil servants. For some groups the episodic contact which takes place on such issues is part of a close, continuous and stable relationship with government.

Personal contacts and informal links

An analysis of formal contacts between groups and the executive does not tell us the whole story. Pressure groups and government organisations are also linked by informal contacts on a personal level.

Much seems to depend on the ability of the groups to cultivate a routine working relationship with civil servants working in the government departments. Indeed, some groups are in contact with the same civil servants on a regular basis, in some cases daily. Where contact is frequent, discussions may be conducted over the telephone, though on issues of importance a meeting will usually be arranged in Whitehall. In some cases groups allow civil servants to attend their own meetings as observers. MIND, the NSPCC and the National Association for the Care and Resettlement of Offenders (NACRO) all allow government observers either to attend meetings of the council or particular specialist committees.

Those civil servants who occupy the lower end of the senior policy grades of the service – the principal and assistant secretary grades – are in the best position to develop a close and continuous relationship with groups (Johnstone, 1984; Miller, 1990). They are more familiar with the details of policy issues and frequently brief their senior colleagues. Most groups find it impossible to build such a relationship with ministers and senior civil servants, who are only able to deal with the most politically salient issues.

The survey by Baggott (1992) indicated the extent of contact between civil servants and pressure groups. Exhibit 5.2 shows the main results. Note that it is the lower ranks of the senior civil service which are most frequently in touch with pressure groups.

The routine nature of this relationship is evident from the table.

Exhibit 5.2 **Contacts between pressure groups and decision-makers**

Institution/office	% of groups in contact at least		
	once a week	once a month	once a year
Prime Minister/PM Office	1	11	53
Cabinet ministers	8	37	81
Junior ministers	11	49	86
Senior higher civil servants*	19	50	82
Junior higher civil servants**	34	67	85
MPs	31	61	89
Peers	18	50	84
Media	81	94	98

* Permanent Secretary, Deputy Secretary, Under-Secretary
** Assistant Secretary and Principal

Source: Baggott (1992)

This is not to underestimate the importance of contact with ministers. A survey undertaken by the Study of Parliament Group (Rush, 1990a) revealed that ministers were seen by most groups (31.6 per cent) as the most important in terms of influencing policy. Civil servants were ranked as the most important contact by 28.5 per cent of the groups surveyed. Baggott's (1992) survey also found that groups regarded ministers, and in particular the prime minister, as the most important contact in terms of influencing policy.

Face-to-face contact with civil servants or ministers can take place in a variety of settings. Meetings may be arranged, either with civil servants alone, or with ministerial participation. Other settings are less formal, but nevertheless are important. Ministers or civil servants may meet pressure-group leaders over lunch or dinner, or they may be involved at 'behind the scenes' discussions at conferences and other special events to which they have been invited.

Personal networks are also regarded as important in the maintenance of group–executive relations. Shared educational backgrounds, friendships and common personal interests may all contribute to effective communication between groups and the executive. The actual impact of these factors is difficult to research and the evidence rather anecdotal. Thomas (1983) for example, believes that much of the influence of the British Field Sports Society upon the government's attitude towards hunting has been derived from its links with the establishment, while Grant and Marsh (1977) found that the relationship between industrialists in the CBI and senior ministers and civil servants was enhanced by their similar social backgrounds. It is clear, nevertheless, that personal networks strengthen the group–executive relationship. As we shall see in the next section, the mobility between groups and the executive may also play a part in building informal contacts.

Knowledge and mobility
Pressure groups are keen to employ personnel with knowledge of the corridors of power, such as former civil servants. For example, the director of the Association of British Pharmaceutical Industries, Dr John Griffin, was formerly a senior civil servant in the Medicines Division of the Department of Health and Social Security. Another former civil servant, Dr George Rae, left his job at the Department of the Environment in 1990 to take up a post with Ocean Environment, a waste disposal firm. Around the same time, British Airways appointed David Holmes, a former deputy secretary at the Department of Transport, as director of government and industry affairs.

Former civil servants have to abide by certain rules when taking up outside appointments. Senior officials (Permanent Secretary, Deputy Secretary and Under Secretary grades) must ask permission to take jobs within two years of leaving the Civil Service. The highest ranking civil servants – the Permanent Secretaries – must wait a minimum of three months before taking outside employment. Potentially controversial cases are vetted by an Advisory Committee on Business Appointments, which reports to the prime minister. Lower-ranking civil servants who have had access to commercially sensitive information, or who have had close links with an outside organisations during their Civil Service career, are also open to scrutiny.

Nevertheless, some continue to believe that the system is open to abuse. Both the Defence Select Committee (1988) and the Treasury and Civil Service Select Committee (1984, 1991) have called for tighter rules, but apart from the closure of one particular loophole – there is now a requirement that civil servants must report job offers from firms with a commercial interest in their work – the government has been unwilling to respond. However in view of the continuing concern about the employment of former civil servants, the government has allowed the issue to fall within the remit of the Nolan Committee on Standards in Public Life, established in 1994 (see Exhibit 7.4).

In recent years the government has also encouraged secondment between the Civil Service and outside organisations. By 1990 there were 1,502 secondments. The aim behind this is to make the Civil Service less insular: to expose it to fresh ideas. During the Thatcher period around two-thirds of inward secondments (i.e. into the Civil Service from outside), were from business and industrial organisations. Individuals are seconded for short periods, though in some cases the appointment is permanent. In some cases, particularly with short-term secondments, the individuals will return to their original employers. The problem is that no clear safeguards exist to guarantee that individuals on short-term secondment will not use the knowledge acquired while working in government to the advantage of their employers. The business appointment rules do not apply on their return to their original employer. A similar problem occurs with ministerial advisers who are also exempt from these rules.

Worries have also been expressed about the hiring of former ministers by outside groups. Although ministers should relinquish their outside interests when appointed, there are no rules to stop them from taking up posts with business or other pressure groups when they resigned (see Chapter 7). Norman Tebbit, for example, who as Trade and Industry minister had the task of privatising British Telecom, later joined the company as a non-executive director. In the period 1990–93, eleven recently retired ministers acquired between them twenty-eight company directorships. (*Observer*, 5 September 1993, p.7). Even the former Prime Minister, Baroness Thatcher, took up a political consultancy with Philip Morris, an American food and tobacco conglomerate, at a reported fee of over £500,000. While there is no suggestion of any impropriety in the acceptance of such jobs, these cases led to calls for rules on the employment of former ministers. Following the recommendations of the Nolan Committee on Standards in Public Life (see exhibit 7.4), the government accepted the need for regulations similar to those applied to senior civil servants.

By employing former ministers and civil servants, groups can acquire greater knowledge about the workings of central government. This can give them an advantage over others that do not have this resource. Obviously business groups are in a better position to employ ex-ministers and former civil servants, given their financial resources. Less wealthy groups can enlist the help of former ministers and civil servants by offering them honorary posts with the organisation. Lord Ennals for example, the former health minister, was the president of the mental health charity, MIND, while former ministers Lord Howe and Shirley Williams have both served as vice-presidents of the Consumers' Association.

Stable relationships

The continuity and stability of the relationship between groups and government sets the context for their interaction on specific issues. This has long been recognised, though in recent years there has been much more academic interest in these relationships and a clearer attempt to locate them in a theoretical and conceptual context (see Chapter 2 above).

At the heart of this approach lies the concept of *policy network* (Marsh and Rhodes, 1992a; Smith, 1993). As already mentioned in Chapter 2, policy networks describe the range of relationships which exist between groups and government. Policy networks are also regarded by their exponents as an explanatory tool as well as a descriptive device. They claim that pressures both within and outside these networks can promote changes both in government–group relations and in policy.

The main distinction made is that between policy communities and issue networks (see Exhibit 2.5). Issue networks are more fragmented and open, links between groups and government are not close and the opportunities for co-operation limited. Policy communities, on the other hand, are relatively exclusive. Groups have privileged links with government and there is a great deal of trust and co-operation between the two. Policy communities are often focused on a particular government department or agency, and there is a stable and negotiated policy environment. Any conflict which does arise is managed within an agreed framework.

There are parallels between the policy networks approach, and the distinction made by Wyn Grant, also noted in Chapter 2, between insider and outsider groups. The former have a certain privileged status related to their close and stable relationships with government. Others do not have the same kind of status and this is reflected in difficulties of access and so on.

The focus on privileged status and on the stable relationships between government and groups lead to a number of important questions. What determines the status of different groups? How is it that some groups enter into a stable relationship and others do not? How does the possession of privileged status and the establishment of a good working relationship with government advantage the group in question?

Some groups find it much easier than others to establish and maintain a close and harmonious relationship with government. There are two main factors which help a group to build such a relationship: first, the extent to which it is seen by government as legitimate; second, the extent to which it is able to co-operate with government.

A legitimate group is one that is able to speak authoritatively for a particular interest or cause. By consulting such groups government can benefit in two main ways. It may derive information about the policy-making environment which it could not obtain through other channels. Or, by consulting with legitimate groups and securing their consent, the government can secure a wider support for its policies, not only amongst the group members and supporters but also from the wider public.

Groups acquire legitimacy in a number of ways. It can be derived from the representational function of the group. If a group represents a large proportion of people in a particular social, economic or occupational section of society – as do the NFU and the BMA, for example – they are more likely to be seen by government as legitimate. The extent to which groups are seen as representative may also be gauged by the quality of democratic mechanisms and procedures within the group (see Chapter 4 above).

It is much more difficult for cause groups to be legitimate in this sense, for they do not claim to represent a particular section of society. For such groups, legitimacy is seen more in terms of public support. As Thomas (1983, p.254) notes in the context of the politics of hunting, cause groups have to be in harmony with public sentiments and express them in an acceptable way if they are to be regarded as legitimate. Legitimacy can also be acquired by building credibility among ministers and their officials. It is possible to achieve this by presenting consistent and well-argued views backed with good quality research (Whiteley and Winyard, 1987). Credibility depends crucially on the knowledge and expertise of the group and its ability to express itself clearly. Groups must be prepared to work with government rather than against it. In addition to establishing legitimacy, groups must be able to co-operate with government in a number of ways. Forms of co-operation include providing advice, assisting with policy implementation, and also what could be called 'obeying the rules of engagement'.

Groups provide a wide range of advice and information for government departments and agencies. According to Grant (1993), the provision of information about the policy environment is particularly useful to government. Trade associations and firms have a mass of information at their disposal which may forewarn government of a political problem or assist in the routine conduct of policy-making.

Other groups are also in a position to provide expert advice and information. Professional groups, such as those representing doctors, lawyers and so on are obvious sources of expertise. Many cause groups, such as the RSPCA, Shelter and the Child Poverty Action Group, for example, are also considered 'experts' in their field and are highly regarded by government officials as sources of information. Such organisations frequently collect information during the course of their work which is of use to government when formulating policies. Often groups undertake research specifically for the purpose of influencing the policy formation process. For example, in 1990 Age Concern undertook a special study into particular problems faced by elderly people from ethnic minorities for precisely this reason (Age Concern, 1990).

Government may also enlist the co-operation of groups in an attempt to ensure that a particular policy is properly implemented. Groups are able to inform their members about government policy and may even urge their compliance. They also monitor the impact of policy and inform government of the extent to which objectives are being achieved, which can lead to a further modification of policy.

In many cases a policy will not require legislation, government instead relying on pressure groups in the field to take action. Lowe and Goyder (1983), for example, note how the government has used the National Trust as a means of implementing policies in areas of scenic protection, historic preservation, nature conservation and countryside recreation. This has enabled the Trust to establish a closer and more intimate relationship with government compared with other environmental and conservation groups. There are many examples of groups undertaking action on behalf of government in this way. This often involves a group persuading its members to change their behaviour in a significant way. For example, in 1980 the British Aerosol Manufacturers' Association persuaded its members to reduce by 30 per cent the use of environmentally harmful Chloroflourocarbon gases (CFCs) following pressure from the Department of the Environment (Grant and Sargent, 1987).

Groups may be useful to government in providing expertise and by co-operating with implementation of policy. But they also have to obey the 'rules of engagement' in their dealings with government. It is particularly important that groups do not jeopardise their relationship with government by attacking government policy openly. Groups that seek to embarrass government rarely have a close relationship with it. Ryan (1978, 1983), in a study of the penal lobby, distinguishes between those groups which government finds acceptable and those which are not. Two 'unacceptable' groups – Radical Alternatives to Prison (RAP) and PROP, a prisoners' rights organisation – were not consulted by the Home Office on penal policy. The department's relationship with RAP was described as 'frosty', largely in view of its criticisms of government policy, while PROP was disliked even more by the government, which adopted a deliberate policy of exclusion towards it.

This is not to say that groups having a poor or distant relationship with government are without influence. Indeed, the point made by Ryan is that such groups can often have an impact on policy by challenging the prevailing *policy paradigms*. By concentrating on informing and educating public opinion, such groups may force government and the more privileged groups to reconsider their policies. Other groups have adopted this strategy, with some success. Environmental groups such as Greenpeace and Friends of the Earth, though consulted by government departments and agencies on occasion, have tended to avoid being too closely associated with them. Yet these groups have exerted a great deal of influence over policy in recent years by raising public concern about issues and raising the profile of debates about the environment.

Nevertheless, most observers agree that a close and harmonious relationship with government is advantageous in terms of achieving influence over policy. Indeed, such a relationship has several specific advantages for the groups concerned. It is a useful way of keeping an ear to the ground about policy developments in central government (Miller, 1990). It enables groups to express an opinion about policies at an early stage in their development. This may save much effort at a later stage when the government's policy has become more concrete. Pressure groups can therefore benefit by getting their views in early through established contacts within government. Or as Miller puts it, 'a battering ram is not needed if you can walk through the door' (1990, p.212).

Some groups have achieved a high degree of success by achieving *client group status*. This is where a group is locked into a very close relationship with government. Examples from the post-war period include that between the Department of Health and BMA and that between the Ministry of Agriculture and the NFU. In each case the group has been seen as the principal representative of interests whose co-operation is essential to the achievement of the government's policy objectives. But such a relationship also has its dangers. Groups which are enmeshed in such a relationship are often reluctant to jeopardise their status by openly criticising policy, and this leaves them open to manipulation by the government. In the case of the NFU, for example, Self and Storing warned over twenty years ago that its close relationship with government could prove debilitating, while more recently Charlesworth et al. (1990, p.8) have commented that 'the NFU is beginning to pay the price for its success in maintaining its close relationship with the state'. Furthermore, as experience of the case of the BMA illustrates (see Chapter 6) client group status has not prevented recent governments from challenging well-established interests.

Conclusions

Jordan and Richardson (1987a, p.127) rightly point out that decisions about who is consulted raise constitutional issues. For them the activities of civil servants and ministers, in consulting certain groups and excluding others, represent a revealed constitution which advantages some at the expense of others. Others have also pointed out the 'structured inequalities' which exist in policy communities (Marsh and Rhodes, 1992a; Smith, 1993). Yet, as we have suggested, this does not necessarily mean that 'outsider' groups will always lack influence. We have also seen that in some cases a close relationship with government can inhibit the achievement of a group's objectives. As McKenzie (1958) pointed out, in pressure-group politics access does not always equate with influence. The relationship between groups and the executive is nevertheless important. It is also dynamic. Changes in the political environment can have a considerable impact upon these relationships. Governments have different ideologies, programmes and styles which favour some groups at the expense of others. The impact of such changes is explored in the next chapter.

6

Trends in government–group relationships

The links between the executive and pressure groups, discussed in the previous chapter, have a certain durability. However, they are not immutable. Changes in the political environment, such as a change of government, can have an impact on these relationships, to an extent affecting the influence of certain pressure groups. In this chapter we shall focus on the consequences of a change in government, by first of all setting out the possible effects, and then analysing the actual trends in government–group relationships over the post-war period.

Governments and pressure groups

A change of government might affect the world of pressure groups in a number of ways. First, a new government may adopt fresh policies and programmes, and these could lead to the creation of a new pattern of relationships between government and groups. Secondly, an incoming government might adopt a different style of policy-making, which deals with groups and their demands in a different way. Thirdly, some groups are not neutral in party-political terms and have a better relationship with some parties than with others. If one party replaces another in government it is likely that some groups will be advantaged at the expense of others.

Programmes and policies

The priorities adopted by government have a significant impact upon its relationships with particular groups. A group whose co-operation is essential to the success of the policy will tend be drawn into a closer relationship with government, creating opportunities for that group to shape the details of the policy. New priorities imply a different pattern of dependence on groups – for advice, information, approval, assistance with implementation and so on. By the same token, where government downgrades a particular policy, groups which have a key role in relation to it are likely to become more distant. Although a change of government has the potential to alter group–government relationships in this way, there are limits. Indeed, there is often much continuity in policy despite a change of government and the declared changes in policy which follow (Rose, 1984; Marsh and Rhodes, 1992b). Furthermore, one should note that shifts in policy can take place within the lifetime of a government, and this too may alter group–government relationships.

Policy-making style

Governments may adopt different styles of policy-making. They may adopt an open style, where outside interests are fully consulted, or a closed style, where the main decisions are determined by a few participants. Yet it is sometimes difficult to establish whether a particular government has an overall policy style. For example, the prime minister may adopt a forceful and dogmatic approach, while departmental ministers consult widely and build support for their policies among pressure groups. Furthermore, the government may decide some issues in a rather closed fashion, while others are resolved more openly. Indeed, there is likely to be much continuity between governments in this respect. Some issues, such as defence, law and order, security and foreign affairs are almost always determined 'behind closed doors', while others, such as moral issues like capital punishment and abortion, tend to be decided in a more open fashion.

A further problem is that it is often difficult to separate policy style from political rhetoric. The government often presents a certain style to suit political circumstances. On some occasions governments like to be portrayed as 'caring' and 'listening', while on others they wish to be seen as 'tough' or 'impartial'. While these styles imply different group–government relationships, in practice the relationships may stay much the same.

Party allegiance
Certain groups may be favoured by government because they are closely associated with the governing party. Alternatively, groups may be discriminated against by government because of their association with opposition parties. While most pressure groups avoid being closely and exclusively linked to a particular party, some cannot remain neutral and some choose not to do so.

The best example of a partisan group is the trade union movement. The Labour Party was created by the trade unions and still receives most of its funds from this source. Trade unionists play a major role in the party, not only as members but as decision-makers. The trade unions are involved at all levels of decision-making, from the selection of candidates to the selection of the leader. Recent reforms – such as changes to the party conference block vote and the introduction of OMOV (one member, one vote) procedures for the selection of election candidates – seek to distance the unions publicly from the party, though their impact on trade union influence within the party has yet to be evaluated.

Meanwhile, business organisations are closer to the Conservative Party than to the other political parties. Many businesses donate funds to the Party. In addition, many business people play an active role in Conservative Party politics at all levels, particularly in the constituencies. However, it would be a mistake to see this relationship as a parallel to the Labour–trade union axis. As Grant (1993, p.131) observes, 'the Conservative Party is the party closest to business in Britain, but that does not mean that it is a party of business, let alone a party for business'. Indeed, over the last decade or so important business interests – particularly manufacturing – have made clear their dissatisfaction with the economic and industrial policies of the Conservative government. The government has faced criticism not only about its management of the economy, but over specific policies such as the introduction of business rates and its attempts to bring more competition into the brewing industry (see Exhibit 7.1).

Even so, one cannot deny that business gains a broad political advantage from a Conservative government compared with other parties. As we shall see later in this chapter, some business organisations have benefited considerably from the domination of the Conservative Party. By the same token, few doubt that the trade unions have suffered a dramatic loss of influence. This will also be investigated later.

Other groups are also closer to some parties. Right-wing ideological groups and 'think tanks' are closely associated with the Conservative Party, while others, such as the peace movement, are more closely associated with the Labour and Liberal Parties. However, most groups, even where they have an affinity for one particular party, tend to declare their impartiality. Political realities mean that groups have to work with governments which may not be favourably disposed towards them. Yet they can still be influential, as illustrated by the long-running, and so far successful, campaign by the Child Poverty Action Group to prevent the abolition of Child Benefit. For a group to declare openly its party political allegiance can be at the very least counter-productive. Such an open stance may also deter support from voters and members of other parties who might have sympathy with the group's aims. Furthermore, many groups are registered charities, a status which could be challenged if they are seen to indulge in party politics.

Trends in government–group relationships

Having explored the potential impact of a change in government, let us now look at the relationships between government and groups in the post-war period. For the purposes of analysis, we shall divide this into three distinct periods: the era of consensus politics, the Thatcher years, and the Major government's term of office up to the end of 1994.

The post-war period

The post-war period, until the 1970s, was characterised by broadly harmonious relationships between government and pressure groups. As Stewart observed, relationships were generally good, with groups accepting 'consultation before legislation as part of the established order of things' (Stewart 1958, p.17). Various procedures had been created or adapted to accommodate the needs of both government and groups. Some were open to a wide range of groups (and also individuals) who might wish to comment. Long-established institutional devices such as Royal Commissions and departmental committees of inquiry were able to collect views on issues of concern. The introduction of Green Papers in the late 1960s provided an added opportunity to comment on policy options before they were officially adopted by government.

Alongside these relatively open channels, the main producer interest groups, such as the professions, business organisations and the trade unions, enjoyed a more exclusive relationship with the executive. They were represented on a growing number of advisory committees and other official bodies which allowed for an exchange of views on specific issues. The post-war period saw the growth of tripartite institutions, such as the National Economic Development Committee, which contained representatives from government, industry and the unions. Producer groups also operated through informal arrangements, in the form of personal contacts with ministers and civil servants. Such privileged access did not belong solely to the most powerful interest groups in this period, Some cause groups, particularly those recognised by government as having a great deal of knowledge about a particular policy area (for example, the Howard League for Penal Reform on policies on crime and punishment), were also brought into a close working relationship.

There are a number of reasons why some groups were drawn into these relationships. First of all, the growing post-war state created a mutual dependence between government and groups (Finer, 1958, pp.30–1). Government responsibility for managing the economy required the co-operation of the trade unions and employers, while the welfare state created a dependence on others such as the professions, who delivered services, and local authorities, who administered them. Another factor was that policy debates were generally conducted in a climate of consensus. Governments sought co-operation and aimed to minimise discontent through consultation. At the same time, those pressure groups which had the ear of government realised the benefits of maintaining a good relationship and were, for the most part, willing to compromise by limiting their demands.

Government–group relationships were not, however, beyond reproach even in the heyday of consensus politics. Open forms of consultation, such as Royal Commissions, were seen by some as excuses for inaction, as we saw in the previous chapter. Meanwhile, the close relationships between government and certain groups were criticised, particularly by those which lacked privileged access. Criticism of the consultation process was not confined to groups which were disgruntled or excluded. The Fulton Committee's report on the Civil Service (1968), for example, found that the quality of consultation varied considerably and was too often perfunctory. Some MPs, on the other hand, took a different view. They believed government was engaged in too much consultation with outside interests, to a degree that threatened to undermine the role of Parliament.

Moreover, there were examples of the consultation process failing to produce a compromise. On occasion even the most harmonious relationships broke down, as in 1965 when the BMA became involved in a heated row with the Ministry of Health over the remuneration of general practitioners. At one stage the BMA Council collected undated letters of resignation from the NHS from its GP members in an effort to place pressure on the department (Grey-Turner and Sutherland, 1982, p.155). There were disputes of similar magnitude during the 1960s between those other famous 'partners', the NFU and the Ministry of Agriculture. Yet such breaches were the exception and, in general, conflict was well-managed. The 1970s, however, saw a greater degree of conflict. Economic crises and the decline of consensus politics created a climate in which it proved difficult to secure agreement on key policies. Relationships between government and the trade unions, for example, became very difficult as incomes policies and industrial relations policies bred discontent. Although confrontational strategies by producer interest groups (and by government itself) became more evident in this period, the accommodation of pressure groups through processes of consultation and negotiation nevertheless remained the dominant feature of the government's policy style, irrespective of which party was in power (Richardson and Jordan, 1979).

The Thatcher government and pressure groups
In 1979 the Thatcher government came to power with a new agenda and a confrontational political style. Although confrontation had been increasingly evident since the 1960s, the Thatcher government was remarkable in that it appeared to adopt a hostile stance towards pressure groups as a matter of policy. As we saw in Chapter 3, the rhetoric of the Thatcher government was in tune with the New Right view of pressure groups which, in contrast to the traditional Tory perspective, sees pressure groups as a malign force. In addition, certain policies of the Thatcher government were explicitly and deliberately provocative to certain groups, undermining long-established relationships with government. The Thatcher government also had considerable political resources to bolster its approach. Large majorities in the Commons, a feeble and divided opposition and a supportive press enabled it to confront pressure groups successfully.

The consultation process: advisory bodies
The Thatcher government's attitude towards pressure groups was reflected by a shift in emphasis within the consultation process. No new Royal Commissions were appointed. The number of departmental committees of inquiry also declined. Between 1980 and 1985 an average of seven committees were set up each year, compared with around ten a year between 1974 and 1980 (Hennessy, 1986). Some advisory and consultation procedures were dismantled as part of the government's attack on quasi-government bodies: between 1980 and 1990 the number of advisory

committees fell by a third. Surprisingly, many of the tripartite
institutions survived the axe during the 1980s. The National Economic Development Council (NEDC) remained, but was down-
graded. In 1987 its meetings were reduced in number from ten to
four per year, with the Chancellor of the Exchequer only attending once a year, while the number of NEDC committees (focusing on particular sectors of the economy) was cut by half. The
NEDC was later abolished by the Major government. Another
agency, the Manpower Services Commission (MSC), thrived
during the 1980s as the government agency responsible for training, but it was seen increasingly as an arm of central government
rather than a quasi-autonomous tripartite body. The position of
the trade unions and the local authorities on the MSC weakened
significantly. It eventually succumbed, being succeeded by the
Training Commission in 1988, an arrangement which subsequently failed when the unions refused to co-operate with the
government's new training programme for the long-term un-
employed.

The Thatcher government's hostility to 1970s-style corporatism is legendary. Nevertheless, her government did adopt a
type of corporatism in spite of this, though it was far more covert
and selective than had been practised before (Perkin, 1989). New
institutions, incorporating particular interests, were created to
formulate and implement policies. They included a number of
new advisory committees. As a result the decline in their number
slowed towards the end of the decade. Indeed, in 1988 and again
in 1990 the number of advisory committees actually increased.
One of the new organisations established to give advice to the
government was the National Curriculum Council (NCC), set up
by the 1988 Education Reform Act (Graham and Tytler, 1993).
It had a number of subject groups whose membership deliberately
excluded those with ideas the government disliked, namely, the
so-called educational establishment, the local education authorities and teachers' unions. This was a means of distancing government from such groups, while enhancing the role of the
independent schools and right-wing educational pressure groups
which, in constrast, were well represented. The NCC, it should

be noted, has since been merged with another body established by the 1988 Act – the Schools Examinations and Assessments Council – whose task it was to advise government on the testing of pupils, to form a new body, the Schools Curriculum and Assessment Authority.

Consultative documents
The Thatcher government retained most of the procedural formalities of the consultative process. It continued to issue consultative documents, including Green Papers, on proposed legislation and other policy initiatives. The number of consultative documents received by the House of Commons Public Information Office rose from an average of 28.6 a year under the Callaghan government to 277 a year during Thatcher's third term (see Exhibit 6.1). However, care should be taken when interpreting these figures. Although the Public Information Office is the best source of information regarding consultative documents, it does not receive some of the more obscure ones. It is therefore possible that the increase in the number of documents may reflect improvements in the collection of information and, in particular, the greater willingness of government departments to circulate consultative documents more widely than before.

One should also note that the Thatcher government legislated more than its predecessors, passing around 1,500 pages of primary legislation a year in the 1980s (compared with fewer than 1,100 pages a year by the 1974–79 Labour government). The apparent rise in the number of consultative documents has to be seen in this context. Moreover, the documents issued by the Thatcher government varied considerably in purpose and importance. Many pressure groups complained that most were in reality statements of intent, and that the procedure was rarely used to garner views on what could be done to tackle a particular problem (Hansard Society, 1993). Another complaint was that the Thatcher government tended to use low-profile consultative documents rather than Green Papers, published in the form of a Command Paper or by Her Majesty's Stationery Office (HMSO). During Thatcher's first term there was a slight fall in the number of 'high profile' Green Papers: an average of eight per year were issued in this period, compared with an average of 9.6 per year during the last three years of the previous Labour government. However, this decline was reversed in Thatcher's second term when an average of 10.7 Green Papers a year were issued and in the third term where the average rose to 12.3 a year. Of course, the consultation process depends more upon a genuine willingness on the part of government to absorb comments than upon how many documents are produced. Indeed, one of the criticisms levelled at the Thatcher government was that it did not allow enough time for proper consultation on important reforms.

Exhibit 6.1 **Green Papers and other consultative documents**

	Green Papers		Other consultative documents	
	Numbers	Average per year	Numbers	Average per year
1967–75	29	3.2	–	–
1976–78	29	9.6	86	28.6
1979–83	40	8.0	412	82.4
1984–87	46	10.7	685	171.3
1988–90	38	12.6	831	277.0
1991–93	31	10.3	859	286.3

Sources: Hansard Society (1993); House of Commons Public Information Office; Jordan (1977); Silkin (1973)

In fact, one finds that during the 1980s consultation periods varied considerably even on issues of similar importance and complexity. For example, three months were allotted for the Green Paper on social security in 1985, while only eight weeks were set aside for comments on the Education Reform Bill two years later. In most cases, however, consultation periods for high profile Green Papers were not different from previous administrations.

The average consultation period for Green Papers in the period 1984–90 was sixteen weeks, comparable with the three-month deadlines common in the 1970s. However, in a quarter of cases from the 1984–90 sample, deadlines of ten weeks or fewer had been set.

An in-depth analysis of all consultative documents issued to the House of Commons' Public Information Office (i.e. high profile Green Papers plus other consultation papers) in the period 1 December 1988 to 31 May 1989 also reveals quite short deadlines in some cases. Of the 140 documents issued in this period, 129 had deadlines set for comments. Of these 16.3 per cent had deadlines of twenty days or less, and almost two-thirds had deadlines of forty days or less. The average consultation period for the sample was 39.2 days (see Exhibit 6.2).

Evidence given by a range of pressure groups to the Hansard Society Commission on the Legislative Process also sheds some light on the quality of the consultation process during the Thatcher era. Sifting through this evidence one can find a number of cases where the consultation process appears to have broken down. One striking example was the Housing Bill of 1988, which was given its second reading before the end of the specified consultation period. The Commission concluded that in general there was a 'substantial, objective evidence of failure to consult, inadequate time for consultation and subsequent unworkability of legislation' (Hansard Society, 1993, p.30). However, it did find some examples of good practice and, in some areas, evidence of improvement. Indeed, some of the groups which submitted evidence expressed their satisfaction with the consultative process. This suggests that the Thatcher government had a variable impact on relationships between groups and the executive, a point we shall return to later in this chapter.

Nevertheless, it does appear that the consultative process deteriorated in several important respects during the 1980s, largely because of the Thatcher government's resistance to adverse comment in the early stages of policy formation. Indeed, it was often committed to reform in the face of intense opposition. For example, of sixty responses to the consultative document on social

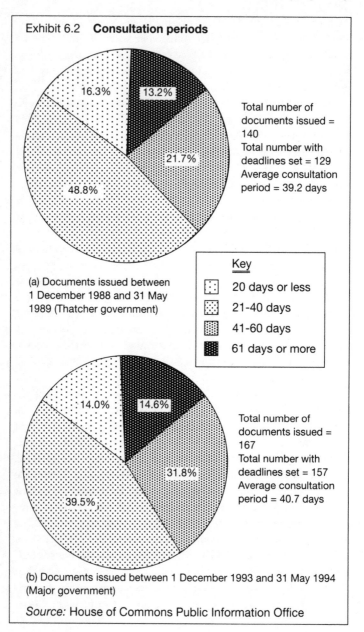

Exhibit 6.2 **Consultation periods**

16.3% 13.2%

21.7%

48.8%

Total number of documents issued = 140
Total number with deadlines set = 129
Average consultation period = 39.2 days

(a) Documents issued between 1 December 1988 and 31 May 1989 (Thatcher government)

Key
[ ] 20 days or less
21-40 days
41-60 days
61 days or more

14.0% 14.6%

31.8%

39.5%

Total number of documents issued = 167
Total number with deadlines set = 157
Average consultation period = 40.7 days

(b) Documents issued between 1 December 1993 and 31 May 1994 (Major government)

Source: House of Commons Public Information Office

security reform in 1985, only two (both right wing organisations: the Monday Club and the Institute of Directors) were unequivocally in support of the proposals (Whiteley and Winyard, 1987). So even where consultation did take place it was often a case of 'going through the motions'.

The consultation process in this period can perhaps be better understood in the light of Sir Douglas Black's (1987) typology of consultation: (1) where government surveys the views of groups and individuals with the intention of modifying its proposals; (2) where the government has little intention of modifying its proposals, though it may be prepared to make minor amendments in the light of views received; (3) where it has a clear idea of the policy required and consults only those who will support it. It appears that the Thatcher government continued to undertake consultation of the second and third type, while the first became less common.

The variable impact of the Thatcher government
Not all pressure groups were affected in the same way. Indeed, some appear to have been unaffected. In one study just under half of the groups surveyed perceived no change in the frequency or effectiveness of contacts with ministers and civil servants during the 1980s (Baggott, 1992). Some were drawn closer to government during this period, while others, in varying degrees, experienced a deterioration in their relationship.

The trade unions suffered the most. In addition to the economic, financial and legislative constraints imposed during the 1980s, they were increasingly excluded from the consultation process. Contacts at prime ministerial level and government-initiated contact declined sharply after 1979 (Mitchell, 1987). Yet the Thatcher government did not sever contact entirely. The unions retained representation on a number of tripartite bodies such as the Health and Safety Commission, the National Economic Development Council and the Manpower Services Commission.

The decline in unions' access and influence was a key feature of the 1980s, but this fate was not an isolated experience. Other lobbies such as doctors, teachers, broadcasters, lawyers and local authorities experienced a deterioration in their relationship with government and could not prevent the adoption of radical policies hostile to their interests.

The Thatcher government introduced health service reforms in the face of strong opposition from the medical profession. One was the decision in 1985 to remove certain medicines from the NHS list without first consulting the BMA, which would have been normal practice in previous years. However, the government did accept a number of amendments at a later stage to minimise opposition from the doctors. Another serious dispute occurred later in the decade over the introduction of a new contract for GPs which tied their pay more closely to specific tasks performed. In this case there was quite a lot of consultation. Many of the changes had been outlined in a Green Paper and some controversial proposals had been diluted, but the broad policy aims remained and the profession continued to campaign against the government's proposals. The BMA did succeed in negotiating a number of small changes to the detail of the contract. However, a majority of GPs voted against it and it was subsequently imposed upon them by the government.

The NHS reforms introduced in 1989 created even more acrimony. The policy was drawn up by a small committee of Health and Treasury ministers and special advisers, chaired by Mrs Thatcher. The profession's representatives were not consulted at this level, though they were invited to submit their proposals directly to the Secretary of State for Health. When the government's plans for reform were published, they contained proposals to establish a competitive market for health care within the NHS. The doctors and other health professionals objected to this plan, but despite a great deal of parliamentary lobbying the government's legislation was approved with few concessions.

Other public sector professions also claimed that they were not being sufficiently consulted on important policy decisions. The teachers faced a barrage of reforms in this period, stemming mainly from the 1988 Education Reform Act, and had little opportunity to comment on the government's proposals. This contrasted with the situation under previous governments where their contribution to policy-making at an early stage had been explicitly recognised. The teachers resorted to lobbying against the legislation as it passed through Parliament, but like the doctors had little success given the government's large parliamentary majority.

The broadcasting lobby was another which felt the force of Thatcherism. The Broadcasting Act of 1990, which sought to introduce greater competition and less regulation into this field, was heavily criticised by most broadcasting organisations. Yet, unlike the NHS internal market reforms and the education reforms, there was prior consultation, including a Green Paper on radio broadcasting and an official inquiry into the future of the BBC (the Peacock report). The broadcasting lobby was therefore able to comment on the government's proposals at an early stage and secured many important amendments both before, during and after the passage of the government's Bill. Indeed, no fewer than 1,356 amendments were made, many in response to pressure from interested organisations and the opposition parties. Some changes were very significant indeed, including amendments strengthening the quality thresholds for the new independent television franchises. Although broadcasting groups complained that there had been insufficient prior consultation, they maintained a close dialogue with ministers during the passage of the legislation which, in parallel with an effective parliamentary campaign, persuaded the government to accept modifications to the Bill. Even so, the broad thrust of the reforms could not be deflected, despite the industry's opposition.

The legal profession was also faced with radical reform. However, these changes were subject to better pre-legislative consultation than was the case with the health, education and broadcasting reforms. The government issued three Green Papers. Extensive consultations led to several key changes to the government's proposals before the Bill was introduced into Parliament. One of the most controversial proposals – to establish an executive committee on legal education and conduct with executive powers – appeared in a diluted form in the subsequent White

Paper. Once again though, the main thrust of the government's reforms – in this case to increase competition while strengthening the regulation of the profession – was carried forward.

The local authorities were subjected to wave after wave of reform during the 1980s. Over 140 Acts of Parliament in the period 1979–92 relate to local government. In previous years the local authority associations had been closely involved in the policy-making process and expected to be fully consulted on matters affecting them. During the 1980s, however, they experienced a serious decline in consultation. Like many of those groups already mentioned, the local authorities focused their lobbying efforts on Parliament in an attempt to secure amendments to bills during their passage and achieved a number of successes, often with the assistance of the House of Lords (Welfare, 1992).

These cases illustrate a deterioration in the relationship between particular groups and the executive, while showing the extent to which this varied, even where groups were equally hostile to government policy. Broadcasters and lawyers were able to maintain a more effective working relationship with government than teachers, doctors, local authorities and trade unions in general. This suggests that neither the style of the Thatcher government, nor the provocative nature of its policies, automatically led to a failure to consult groups and to maintain a good working relationship with them.

Indeed, there was a noticeable variation in the way individual ministers handled pressure groups. Some appeared dismissive of groups and frequently had a poor relationship with them. Indeed, Kenneth Clarke was openly criticised by pressure groups for this reason during his tenure at the departments of Education, Health, and at the Home Office. Interestingly, the same groups reported better relations with some of his immediate predecessors and successors, namely John MacGregor (who preceded Clarke at Education) and William Waldegrave (who replaced him at Health). The local government associations similarly perceived an improvement in relations with the Department of the Environment when Nicholas Ridley was replaced by Chris Patten. Personalities can make a difference. For example, David Mellor, the

Home Office minister responsible for piloting the government's Broadcasting Bill through the Commons in 1989/90, was applauded by many for being prepared to discuss issues extensively with pressure groups and for his willingness to accept constructive amendments. However, the general thrust of government policy in the 1980s and the political style of its leader, limited the ability of ministers to pursue constructive and consensual policy styles.

Yet even where ministers were hostile, some pressure groups found that they could maintain fairly cordial relationships with civil servants. This suggests that the strength of existing links with the executive, through its permanent officials, had a protective effect which in some cases prevented a complete breakdown of the relationship. The BMA, for example, contrasted its dealings with ministers during the 1980s (often hostile) with its contact with civil servants (generally cordial). Survey evidence also indicates that many groups which were disadvantaged in the Thatcher era retained effective contacts with civil servants and in some cases improved upon them. According to one survey (Baggott, 1992), among groups representing labour interests (that is trade unions and professional bodies, whose relationships with government appear to have deteriorated most) three-quarters claim not to have experienced a decline in the frequency of their contacts with civil servants during the 1980s, while two-thirds did not perceive a decline in the effectiveness of those contacts. A closer analysis of the data yielded by this research, relating to nineteen groups who claimed that the effectiveness of their links with ministers perceptibly declined during the 1980s, reveals that seven did not experience a decline in the effectiveness of their relationships with civil servants. Although the sample is small, this does suggest that a deterioration in a group's relationship with ministers is not automatically reflected in a similar decline in their relationship with civil servants.

The impact of the Thatcher government on relations between groups and the executive also varied with the stages of policy-making process. As mentioned earlier, some pressure groups found it difficult to influence the policy process at an early stage, and prior consultation, where it did take place, was often limited. Most groups also faced difficulties getting their views across at the legislative stage. However, the Thatcher government did not have an absolute grip on the legislative process, despite its large majorities in the House of Commons. As the broadcasting case illustrated, pressure could still be effective at this stage. The House of Lords also inflicted regular defeats on the government during the 1980s. Often such defeats were inspired by groups deliberately excluded by the government from the consultation process. For example the Lords' amendment to the 1988 Education Bill, altering the government's rules on parental ballots for school 'opt-outs', was urged by the teachers' unions and the local authority associations (see p.163 below).

Furthermore, once legislation had been passed, the government was rarely able to ignore groups at the implementation stage. Indeed, the traditional process of negotiation between groups and government tended to reassert itself over practical issues of implementation (Richardson, 1990). In the case of education, for example, the government was willing to make a number of changes to pupil assessment and to the national curriculum in the light of criticisms by teachers and their representatives. Its dependence on the co-operation of the teaching profession weakened its position at this vital stage. Later, as we shall see, the teachers' unions boycotted assessment and their protests resulted in further changes to the regime.

Who benefited?

Let us now consider those groups which perceived an improvement in their relationship with the executive during the 1980s, either because they supported the aims and policies of the Thatcher government, or because they could assist the development and implementation of these policies. These included business organisations, right-wing think tanks and conservative moral groups.

During the 1980s many business organisations entered into a closer relationship with government as advisers and consultants on the practical implementation of policies. For example, the advertising industry and the financial sector were, through their expertise, able to exert considerable influence over the details of the government's privatisation programme. This was illustrated by the withdrawal of nuclear power from the electricity privatisation plans in 1989, a sharp reversal in official policy prompted by the government's own financial advisers. However, the influence of consultancy firms such as solicitors, accountants, merchant banks and management consultants has not been confined to the work for which they are paid, though this has given them valuable experience and helped them to develop useful contacts when lobbying on issues affecting their broader interests.

Other private sector lobbies also found themselves drawn closer to government as a result of policies which sought to increase their role in the delivery of public services. These included the independent schools, private health providers and companies tendering for public sector contracts. The private sector in general enjoyed increased access to government during the Thatcher era (Grant, 1993). This was enhanced by close personal relationships between businessmen and senior members of the government, such as the rapport which existed between Lord King of British Airways and Margaret Thatcher. The acceptance of company directorships by former Cabinet ministers further strengthened these links (see pp.95–6 above). Government also turned increasingly to businessmen for specialist advice: including the Prime Minister herself who used Lord Rayner (Marks and Spencers) and Sir Robin Ibbs (ICI) as efficiency advisers, and Sir Roy Griffiths (Sainsbury's) as adviser on health policy. Inward and outward secondments between the Civil Service and business increased considerably in this period, strengthening these networks (see p.95 above).

Not all business organisations enjoyed a cordial relationship with government, however. For example, farmers and the fishing industry frequently expressed their unhappiness with policy. Even the brewing industry, one of the most powerful lobbies in the country, had to fight a vigorous campaign during the late 1980s to persuade the government to dilute its plans for greater competition in the industry. Its members did prompt the government to think again on this issue, but the remarkable thing was that such a powerful and well-connected lobby had to work so hard to persuade ministers to back down (see Exhibit 7.1).

What about business associations? The CBI had a difficult relationship with government in the Thatcher era. In 1981 its opposition to government policy led its Director-General to declare 'a bare-knuckle fight'. This was not an isolated skirmish: CBI criticism of economic policies was heard throughout the decade. For some ministers, particularly those on the right of the Conservative Party, the CBI was tainted by its involvement with the corporatist politics of the 1970s: they preferred the more individualistic and entrepreneurial spirit of the Institute of Directors. The latter improved its relationship with government during the 1980s, as did the Association of British Chambers of Commerce and other groups specifically representing small businesses, which were very much in tune with the Thatcher government's ideals.

The Thatcher government was also more receptive than previous governments to the views of right-wing ideological and conservative moral groups. During the 1980s these enjoyed greater access to ministers and exerted considerable influence over policy. Right-wing think tanks such as the Centre for Policy Studies, the Adam Smith Institute and the Institute for Economic Affairs became a rich source of ideas for the government, playing a key role in health service reform (GP fundholding, the internal market, trust hospitals) and education (opting out, national curriculum testing), as well as in the field of privatisation and contracting out. However, though their ideas have often had a considerable impact on policy formation, the think tanks have often expressed dissatisfaction with the way in which reforms have been implemented, reflecting their weakness in influencing policy at this stage.

During the 1980s the government was also more open than its predecessors to lobbying from conservative moral groups such as the Conservative Family Campaign and the National Viewers' and Listeners' Association. A number of reforms illustrate the growing influence of such groups: the establishment of the Broadcasting Standards Council, restrictions on video recordings; new controls on sex education; and an amendment to the 1989 Local Government Act which outlawed the promotion of homosexuality by local authorities. However, one should not overestimate the importance of these groups, despite their rising profile (Durham, 1989). The moral issues they raised were not central to the Thatcherite agenda. Moreover, their main successes came at the parliamentary stage, rather than through Whitehall. Like the think tanks, they have often been disappointed at the way in which the reforms they have proposed have been implemented.

In summary, the Thatcher government did have a significant impact upon relationships between pressure groups and the executive. It presented a challenge to the philosophy of consultation. Its style and policies brought it into conflict with powerful groups which would normally have expected to be consulted earlier and more extensively than was the case. However, there was much variation in the experience of these groups, with some being more disadvantaged than others. Relationships between the executive and pressure groups also depended on a number of other factors, such as the particular stage of policy-making, the character of individual ministers and the strength of existing relationships with civil servants. Similarly, while the Thatcher government was broadly favourable towards some groups – those representing business, right-wing think tanks and conservative moral groups – there is evidence of a variable impact here too; some groups experiencing greater improvements in their links with government than others and some actually experiencing a deterioration.

The focus upon 'winners' and 'losers' is understandable, but misleading when looking at the broad impact of the Thatcher government upon groups. There was, it seems, a degree of continuity between the Thatcher government and its predecessors. The evidence suggests that in a large proportion of cases the relationship between groups and the executive neither improved nor deteriorated. There was a continued reliance on the procedures of consultation in the majority of cases. Other continuities can be found in the growing confrontation between government and groups and the criticism of consultation processes in the immediate pre-Thatcher period. On the other hand, these should not obscure the very significant changes in emphasis which occurred in the 1980s. The Thatcher government adapted consultative processes, challenging the philosophy of consultation explicitly in many key policy areas, particularly at the earlier stages of the policy process.

The Major government

The replacement of Mrs Thatcher by John Major in 1990 was heralded as a change in style at the top. Major's style was portrayed as a return to 'One Nation Toryism', despite the uncertainties about his ideological position within the Conservative Party. Initially, he seemed to be a more convincing supporter of public services and the welfare state as well as less dogmatic on privatisation. He also appeared to have a more flexible, pragmatic and consensual approach. There were clear signs of a re-emphasis on the philosophy of consultation. The Major government offered an olive branch to many groups which had been excluded in the previous decade, such as the trade unions, the doctors, the teachers and the local authority associations. Ministerial speeches began to emphasise the importance of these groups as partners rather than as opponents.

A survey of pressure groups undertaken a year after Major's accession revealed that many pressure groups (38 per cent of respondents) believed that the political environment had improved since the departure of Thatcher (Baggott, 1992). Most of these claimed that the new government was more sensitive and sympathetic, more willing to listen to their views and more ready to grant access to senior decision-makers. Very few groups (4 per cent) believed that the political environment had deteriorated, while the majority (58 per cent) did not perceive any significant change, again reflecting the stability of most relationships between groups and the executive.

One has to bear in mind, however, that Major came to power in a pre-election period. Though the general election did not take place until April 1992, it had been expected for well over a year.

In this politically sensitive period, the government went out of its way to appear open to concerns raised by groups. The poll tax was abolished; pre-election 'sweeteners' totalled almost £3 billion, including orders for military equipment, a plan for nature conservation in England, and various subsidies, grants or other financial concessions. In addition the government conceded to a number of campaigns which it had previously opposed. For example, compensation for haemophiliacs infected by HIV-contaminated products was increased after the government had earlier refused anything more than a small *ex gratia* payment (Ashley, 1994). The government also increased the resources available to the Social Fund – a part of the social security system which had attracted particularly heavy criticism from the poverty lobby.

After the election
The general election of 1992 left the government with a much smaller majority, making it far more vulnerable to parliamentary pressure and backbench rebellions. It was expected that this would place even greater emphasis upon a political strategy that involved rather than excluded pressure groups. Most thought that, irrespective of the government's style or ideological standpoint, it would have to consult more thoroughly and rebuild relationships with particular groups.

The record of the Major government in this respect is difficult to measure. We are dealing with a much shorter time period than the Thatcher era. Nevertheless there are fragments of evidence that we can consider. First of all, we can look at the numbers of consultation papers issued by the Major government. This is a crude indicator, as already noted, but it does give a rough guide to the willingness of a government to consult. Under Major, the number of consultative documents received by the Public Information Office of the House of Commons rose to an average of 286.3 a year (see Exhibit 6.1) compared with an annual average of 82.4, 171.3 and 277 for Thatcher's first, second and third terms, respectively. However, there was at the same time a decline in 'high profile' Green Papers: down to 10.3 a year compared with 12.6 in Thatcher's third term.

How do consultation periods compare with the Thatcher era? An analysis of a sample relating to a three-month period between 1 December 1993 and 31 May 1994 found that of the 167 documents concerned, 157 had specified deadlines for comments. Of these 14 per cent had deadlines of twenty days or less, while just over half (53.5 per cent) had deadlines of forty days or less. Although this seems to indicate a slightly more generous approach, the average consultation period of the Major sample was 40.7 days, only 1.5 days longer than in the Thatcher sample taken five years earlier. This suggests more continuity than change.

The Major government did depart from the practice of its predecessor by appointing a new Royal Commission (on Criminal Justice) in 1991, but this did not signal a shift back to the use of commissions and committees of inquiry on the scale that some expected. No further Royal Commissions have been created. Only six committees of inquiry were created in 1992 and three in 1993. Their number is therefore lower than in the 1980s and represents about half the annual average of the 1970s. Furthermore, the fall in the number of advisory committees, which actually slowed down and then reversed in the last years of the Thatcher government, has since regained impetus. Their number declined from 971 (1990) to 829 (1993).

The impact on particular groups

Further evidence can be gleaned by looking at groups whose relationships with government deteriorated in the 1980s: trade unions, the medical profession, teachers and local authorities. There were initial signs of an improved relationship between government and the trade union movement, reflected in meetings between the two in the period after Thatcher's departure. Contact with ministers, which was virtually non-existent during the latter part of the 1980s, also increased in frequency during the early 1990s. Both ministers and senior trade unionists began to drop their mutually hostile stance in public. There were also signs of improved co-operation, such as the development of a new apprenticeship scheme, announced in the November 1993 budget. However, talk of a new partnership was premature. The National

Economic Development Council, the last vestige of post-war corporatism, was abolished in 1992. This act perhaps symbolised the
Conservatives' true feelings about the value of partnership with
the trade unions. Meanwhile, government policy continued to
restrict trade union activities along the lines set by its predecessor and indeed sought to deregulate pay and conditions even further. In addition, the government remained at odds with the
social and economic policies of the trade union movement, while
the imposition of a public sector pay freeze has brought further
criticism from this quarter. There was also increased conflict with
particular sections of the trade union movement, the most notable
being the clash with the miners during 1992/3 over the pit closure programme (see Exhibit 6.3).

Exhibit 6.3 **The pit closure programme**

The decision in 1992 to close thirty-one pits with the loss of
30,000 mining jobs was not simply a matter for the miners'
unions, British Coal and the government. It brought protests,
from miners, from the media, the general public and even
from Tory MPs, whose rebellion threatened the government's
slim parliamentary majority. The government responded with
a White Paper, published in March 1993, which offered subsidies to those pits which could prove their commercial viabil-
ity. But it refused to intervene more widely in the energy
market, for example, by restricting the use of other fuels by
power stations. Most observers agreed that unless this was
done the energy market would still be weighted against the
British coal industry, making the pits commercially unviable.
Their analysis proved correct. By late 1993, even some of the
pits which were thought to have been saved began to close.
By December 1994, of the twelve pits which had apparently
been reprieved by the government's White Paper only four
now remained in production. By now the protests were
smaller, localised and muted. Despite the scale of opposition
to the government's policy, the programme of closures was

carried through largely as intended.

The Major government faced other battles throughout the public sector, arising largely from the implementation of the policies of its predecessor. The doctors' organisations have continued to oppose the NHS internal market, despite various attempts to pacify them. Relations between the medical profession and the government thawed slightly following the departure of Mrs Thatcher, and the replacement of Kenneth Clarke, the Secretary of State for Health, first by William Waldegrave and then Virginia Bottomley.

Clarke's successors appeared more willing to modify the reforms at the implementation stage. Concern among doctors that the reforms were producing a two-tier system of health care led to new rules on admitting patients to hospital. Sensing a new mood of co-operation, most observers believed that the formerly close relationship between the government and the medical profession was being re-established. However, it appears that relations were still strained. Although the BMA dropped its opposition to some government policies (such as GP fundholding, for example), it remained highly critical of the impact of the internal market. Although access to decision-makers improved, the BMA continued to protest that it was not fully consulted on policy matters. In January 1994 its chairman was asked to raise this problem with the Secretary of State. One particular concern has been the short time allowed for comments on consultative documents. For example, it was reported in the medical press that the Department of Health requested comments from the BMA on a twenty-page document (on the subject of clinical audit) within twenty-four hours! (*British Medical Journal*, 1994.)

Following Thatcher's departure, it appeared that the government and the teaching profession would be able to work together in a more constructive way. But, after early attempts to rebuild relationships, hostilities resumed. This culminated in the teachers' boycott of the standard assessment tasks (SATs) which had been introduced by the 1988 Education Reform Act. Many changes had been made to the detail of the national curriculum and the SATs, some in line with the criticisms of teachers. These concessions did not go far enough, however, and the teachers' unions threatened a boycott of the tests which were due to take place during the summer of 1993. The government offered further concessions by agreeing to a review of the national curriculum that would include in its remit the possible slimming down of the curriculum and assessment process. The unions were strengthened by membership ballots and by the failure of attempts to obtain a High Court injunction against the boycott. Criticism from other quarters mounted as parents, governors and even the independent schools and some of the government's own advisers expressed their dissatisfaction with the tests. The government responded with even more concessions – in the form of a simplified system of tests in the following year. Nevertheless, the boycott went ahead and was successful, with only 5 per cent of secondary schools administering the tests.

When the review was published in January 1994 the result was seen very much as a victory for the teachers. The government accepted proposals to cut back the elaborate testing system, and to simplify the national curriculum in order to give schools more flexibility. It also agreed to involve teachers, nominated by teacher and subject associations, on the working parties established to shape the new curriculum. Far from being further alienated by opposing government policy, as one might have expected, the teachers appeared to have achieved greater influence through their action. The relationship between their unions and ministers, in view of the government's embarrassment at losing the confrontation, nevertheless remained cool.

We turn now to the local authority associations, another group which was excluded in the 1980s. In 1991 the Major government initiated consultation on three areas of reform: the internal workings, the structure and the financing of local government. Aside from this process, the associations claim to have experienced an improvement in their relationship with government in recent years. Their chairmen now meet formally with the Secretary of State for the Environment on two or three occasions a year, a practice which began in 1992. The associations also believe that government is now more willing to listen to their views, and can point to instances where they have been able to persuade it to change its mind. For example, on the subject of compulsory competitive tendering, the local authority associations have been able to delay and dilute the government's original plans. However, there is still much disagreement and the pre-Thatcher relationship has not as yet returned. In particular, there has been a great deal of conflict on a number of issues, including expenditure restrictions, changes to police authorities, housing and education policies.

These cases indicate that the governments expressed willingness to rebuild relationships has been reflected by increased contact between ministers and pressure group leaders. However, there are few signs that the government has taken these groups into its confidence. Consultation in some respects appeared to have improved slightly, but prior consultation has been patchy and lacking on some key issues. Moreover, confrontation has continued in a number of areas as the Major government has struggled to implement policies devised by its predecessor. As the battle over the national curriculum and assessment illustrated, this government has not been afraid of brinkmanship – adopting a Thatcherite style of confrontation, but with fewer political resources in terms of parliamentary, media and public support.

The case of law and order

A similar pattern can be found in other policy areas. Law and order, for example, has been the subject of a number of reforms in the post-Thatcher era. In the 1980s the government's relationships with most of the prominent groups in this field were relatively good: even the battle with the lawyers was conducted both with civility and a considerable degree of consultation, as we saw earlier. As also noted, the Major government appointed a Royal Commission in 1991 to examine the criminal justice system, allowing all interested parties to put their case. Yet, it also initiated a number of policies which appeared to be based on a rejection of the advice of the Royal Commission and of many pressure groups in this field. At the same time, the way in which government was making policy in this area revealed a deterioration in the consultative process.

The repeal of the provisions of the Criminal Justice Act of 1991 relating to a unit fine scheme for offenders, provides an example. The scheme, which was intended to relate fines to offenders' incomes, had not been clearly thought through and when implemented threw up a number of problems. Groups such as the Magistrates' Association lobbied for reform and discussed with the Home Office various ways of improving it. Further consultations were planned, but there then followed a sudden reversal of policy when, without warning, the government announced the complete abolition of the scheme. Better consultation might have enabled government to avoid some of the problems of the scheme while retaining its positive features.

Proper consultation appears to have been lacking when the government publicly backed the principles outlined in the Sheehy report on police pay and conditions in 1993. However, under pressure from the police associations it diluted some of the most contentious proposals, such as the introduction of fixed-term contracts and performance-related pay. The move was widely seen as a U-turn, though in fact ministers did press ahead with some of the report's controversial recommendations, such as the abolition of certain ranks in the police force.

Defeats on the Police and Magistrates' Courts Bill during the 1993/4 parliamentary session provide a further indication of the government's approach in this field. Many of the provisions of this Bill were heavily criticised by the police, magistrates and the local authorities among others. Once again, it appeared that government had failed to consult at an early stage, as this lobby with the help of the House of Lords inflicted a series of defeats on the Bill, including a staged retreat from plans to alter the composition of police authorities. Similarly, many aspects of the Criminal Justice and Public Order Bill, introduced during the same parliamentary session, rejected the views of the law and order lobby. It was heavily criticised and faced a very rough ride indeed through Parliament.

Whether or not the Major government won or lost on these issues is not the main point. What is more important is the way in which it adopted an approach to policy-making which is not dissimilar from that of its predecessor: attempting to ride roughshod over interested parties, failing to consult adequately, and grudgingly giving concessions when the forces rallied against it proved too strong. The examples taken from law and order are not exceptional: one can name a host of others from this period, such as the privatisation of British Rail, the reform of the Child Support Agency, the D-Day commemorations and the curtailing of the roads programme (see Exhibit 8.3).

Thatcher's beneficiaries

Finally, what of the impact of the Major government's approach upon those groups which benefited during the Thatcher period? The think tanks and moral groups were initially concerned that it might seek to distance itself from them. These fears have proved largely unfounded. The think tanks, for example, have continued to influence policies such as market testing of public services and the Citizen's Charter. Meanwhile, the government's 'Back to Basics' policy appeared to reflect in some respects the political agenda of the moral right.

Business groups continued to exercise considerable influence, as illustrated by the deregulation initiative, for example, where businessmen and women were appointed to the task forces set up to recommend changes in the law. However, since the Major government came to power, there has been a shift in the balance of power between the business organisations. Some claim to have lost influence as a direct result of Thatcher's departure including, for example, companies like British Airways (which, as noted earlier, had built up a strong personal link with the former Prime Minister). Others, however, tell a different story. For example, relations between the government and the CBI have been much more cordial in recent years than in the Thatcher era.

Conclusions

We have seen that changes in government can weaken the influence of some groups and strengthen the hand of others. The successive election victories of the Conservative Party seems to have benefited groups which share its broad ideological vision and disadvantaged others, which do not. There is also some evidence that new priorities draw some groups closer to government, while others become more distant. Furthermore, the style of government seems to be an important factor in shaping the group–government relationship although, as we have seen, rhetoric and practice are not always matched. In this context one should also note that ministerial changes can have an impact given the different styles, personalities and prejudices of individual ministers.

The web of contacts between groups and government is, however, complex. Government is locked into the world of pressure groups through a variety of formal and informal relationships. Some of these are stable and can survive changes in government. It is very difficult for any new government to transform these arrangements and there is likely to be an element of continuity. Even the Thatcher government adapted government-group relations rather than sought a complete transformation of them, while the Major government, despite the suggestion that it would adopt a more consensual and consultative style of policy-making, has attempted to continue along the lines set by its predecessor in many respects.

7

Lobbying Parliament

Surveys have confirmed the importance of Parliament as a focal point for pressure-group lobbying. The Study of Parliament Group found that three quarters of the groups examined had regular or frequent contact with MPs while 59 per cent had regular or frequent contact with members of the House of Lords (Rush, 1990a). Another recent survey (Baggott, 1992) has also revealed high levels of contact between Parliament and pressure groups, finding that almost a third of groups were in contact with MPs at least once a week, while over 60 per cent had contact at least once a month (see Exhibit 5.2). Survey evidence also shows that parliamentary lobbying has increased in recent years. According to the survey undertaken by Baggott, 45 per cent of groups reported an increase in their contact with the House of Commons in the 1980s while 37 per cent reported an increase in their contact with the House of Lords. There is also considerable anecdotal evidence of an increase in lobbying, reflected in the observations of MPs themselves (House of Commons, 1990).

This chapter explores the nature and extent of parliamentary lobbying in some detail. First of all, we shall look at the reasons why groups lobby Parliament and why this appears to be on the increase. Secondly, we shall explore the various channels which groups may use when seeking to influence Parliament, along with some suggestions about how pressure groups might be more effectively integrated in the processes of scrutiny and legislation. This is followed by a discussion of the background and interests of MPs, where we shall take the opportunity to examine the concern which has surrounded MPs' outside interests in recent years, in particular their pecuniary interests, and related issues raised by the growth of commercial lobbyists. Finally, we examine the relationships between groups and the House of Lords, which has been an increasingly important focus for lobbying over the last two decades.

Why do groups lobby Parliament?

At the heart of any discussion of the relationship between pressure groups and Parliament lies a conundrum. If policy-making is dominated by the executive arm of government, why do pressure groups invest so much time and effort in parliamentary lobbying? Rush (1990b) has set out three possible explanations. First, that outside organisations fail to perceive Parliament's place in the policy-making process, believing it to have more influence over policy than is actually the case. Second, that Parliament is used when pressure elsewhere has failed, and is therefore a kind of last resort for those unable to influence ministers and senior civil servants. The third explanation is that Parliament does have an impact on policy. In other words, groups that lobby Parliament are not labouring under a delusion, nor are they by definition excluded from the higher echelons of the decision-making process. Rather, they deliberately choose a strategy which involves parliamentary lobbying because they correctly believe that this will bring benefits in terms of policy.

One can find evidence to support all three contentions. There are undoubtedly some politically naive groups which believe that Parliament is all-powerful, and that by simply lobbying MPs they will be able to secure their objectives. But even the least experienced groups, whose foray into the political arena is brief, will quickly learn that Parliament is not all-powerful. Naivety alone cannot explain the scale of parliamentary lobbying which exists.

The second explanation has a more solid foundation. Samuel Finer (1958) identified a law of inverse proportion: the closer and more exclusive a group's relationship with the executive, the less use it will make of Parliament. By the same token, groups which do not enjoy such a relationship with the executive are forced to take up their case through parliamentary or other channels. Wyn Grant's distinction between insider and outsider groups (see p.14–20 above) has similar implications. Here it is assumed that the gains offered by an insider strategy, coupled with the requirements of the consultative process, will lead groups who are willing and able to establish good contacts with the executive to focus their efforts there. The implication is that insider groups will spend relatively less time on other strategies such as parliamentary lobbying which will be pursued to a greater extent by outsider groups.

Is parliamentary lobbying a second-best strategy, reserved for those groups which lack good executive contacts? Certainly Parliament is more open and accessible than Whitehall. For those groups which are unable to influence ministers or civil servants directly, parliamentary lobbying is usually regarded as the next best alternative. Notably, those groups which experienced a degree of exclusion from key policy discussions during the 1980s, such as the trade unions, certain public sector professions and the local authorities, expanded their lobbying efforts in Parliament during this period (Baggott, 1992; see also Chapter 6 above).

It would, however, be a mistake to see Parliament as merely a resort for those groups which are out of favour. Indeed, it appears that even groups which enjoy a good relationship with the executive feel that it is important to maintain a significant parliamentary presence. According to Judge (1990) insider groups have a higher frequency of contact with Parliament (86 per cent of insider groups had regular or frequent contact with MPs compared with 67 per cent of outsider groups) and are generally more active in Parliament (except in their contact with the House of Lords and with all-party backbench groups). The survey by Baggott (1992) also showed that insider groups have more frequent contact with Parliament than outsider groups: 72 per cent of insider groups had contact with MPs at least once a month compared with 51 per cent of outsider groups. Insider groups were also more frequently in touch with the House of Lords (63 per cent of insider groups, but only 36 per cent of outsider groups, had at least monthly contact with peers).

It is easy to understand why insider groups do not wish to neglect Parliament. Circumstances can change. There may be a change of government, a ministerial reshuffle or the entry of new issues on to the political agenda. Such changes can bring in new ideas and policies which threaten even the most well-connected groups. Even where the relationship between the executive and the groups remains generally good, it is often very useful to have a parliamentary base from which to launch campaigns on specific issues where insider strategies have so far proved ineffective, or to supplement lobbying through insider channels, as the case of the brewing industry clearly illustrates (see Exhibit 7.1).

Exhibit 7.1 **The brewers and the Monopolies Commission**

In March 1989, after over two years of research, the Monopolies and Mergers Commission presented its report on the brewing industry to the Secretary of State for Trade and Industry, Lord Young. The report called for large brewers owning more than 2,000 public houses to sell off their remaining estate. It also called for more freedom for publicans to stock drinks of their own choice rather than being 'tied' to one particular brewer. Lord Young warmly received the report and said he was minded to implement the proposals. He was supported by consumer groups (such as the Consumers' Association and the Campaign for Real Ale) and by some of the smaller brewing companies. The larger brewers, however, were extremely hostile to the plan. They had well-established links with a number of government departments, including the Department of Trade and Industry (DTI) itself and the Ministry of Agriculture, Fisheries and Food (MAFF, which shared the brewers' hostility to the plan). But much needed to be done to change the DTI's position. The brewers adopted a twin strategy aimed at building broad support for their position. They employed a PR company (Paragon Communications) to undertake a high profile publicity campaign against the plans involving advertisements in the national press. The brewing companies lobbied Parliament, courting the support of individual MPs, the Conservative 1922 Committee and the relevant party subject committees. As a major funder of the Tory Party at a local and national level, the brewers' views could not be ignored. MPs and peers introduced debates in Parliament and raised parliamentary questions on the issue. Over 100 Conservative backbenchers supported an Early Day Motion condemning the Monopolies and Mergers Commission's report. In addition, Lord Young faced a great deal of pressure from within the Conservative Party in Parliament on this issue, particularly from the Party's backbench committee on trade and industry.

This intense pressure forced ministers at the DTI to rethink their position. A compromise plan was put forward in July 1989. The brewers could keep more of their pubs and would not be forced to sell any 'surplus', but would instead operate these outlets at arms' length. The brewers were relieved at the outcome. Their shares rose on the Stock Exchange following the news of the DTI's compromise.

There are other reasons why insider groups may wish to build support among MPs. The prestige of having friends in Parliament should not be underestimated. Groups often gain both credibility and publicity from MPs speaking out on their behalf. In addition, MPs can be useful informants. They can act as the eyes and ears of pressure groups within Parliament itself, monitoring political developments and advising on strategy. Some MPs – particularly those on the government backbenches – are also linked to political and social networks which include senior decision-makers within the executive. These networks can be useful both as means of applying pressure and as sources of information. Thus by cultivating close relationships with certain MPs, groups may improve their knowledge about what is going on in the corridors of power as well as their influence over decisions.

Influencing policy

There are a number of circumstances where Parliament can be influential over policy. Although occasions when MPs are freed from the constraints of party discipline are few and far between, there have been several cases in recent years when free votes have been allowed on important issues such as abortion, embryo research, the restoration of the death penalty and the lowering of the age of consent for homosexuals (see Exhibit 7.2). Once a free vote has been permitted, individual MPs are less constrained on how they vote and are generally more open to pressure-group lobbying. However, one should bear in mind that even in the absence of the whip, other constraints may still make it difficult for groups to influence the way in which MPs vote. As Marsh and Read (1988) have made clear, party allegiance is still the best predictor of how an MP will vote even on an unwhipped vote. There are other factors which also affect the outcome, such as current political circumstances, the views of constituents, the constituency party and colleagues, all of which may shape an MP's judgement. Furthermore, it should be recognised that the decision to allow such a vote to take place is largely determined by the government.Therefore, pressure groups and their supporters in Parliament have to persuade the government that a free vote is desirable.

Exhibit 7.2 **Homosexual law reform**

During the passage of the Criminal Justice and Public Order Bill of 1994, Edwina Currie MP tabled an amendment reducing the age of consent for homosexuals from 21 to 16. The government permitted a free vote on the issue. On 21 February, the amendment was defeated by 307 votes to 280. However, a compromise vote, reducing the age of consent to 18, was carried by 427 votes to 162. As the vote was unwhipped,

the pressure groups involved had plenty of scope for persuading MPs to support their views. However, there were
other important factors which shaped the final outcome.
Many MPs were subjected to pressure from constituents
opposed to liberalisation. In addition, it appears that the
broader political environment affected the vote of Conservative MPs, whose support for the age limit of 16 would have
been decisive. In the months preceding the vote, moral issues
had been at the top of the political agenda, with the government's reiteration of family values being followed by a series
of sex scandals involving Tory MPs. This produced a feeling
of caution on the Conservative benches and created a certain
amount of resistance to Currie's amendment. In the event
only forty-two Tory MPs actually supported the amendment.

The main pressure groups in favour of lowering the age of
consent to 16 involved groups representing gay people,
including Stonewall, OutRage and Torche (the Tory Campaign
for Homosexual Equality). The age limit of 16 was also supported by a range of professional bodies involved in the provision of health and social services, including the BMA, the
Royal College of Psychiatrists, the British Association of
Social Workers and the Health Education Authority. Some
church leaders were also in favour of a lowering of the age of
consent, although the Catholic Church advocated caution.
Other groups were more overtly opposed to change, though
these were in a minority. They included right-wing moral
groups such as the Conservative Family Campaign and
Family and Youth Concern.

Although the gay lobby were very disappointed that they
failed to achieve their primary aim, they nevertheless won a
compromise and came close to a famous victory in circumstances that were far from favourable. Stonewall's campaign
in particular was well-organised. It worked closely with MPs
who openly supported its line, while targeting those who
appeared to be undecided. Its individual supporters, numbering around 10,000, were urged to contact their MPs directly,

to put their case. Stonewall also organised a mass lobby of Parliament on the day of the debate. This latter tactic was, however, regarded by some MPs as counter-productive. But it was perhaps the more aggressive lobbying of some of the other, more militant gay groups – involving alleged threats to expose gay MPs – which may have turned wavering MPs against them, and which, in the circumstances, led to their defeat on the main amendment.

Source: Read, Marsh and Richards (1994)

Private members' legislation, which provides further opportunities for groups to build cross-party support in an effort to change the law, also depends upon the government consenting to the measures in question. For example, David Steel's Termination of Pregnancy Act of 1967, promoted by the pro-abortion lobby, would not have become law without the approval of the then Labour government. Any government, provided that it has a majority, can block the progress of bills which it dislikes, even when there is a considerable amount of parliamentary support for them. This is usually achieved by refusing to allocate the bill sufficient time, or by getting government backbenchers to sabotage it. The latter strategy was in evidence in 1994 when the Department of Social Security was found to have played a major role in wrecking a private member's bill which aimed to extend the rights of disabled people. The Civil Rights (Disabled Persons) Bill fell as a result of damaging amendments, drawn up by the Department of Health itself, but tabled by Conservative MPs.

In the case of government bills the strict imposition of party discipline makes it difficult for pressure groups to persuade MPs, especially government backbenchers, to take a different line from that of their party leadership. However, on rare occasions, parliamentary lobbying has induced rebellions on such a scale that the government has had to withdraw a bill, as the case of the Shops Bill illustrated (see Exhibit 4.4). Usually, when faced with such discontent among its own backbenchers, the government will produce a compromise in order to win their support. This usually takes the form of a government amendment to its own bill, reflecting the concerns expressed by potential rebels. Amendments to government bills by the House of Lords have on some occasions produced a similar response, as we shall see in later in this chapter.

Although MPs can in certain circumstances have a direct impact on government policy and legislation, the scope for achieving even a modification of the government's position is fairly limited on the vast majority of issues. As long as the government has a majority its view will generally prevail on the key issues. Indeed, if the direct impact of Parliament upon legislation were the sole reason why groups lobbied MPs, it is doubtful that the scale of parliamentary lobbying would be at its present level. Yet pressure groups are not only interested in the impact of MPs on legislation. They are aware that MPs can raise issues, thereby helping to influence the political agenda. In the longer term the sentiments expressed in Parliament can filter through into government policy, providing a further incentive for groups to build and maintain support among MPs.

Raising issues

MPs can raise issues in Parliament on behalf of groups in many ways (Dubs, 1989). Parliamentary questions – particularly oral questions – have a high profile and often attract the attention of the media. Questions, whether written or oral, will often set off alarm bells in the government department to which they are addressed, while a series of questions from different MPs on the same subject will further concentrate the minds of ministers and civil servants on the issue. The department concerned will be keen to know what has prompted the questions and whether or not it is part of a broader lobbying campaign. Parliamentary questions can also be used to embarrass the government, but rarely on their own bring about a change in policy.

Early Day Motions are often used to express support or opposition for a policy. Individual MPs allow their names to be associated with a particular motion which is posted on the House of

Commons Order Paper. If a motion attracts a large number of supporters this obviously attracts the government's attention, particularly if they are drawn from its own backbenches. An Early Day Motion was used to good effect by the MPs involved in the brewers' campaign against the government's proposed reforms of the industry (see Exhibit 7.1). Along with other expressions of discontent, this action demonstrated the level of backbench opposition to the government's proposals.

A further option for MPs who wish to raise issues on behalf of a pressure group is the initiation of debates. These tend to get little publicity, however, and rarely provoke government into action. Even so, the short adjournment debates, initiated by backbench MPs at the end of each parliamentary day, are sometimes quite useful as part of a broader campaign of raising government awareness of a particular issue.

MPs may also introduce private members' legislation as a means of highlighting a particular issue. For reasons mentioned earlier, the vast majority of these bills fail. Indeed, most are introduced without any real hope of success, but with a clear intention to raise the profile of an issue. In some circumstances the government is persuaded to introduce its own proposals. For example, following the furore surrounding the defeat of the Bill on the rights of disabled people discussed above, the government introduced a consultation paper on discrimination against the disabled with a view to bringing forward its own legislation.

Finally, we should note the important role of parliamentary committees in raising issues, particularly the departmental select committees (Drewry, 1989). These scrutinise the main policy issues facing particular government departments. They take evidence from the government itself, independent experts and interested organisations. Their reports often attract a great deal of publicity, and in some cases the government has responded positively to their recommendations. Even where government rejects their recommendations, the committees nevertheless perform a useful role in promoting debate. The select committees represent an increasingly important interface between groups and Parliament, as we shall see later in this chapter.

To summarise, the dominance of the executive does not mean that Parliament should be neglected. Even those groups which have a close and effective working relationship with the executive recognise the importance of a significant parliamentary presence. It is not simply a last resort for those unable to influence government through other channels. Although the direct influence of Parliament on policy and legislation may be small, there are circumstances where pressure from backbench MPs can be effective in modifying the government's position. Moreover, Parliament plays an important role in raising issues of concern and thereby helps shape the wider political agenda.

Most groups are aware of this although, as the Shops Bill example in Chapter 4 illustrated, some may be complacent about parliamentary lobbying when they firmly believe the executive to be on their side. Surveys reveal a high level of satisfaction among groups regarding their parliamentary contacts. The Study of Parliament Group found that 93 per cent of respondents believed their contacts with MPs were either useful or very useful. A slightly lower proportion (82 per cent) rated their contact with peers as useful or very useful. Just over half the groups judged their efforts in trying to influence legislation before Parliament as quite successful or very successful. According to the survey by Baggott (1992), it appears that Parliament is becoming even more highly rated by some groups as a focal point for lobbying. This survey found that a third of groups perceived an improvement in the effectiveness of their contacts with MPs during the 1980s, while only 13 per cent perceived a decrease in effectiveness. A third of groups also believed that the effectiveness of contact with the House of Lords had improved during the same period, while only 11 per cent perceived a decline in effectiveness of these contacts.

Influencing Members of Parliament

The ways in which pressure groups lobby MPs can be divided into two main categories: approaches to MPs on an individual basis; and approaches to MPs who are members of a formal committee or group. In practice groups tend to pursue both strategies at the same time. Nevertheless, the distinction is useful in setting out the various options open to them when lobbying Parliament. In this section we shall confine our analysis to the House of Commons; the lobbying of peers is considered separately towards the end of the chapter.

MPs are extremely accessible. They are lobbied in person at the House or in their constituency surgeries. They may meet group leaders for discussions, sometimes informally over lunch or dinner. They also receive written communication from groups and individuals, with some MPs receiving as many as 10,000 letters a year. Despite the accessibility of MPs, there are pitfalls in lobbying them as individuals (see Dubs, 1989; Miller, 1990). It is widely accepted that the practice of wining and dining MPs, though providing a useful opportunity to make a case, does not necessarily produce results. Most agree that it is the quality of the case rather than the quality of the food that is important. Another tactic which often fails is the mass lobby, where hundreds of people descend on Parliament to buttonhole their MPs in an attempt to win support. In order to be effective, mass lobbies have to be extremely well-organised in order to ensure that those involved actually do see their MP and get their view across. To maximise the impact of a mass lobby, it is also important to attract as much publicity as possible in the media and this depends very much on other events happening on the day, which cannot easily be predicted beforehand.

Mass letter writing campaigns can be effective, particularly if the letters are directed by constituents to their own MPs or by ordinary rank-and-file members of a particular group to MPs with an obvious interest in the issue in question. Letters from organisations are also treated with respect as long they are personalised. However, MPs are particularly suspicious of impersonal, glossy brochures which have obviously been sent out *en masse* to all members. It is important to recognise that at least half of MPs' mail is thrown in the bin, much of it unopened (Public Policy Consultants, 1988). Given the pressure of work facing MPs, and the volume of mail they receive, it is extremely important that any communication is short and to the point. Perhaps the most effective form of written communication which a group can provide is a short, well-researched briefing paper on a particular issue, which MPs can actually draw upon when participating in parliamentary debates.

The choice of who to lobby is also an important one. Groups must recognise their friends and enemies in the House. Many groups actually keep lists of MPs who are known to be on their side; some also have blacklists of MPs who are opposed to the group's aims. Most are able to build links with MPs should they wish to do so. As Richards (1972) once remarked, there are few outside interests that cannot find a friend in the House of Commons when they need to. In seeking allies groups will familiarise themselves with the interests of MPs which, as we shall see in a later section, are many and varied. They may even invite MPs to join their groups, or if they can afford it may sponsor an MP or hire one as a political adviser.

Obtaining the support of allies is the easy part. The real battle often involves winning over MPs who are neutral, or even hostile, to the group's aims. Groups have to demonstrate the widest possible support for their viewpoint. This often means that neutral MPs have to be persuaded to support the campaign while potential opponents are placated. In some circumstances seeking support from normally hostile quarters is not just desirable but essential. For example, during the 1980s the Child Poverty Action Group (CPAG) and many other welfare groups focused their attention on building support among backbench Tory MPs. This strategy proved difficult given the Conservative government's ideological hostility to the welfare state. Yet it was vital in the light of the large majority which the government enjoyed. Only by raising doubts on the backbenches could these groups hope to modify government policy. Indeed, in a number of cases, such as the retention of Child Benefit and changes in housing benefit rules, the welfare groups managed to secure valuable support from the Tory backbenches.

Influencing committees

Pressure groups lobby MPs on a collective as well as an individual basis. Committees of MPs often represent a useful target for lobbying, although informal groupings (i.e. of MPs with a similar ideological position, or with similar personal and political interests) can also be a useful focal point. There are four main types of formal committee which we shall consider: party subject committees; all-party committees; standing committees; and select committees.

Within each of the main parliamentary parties there are subject committees which focus on a particular policy area or government function, such as education, foreign affairs, social services and so on (see J. B. Jones, 1990). MPs with an interest in a policy area may attend meetings of the relevant committee, which often take the form of presentations by outside organisations. The party subject committees have a low profile and if lobbied in isolation are fairly ineffective. However, groups do find them useful as part of a broader parliamentary campaign. The Study of Parliament Group found that over 40 per cent of the groups they examined had been in contact with them, and that 73 per cent found them useful or very useful. Miller (1990) believes that at a time of large government majorities they provide a powerful focus for backbench opinion. Indeed, one can point to a number of instances during the 1980s where Conservative Party committees were critical of ministerial decisions. In some cases – notably the government's climb-down on increased parental contributions to student grants in 1984, and the watering down of the proposals on the brewing industry (see Exhibit 7.1) later in the decade – committees played a role in changing government policy.

The membership of all-party committees, in contrast, is not confined to MPs of any single party. These committees are particularly useful to pressure groups wishing to build cross-party support. Indeed, in most cases they work very closely with pressure groups, sometimes initiating parliamentary activity such as the tabling of questions and motions on their behalf. Some pressure groups support the work of an all-party committee by undertaking administrative duties. According to Jones (1990) twenty-five of the 103 all-party committees which existed in 1988 had secretaries or officers who were located outside Westminster. For example, the Animal Welfare All-Party Committee is serviced by the RSPCA, while the secretary of the All-Party Committee on Smoking is none other than the director of the pressure group, Action on Smoking and Health (ASH). Again, the Study of Parliament Group survey revealed a high level of use and satisfaction with the system of all-party committees. Almost half the groups surveyed had contact with these committees and of these over two-thirds found them useful or very useful.

Select committees, particularly the departmental select committees which since 1979 have scrutinised the work of government departments, are increasingly important as a focus for pressure groups. Two-thirds of pressure groups have given evidence to select committees and more than two-fifths of oral and written evidence is submitted to these committees by outside organisations (Rush, 1990c). In addition, groups sometimes have links with members of these committees and their support staff. This does not necessarily mean that committees will be biased towards a particular interest, although it has been alleged that outside organisations are able to influence the choice of topics for inquiry (Burch, 1989).

The value of select committees, in contributing to debates and in shaping the political agenda, should not be underestimated. If pressure groups can influence the recommendations of committees, they can add considerable weight to their case, giving it a certain legitimacy (Judge, 1992). Of course this does not mean that the government will necessarily accept such recommendations once they have received a committee's 'seal of approval'. But where the government rejects recommendations it often has to justify its decision. In this way a committee's support for a particular viewpoint is often useful in putting the issue on the political agenda. Coupled with pressure through other channels, this raises the possibility of a more positive outcome in the longer term. Certainly, pressure groups seem to find the select committee system useful. The survey by the Study of Parliament Group (Rush, 1990a) suggests that the majority of groups believe that they have had some impact on the reports of select committees.

Finally, we turn to the standing committees, whose task it is consider bills in detail. As one might expect, members of standing committees are often lobbied by pressure groups who wish to amend legislation. Pressure groups frequently brief individual MPs on the relevant committee during the passage of a bill. But they are unable, except in very special circumstances, to give evidence to the standing committee as a whole, as they may do in a select committee investigation. Some commentators believe that this is wrong and have proposed changes to improve the contact between standing committees and outside organisations.

Improving representation at the legislative stage
Although pressure groups have a variety of options when putting their case to MPs, there has been a lot of concern in recent years about the quality of some of these channels, particularly with respect to procedures for the scrutiny of legislation which, some believe, do not allow interested organisations sufficient opportunity to consider and comment upon bills. Both the Hansard Society Commission on the Legislative Process (1993) and the Law Society (1992) have recommended changes in parliamentary procedure in order to create a more systematic process of taking evidence from outside organisations. Their recommendations include a greater use of special standing committees – legislative committees which are allowed to take evidence directly from interested groups and individuals. Although a provision for special standing committees has existed since 1980, this is very rarely exercised. Only five special standing committees have actually been established, and none since 1984.

Others, such as Graham Allen, the Labour MP for Nottingham North, would also like to see a better procedure for commenting on proposed legislation (Allen, 1994). He has stated that before a standing committee begins to look at a bill, there should be a six-week period during which interested parties can give evidence. He stresses that these evidence sessions should be informal, public and possibly televised. This would certainly increase the opportunities for groups to make their points in an open manner before bills are considered in detail.

Although the prospect for such reform looks poor in the immediate future, a number of informal arrangements have developed in recent years which have attempted to incorporate more effectively the views of outside organisations when legislation is being considered. One development has been the tabling of amendments to bills by members of departmental select committees (which do take evidence from outside organisations when compiling their reports). This has happened on a number of occasions, notably by the Energy Select Committee on the government's Electricity Bill in 1987. This tactic now has the blessing of the Commons' Procedure Committee and we may see more of it in the future.

A further development which became more evident in the 1980s was the targeting of the committee stage of bills by pressure groups which had been ignored or excluded at the consultation stage. Of course MPs who are members of standing committees have always been a focal point for such groups (Norton, 1990). But in the 1980s this appeared to intensify, largely because of the Thatcher government's greater unwillingness to modify its proposals in prior consultation with so-called 'vested interests' (see Chapter 6). Groups which had been unable to influence government policy through the normal channels began to focus on the parliamentary stage, particularly the committee stage, where they would lobby for detailed amendments. In addition to lobbying MPs on an individual basis, they often systematically targeted particular groups or factions of MPs on standing committees in order to secure support for a particular amendment. In some cases it was the MPs who took the initiative. Believing that the proposals were not as well-informed as they should have been, some actively sought the views of interested organisations. In the case of the Broadcasting Bill in 1990, for example, the Labour MPs on the standing committee took the step of establishing an informal special standing committee of their own, taking evidence from interested groups such as the television companies.

Parliament is highly accessible to pressure groups. But those who are concerned about the quality of links between groups and

Parliament are right to recommend reform, particularly where such changes will allow all interested parties to comment adequately on proposals that affect them. Informal and piecemeal changes of the kind mentioned above may improve the situation, but perhaps the time has now come for systematic reform to ensure that changes are introduced quickly, thoroughly and equitably.

MPs' interests

In contrast, fears have also been expressed that some pressure groups actually have too much influence over MPs. Much of this concern has focused upon pecuniary interests, which some believe are particularly powerful in shaping the judgement of MPs. But any excessively close relationship between an MP and a particular pressure group – even in the absence of financial considerations – could be viewed as potentially damaging, if it dominates the member's judgement over all else.

Yet there are well-rehearsed arguments in favour of MPs having external interests, including links with outside organisations. It is believed that outside interests enable MPs to stay in contact with the 'real world', helping them to assess the impact of their actions on society. Even if it were possible to insulate MPs from the outside world, to prevent them from having close relationships with pressure groups, or to debar them from having external interests, it would not necessarily be desirable to do so. Moves in this direction would probably reduce the accessibility of Parliament, making MPs more remote from society.

MPs' outside contacts and interests can be divided into a number of categories: constituency and personal interests; sponsorship and consultancy; and other economic and financial interests. Let us now examine these more closely.

Constituency and personal interests

Given that MPs represent territorial constituencies, it is not surprising that they are the natural focal point for interests which are geographically concentrated. They seek to advance these local interests by campaigning on behalf of constituents for economic benefits, such as better air, road or rail links, or for economic development funds. They also defend these interests, campaigning against proposals which might affect their constituents. This defensive role has been much in evidence in recent years in the context of NIMBY-ism. Local MPs have been actively involved in local campaigns including the Channel Tunnel rail link, the opposition to the government's road building programme and other environmental issues (see Exhibit 9.2).

MPs often have an interest arising from the concentration of a particular activity in their constituency. Hence industries which are located in a particular area will carry a lot of weight with local MPs. For example, Ivan Lawrence, the MP for Burton on Trent, a major centre for the brewing industry, often speaks out on behalf of this industry. Modern industry, it should be noted, is less geographically concentrated than the old heavy industries such as mining, shipbuilding and so on. Nevertheless, pressure groups wishing to mount an effective parliamentary campaign still focus upon MPs with relevant constituency interests. For example, British Airways tends to have more contact with those MPs who have national and regional airports in their constituency. Meanwhile, the British tourist industry, for similar reasons, tends to focus on MPs representing the major resorts and tourist centres. Targeting is not, however, confined to industrial interests. For example, in recent years NHS workers, campaigning against the government's reforms, have targeted those MPs who have hospitals in their constituency.

MPs also have interests which arise from their personal principles, preferences and experiences. These are often significant in leading MPs to sympathise with and support particular pressure groups. Take Jack (now Lord) Ashley, for example, the former MP for Stoke-on-Trent, whose own experience of hearing disability led him to take a particular interest in the problems facing the disabled. Throughout his long and distinguished career in Parliament he lobbied on behalf of disabled people, particularly those who have been the victims of accidents, medical error or negligence (Ashley, 1994).

Some MPs actually join pressure groups on the strength of a personal interest. For example, Dame Janet Fookes, a Conservative MP who often speaks out on animal welfare issues, has served for a numbers of years on the council of the RSPCA. In such cases MPs often act in the capacity of informal spokesperson for the group. They are able to advise the group on strategy and may table questions and motions or introduce debates and bills on its behalf. For example, Kevin McNamara, who is a vice-chairman of the League Against Cruel Sports, assisted its campaign against fox-hunting by introducing a private member's bill on the subject in 1992, which in fact was only narrowly defeated by 187 votes to 175.

Constituency and personal interests are important, but they are relatively uncontroversial. Indeed, most would agree that it is part of the democratic process that MPs should have such interests and respond to lobbying from pressure groups which share a common concern. There is more disquiet about the financial interests of MPs, and their behaviour in circumstances where their association with external organisations involves payment or other material benefit.

Sponsorship and political consultancy
It is perfectly legitimate for pressure groups to build links with MPs by sponsoring them or by hiring them as political consultants. Exhibit 7.3 gives examples of such links. Sponsorship is a method adopted by the trade unions. Individual trade unions pay money into the MP's constituency fund – there is no personal financial gain to them under this arrangement. In return he or she acts as a political adviser, keeps the union informed on political matters and may also undertake campaigns in Parliament on its behalf. In the 1992 Parliament, 143 Labour MPs (over half the parliamentary Party) were sponsored by trade unions. The Transport and General Workers Union alone sponsors over thirty MPs, a significant bloc within the House of Commons. One example of a trade union-sponsored MP is Dennis Skinner, who represents the mining constituency of Bolsover and is sponsored by the National Union of Mineworkers. In recent years he has been at

the centre of a number of campaigns by the miners, including the opposition mounted against British Coal's pit closure programme in 1992–93 (see Exhibit 6.3).

Exhibit 7.3   **The interests of MPs**

The 1994 *Register of Members' Interests* gives an insight into MPs' links with outside organisations. A few examples are shown below.

Richard Caborn (Lab, Sheffield Central) is sponsored by the Amalgamated Union of Engineering workers.

John Cunningham (Lab, Copeland) is sponsored by General Municipal Boilermakers and Allied Trades Union. He is also an adviser to Albright and Wilson (UK), Hays Chemicals and Centurion Press.

Sir Marcus Fox (Con, Shipley) is a director of Westminster Communications (a public affairs consultancy whose clients include British Gas, the Builders Merchant Federation and Standard Life). Fox also holds directorships in the Care Services Group (contract cleaning services), McCarthy and Stone (sheltered housing), Bristol Port Company, Illingworth Morris (wool textiles), Hartley Investment Trust and Yorkshire Food PLC. He is also a consultant to 3M (UK), which manufactures industrial, consumer and health products, and to Shepherd Construction and Gratte Brothers, a firm of electrical engineers.

Don Foster (Lib, Bath) is an adviser to the Association of Teachers and Lecturers, the National Union of Teachers, Pannel Kerr Fosters (accountants and business planners), and the Institute of Professional Managers and Specialists.

John McWilliam (Lab, Blaydon) is a parliamentary adviser to the Federation of Licensed Victuallers and is sponsored by the National Communications Union.

Paul Marland (Con, West Gloucestershire) is a parliamentary adviser to the British Scrap Metal Federation, Unigate Dairies and the Reclamation Association.

David Willetts (Con, Havant) is a director of Retirement Security (involved in sheltered accommodation), Electra Innvotec (a venture capital company) and Sphere Drake holdings (insurance). He is a consultant to the TI Group (engineering), Healthcall UK (health services) and Kleinwort Benson (financial services).

Source: House of Commons *Register of Members' Interests*, 1994

Businesses and trade associations generally prefer to employ MPs as consultants rather than sponsoring them, though they may from time to time make donations to constituency funds. The usual arrangement is that in return for a fee, the MP will provide information about parliamentary developments, advise on strategy and may also undertake a range of parliamentary activities on the clients' behalf. In 1994, 178 MPs were currently employed as parliamentary consultants or advisers. One of these was Dr Michael Clark, MP for Rochford, who is a parliamentary adviser to British Gas, the Royal Society for Chemistry and the British Chemical Contractors' Association. It not uncommon for MPs to hold more than one consultancy, though it is rare for them to have more than two or three. One of a number of exceptions, Patrick Nicholls, the Member for Teignbridge, declared nine separate consultancies in 1994. In the same year around 400 outside organisations directly employed MPs as political consultants or advisers.

Not all MPs who hold consultancies are employed by business organisations. Some advise professional bodies, such as John Hannam MP, adviser to the Pharmaceutical Society of Great Britain. A number of charities also use MPs as advisers, usually without payment. For example, Geoffrey Dickens MP acted in this capacity for the child protection charity, Childwatch.

Some outside organisations provide other benefits to MPs, including gifts, travel and the provision of office accommodation. One area of concern in recent years has been the provision of research support to MPs by pressure groups. There have been a number of instances where MPs have allegedly used research assistants who are employed by outside organisations. Often these individuals are connected with lobbying firms (whose activities will be discussed later in this chapter), though other pressure groups have also been engaged in this practice. The main worry here is that by employing lobbyists as research assistants MPs are giving particular groups privileged access to Parliament, placing them in a superior position relative to others.

Economic interests

MPs have a wide range of economic interests. Many are company directors. In aggregate the 651 MPs have over 500 seats on the boards of companies. From the point of view of a company, having an MP on the board can be very useful when lobbying, particularly if they are former ministers. As we saw in Chapter 5, there has been little but conscience to stop a minister from taking a post with any organisation after leaving office.

MPs may support business interests in other ways. They may have their own business, or they may have a shareholding in a company. There are no restrictions on ordinary MPs in respect of their business interests. However, ministers must resign their company directorships and relinquish any controlling interest in a company when taking up their appointment. They are also expected 'to order their affairs so that no conflict arises or is thought to arise, between their private interests and their public duties' (Cabinet Office, 1992). However, as Hollingsworth (1991) notes, there are many loopholes. For example, the rules do not apply to companies established in connection with private family estates. As a result much depends on the individual minister's judgement and that of the prime minister.

Many MPs derive an income from other occupations. Some are effectively part-timers, undertaking external work alongside their political duties. An analysis of MPs' occupational backgrounds illustrates the bias towards business and the professions. Among those elected in 1992, the most common backgrounds were company director, lawyer, business consultant, lecturer or teacher, journalist or writer, trade union official and farmer. Of course not all MPs continue their occupations. But many do, particularly lawyers and those involved in business. Obviously where MPs continue an outside occupation they retain a vested interest in issues affecting their work. But even in the case of those who no longer continue to work outside Parliament, occupational background may still be an important factor in shaping their perception of issues. Certainly, any pressure group representing a particular profession or occupation would hope to obtain the support of those MPs drawn from the same background, and at least initially will focus their lobbying efforts here.

Concern about Members' interests

The extent of MPs' financial interests, and the growth of paid political consultancies in particular, has caused the most concern in recent years. These fears have been fuelled by other developments such as the growth of commercial lobbying companies, to be discussed later, which have focused public attention on the system which regulates MPs' external interests.

The conduct of MPs with regard to their external interests is governed by a system of self-regulation established by the House of Commons itself. Although MPs are not strictly speaking above the law, it has been accepted for many years that they are virtually immune from prosecution for corruption and bribery. As Hollingsworth (1991) observes, the political and judicial establishment refuse to accept that an MP lobbying for outside bodies in return for payment is corrupt. This approach contrasts sharply with other democracies, such as the USA and Canada for example, where the possibility of jail sentence awaits representatives who accept money in return for lobbying. It also contrasts with the rules governing local councillors in the UK who are required to declare their interests in a statutory register.

There are rules which require MPs to declare any relevant interest when they speak in debate, in a committee, or when they communicate with ministers, other Members or Crown servants. Since 1975, MPs have also been expected to enter their pecuniary interests and any material benefits received in a *Register of Members' Interests*, if they believe such interests might be believed to influence their thought and actions. In theory, failure to comply with these rules can lead to suspension from the House of Commons. There have been a number of cases in recent years where MPs have been criticised for not playing by the rules, and some have been punished. For example, in 1990 John Browne, the MP for Winchester, was suspended from the House of Commons for omitting to declare a payment from the Saudi Arabian government for a political consultancy. He subsequently stood down as the official Conservative parliamentary candidate for Winchester following pressure from his constituency party.

In another case Michael Mates, the then chairman of the Defence Select Committee, was criticised for not declaring a relationship between his consultancy firm and companies having an interest in an issue under investigation by the select committee. Mates did register his interest and it was accepted that he had not used his position to further his personal interests nor those of the companies concerned. But he was found to have erred by not declaring an interest when asking specific questions during the inquiry.

These and other cases placed the existing rules under the spotlight and led to fresh inquiries by the Select Committee on Members' Interests which investigates breaches of the register. Some of the committee's recommendations have been incorporated into the rules. The requirement for members of select committees to declare their interests has now been clarified. It has also been made clear that members having a conflict of interest during select committee investigations should withdraw from proceedings. The procedures for appointing the chairpersons of select committees have also been altered to enable the disclosure of interests at this stage.

The rules covering the registration of interests for all MPs have also been tightened and clarified. The rules relating to gifts and shareholdings are now much clearer. MPs now have to specify those clients for whom they provide a service, as well as specific Lloyds insurance syndicates of which they are members. In addition, the leading sponsors of Early Day Motions now have to declare their interests.

Despite these improvements, however, declaration still depends on the judgement of each individual member. It is still theoretically possible for MPs to refuse to submit an entry to the register – as Enoch Powell famously did – or to fail to disclose significant pecuniary interests. However, in the present climate those who openly flout the rules increasingly risk unwanted media attention and disciplinary action.

There are those, including a number of MPs, who believe that the rules should be even tighter. Members are still not required to disclose the amounts of remuneration they receive. Investigations into an MP's interests still depend on complaints being made by members of the public. Moreover, where a complaint has been made by a member of the public, the allegation will only be passed to the Select Committee for Members' Interests for investigation if the registrar (of members' interests) agrees that the allegation is substantiated. Nor are MPs prevented from taking part in debates in which they have a pecuniary interest, a rule which applies to councillors and parliamentarians in some other countries, such as Canada.

Despite the tightening up of registration, the concerns regarding MPs' interests have not dissipated. Indeed, in July 1994 it was alleged that two MPs had agreed to table parliamentary questions in return for payment. This was subsequently referred to the Committee of Privileges. The two MPs in question – David Tredinnick and Graham Riddick – were subsequently suspended from the House for 20 days and 10 days respectively. Meanwhile, in October 1994, allegations about ministers accepting material benefits led the Prime Minister to establish a standing committee chaired by Lord Nolan, to make recommendations about rules of conduct for those in public life (see Exhibit 7.4).

Exhibit 7.4 **The Nolan Committee**

The Nolan Committee on Standards in Public Life was
announced by the Prime Minister on 25 October 1994. Its
terms of reference are:

> To examine current concerns about the standards of conduct of all
> holders of public office, including arrangements relating to financial
> and commercial activities, and make recommendations as to any
> changes in present arrangements which might be required to
> ensure the highest standards of propriety in public life.

The committee, set up initially for a period of three years, was
a response to growing public disatisfaction with standards of
behaviour among ministers, civil servants, MPs and other
office-holders such as members of quasi-government bodies.
The Committee's first report was published on 11 May 1995.
The main recommendations concerning MPs and ministers
were as follows: MPs should be prohibited from working for
lobbying companies; there should be clearer description of
MPs' interests in the Register of Members' interests; an independent Parliamentary Commissioner for Standards should
be appointed; a system similar to the Civil Service business
appointments rules should be applied to ministers.

Commercial lobbyists

Some outside organisations wishing to influence the decision-
making process seek professional advice from commercial lobbying firms. These firms provide a range of services, including
political briefings, advice on how to approach decision-makers
and, if required, will lobby on behalf of clients. Lobbying companies can be seen as political middlemen, a bridge between outside interests and decision-makers. Some lobbying firms employ
or retain MPs, who then take up a client's case. Others act mainly
as facilitators, arranging meetings between their clients and ministers, civil servants or MPs.

Lobbying is a growth industry. A few years ago it was estimated that the turnover of lobbying companies was around £10 million per annum, three times greater than in the early 1980s (Grantham, 1989). Some firms have an impressive list of clients. For example, Westminster Communications' clients includes Cellnet and British Rail; and Public Policy Consultants have acted for Proctor and Gamble, the Association of District Councils and Britannia Airways. Another firm, Westminster Strategy, has worked on behalf of the Japanese electronics industry and the certified accountants professional body (Grantham and Seymour-Ure, 1990).

The growth of lobbying firms has caused concern for a number of reasons. First of all, as their services are expensive it is believed that they serve to enhance the position of groups which are already relatively powerful, namely those with financial resources. Secondly, there are worries that the activities undertaken by some firms, particularly where payments are made to MPs, could undermine the independent judgement of decision-makers, leading to the dominance of private over public interests.

However, it is difficult to assess the influence of these political brokers. Some observers believe that their influence is exaggerated and that many of the fears about them are unjustified (Berry, 1992). As commercial organisations, keen to attract clients, perhaps the lobbying firms have themselves contributed to their exaggerated importance. Indeed, as Jordan (1989) has rightly cautioned, 'we need to weigh the impact not count the claims'. There is some evidence to suggest they can be influential, as the case study shown in Exhibit 7.5 shows. But most of the cases where lobbyists claim victory tend to occur on issues of fairly low political significance. It is unlikely that their activities could be successful in the face of strong public opposition. However, many of these companies are also active in public relations, and are therefore skilled in manipulating public opinion.

The concern about the relationship between MPs and these lobbying organisations is perhaps justified. About forty MPs either run their own lobbying companies or act as consultants to such firms. This is not a problem in itself; it is no better or worse than an MP taking on a political consultancy. Indeed, the same

kind of conflict of interest could arise between an MP's constituents and the clients of the lobbying firms for whom he or she
is acting.

But when MPs act on behalf of lobbying companies, there is
more scope for what could be called covert operations. MPs are
now expected to disclose the name of the client when they are
working on behalf of a lobbying company. But they have not
always done so. This has made it very difficult to trace the link
between pressure groups and MPs, even when it is in the public
interest to know of such relationships.

Exhibit 7.5   **Lobbying companies: a successful case**

In 1985 Tottenham Hotspur Football Club hired Profile Public
Relations (PPR) to help persuade ministers to amend a new
law restricting the availability of alcohol at sports grounds.
This legislation banned the consumption of alcohol from any
position which overlooked the pitch. It therefore included
executive boxes, which many soccer clubs had installed as a
means of generating revenue from the growing corporate
hospitality trade. As the provision of alcoholic drinks was
regarded as an essential part of this service, the clubs quite
naturally feared a substantial loss of revenue from this source.
In order to persuade the government to exempt executive
boxes from the legislation, PPR arranged for selected politicians and their advisers to be invited to Tottenham Hotspur's
ground on match days, to see the problem for themselves.
Other activities included a meeting at Westminster, an
adjournment debate in the Commons, and the tabling of an
motion by sympathetic MPs. By April 1986 the argument had
been won. The Home Office minister Giles Shaw introduced
an amendment to the Public Order Bill in the Commons,
which relaxed the controls on the provision of alcohol in executive boxes.

Source: Grantham and Seymour-Ure (1990), pp.71–2

Concern about the growth of political brokers has led to calls for a register of lobbyists as is the case in the USA, Australia and Canada. A registration scheme was backed by the House of Commons Select Committee on Members' Interests in 1991. It recommended a register where lobbying firms would have to disclose their clients, the names of any MPs with a pecuniary interest in the firm and the names of any persons carrying out lobbying activities on the firm's behalf. The House of Commons has not as yet approved the committee's recommendations.[1]

The House of Lords

Most of this chapter has been concerned with the relationship between pressure groups and the House of Commons. But the House of Lords is also a significant target for pressure groups, and during the 1980s provided a valuable ally for groups wishing to amend the government's legislation (Baldwin, 1990). Between 1979 and 1990 the House of Lords defeated the Conservative government on over 150 occasions. Some of these victories were short-lived with the government reversing Lords' amendments when the legislation returned to the Commons. But even these reversals had a publicity value, enabling further discussion of the issue in question. Moreover, in many cases the government had to rethink its plans in the light of defeats in the Upper House. For example, on the Education Reform Bill of 1988 the Lords defeated the government on a clause which determined the procedure by which schools could opt out of local authority control. The Lords inserted an amendment which stated that a majority of eligible parents would have to vote in favour of opting out in order for the ballot to be legitimate. The government later introduced its own compromise amendment by allowing a second ballot in cases where less than half the parents voted in the original ballot.

In addition to the publicity value of government defeats in the House of Lords, there are other ways in which pressure groups may use the chamber to raise issues. Groups can persuade peers to initiate or participate in a debate, to table questions or introduce a private member's bill. They may also give evidence to select committees of the House of Lords. The profile of the Lords has risen in recent years, bringing extra publicity for issues raised there. This raised profile was due in no small measure to the broadcasting of proceedings, through the introduction of television in the mid-1980s, which was extremely helpful in raising public awareness about the work of the chamber.

Pressure groups are well aware of the value of the Upper House. Survey evidence from the Study of Parliament Group showed that 70 per cent of groups had used the House of Lords to make representations and that 59 per cent had regular or frequent contacts with peers (Rush, 1990a). Four out of five groups rated their contacts with the Lords as useful or very useful, and almost a quarter found the Upper House more useful than the Commons when seeking to influence policy. The results from the survey by Baggott (1992) also confirm the importance of the Lords as a focal point for pressure groups. Almost one in five groups was found to be in contact on at least a weekly basis, while half the groups surveyed were in touch with peers on at least a monthly basis (see Exhibit 5.2); 37 per cent of groups claimed to have increased their contact with the Lords during the 1980s, with only 5 per cent perceiving decreased contact. A third of groups believed that their contacts with the House of Lords had become more effective over this period, while only 11 per cent perceived a decrease in effectiveness.

Groups which have not been properly consulted by government, or whose views have been ignored, have found the House of Lords particularly useful. Groups such as local authorities, trade unions and public sector professional bodies found the Lords a useful rallying point during the 1980s when many government reforms in education, health care, social security, employment and local government were based upon a rejection of their views. Peers are more independent-minded than MPs and less fearful of the whips, hence the large number of government defeats mentioned earlier. Since the departure of Mrs Thatcher, the government has retained its confrontational stance in many policy areas, as we saw in Chapter 6. It has also faced opposition from the Lords, being defeated on a number of issues as a result of pressure-group lobbying, most notably in the field of law and order.

Rather like MPs, peers have various interests which make them more sympathetic to some lobbies than others, although they do not of course have constituency interests. Groups wishing to lobby peers will focus their attention, at least in the initial stages of a campaign, upon those whom they believe will be sympathetic to their case. They may target peers who have relevant personal experience or who have previously expressed an interest in the issue in question. Peers also have economic interests, some are company directors, for example. Others are connected with particular groups, such as Baroness Stedman of the Association of County Councils. However, it is a convention that peers speak for themselves and not on behalf of outside interests, so it would be wrong to identify peers as spokespersons for any outside group.

Peers' interests are difficult to analyse as there is no comprehensive register of members' interests for the Lords. However, they can voluntarily declare the subjects in which they are interested, (this information is published in Dod's *Parliamentary Companion*). In addition peers are expected to declare pecuniary interests and by convention should not promote or oppose legislation in areas where they are receiving a fee or reward.

Conclusions

This chapter has shown that Parliament is an important focus for pressure groups, and not simply because it is a last resort for those unable to gain access to the executive. Parliament can have a bearing on important issues, and groups which spurn this channel are mistaken. There are, as we have seen, many avenues which a group can pursue if it wishes to influence Parliament. We have also observed that parliamentarians have a vast range of interests and that most groups can find someone to sympathise with their case. However, the chapter has also identified problems in the relationship between pressure groups and Parliament. Often, groups do not have sufficient opportunity to get their detailed views across, particularly when government legislation is being considered. Moreover, access to Parliament, though fairly open, is far from equal. The vested interests of MPs and their close relationships with some groups creates an uneven playing field, reinforcing a bias in favour of some interests and against others.

Note

1   These recommendations have been overtaken to some extent by Nolan's recommendation that MPs should be barred from working for lobbying companies.

8

Pressure groups, the public and the media

Many decisions, particularly those of a highly technical, specialised or detailed nature, do not enter the public domain. Such
matters are usually resolved by discussions between pressure
groups and the executive arm of government. On many other
issues, however, pressure groups have to demonstrate further
political support for their position. In some cases this can be
achieved through parliamentary lobbying. But there are circumstances where a group must also show that it has even wider
public support. This chapter explores the ways in which pressure
groups claim to represent the public, and the tactics they adopt
to influence public opinion. We begin by examining the representative role of pressure groups. Later, we discuss why groups
wish to influence public opinion, and look at their efforts to build
public support. Finally, we focus on the role of the media in relation to pressure-group campaigns.

Representing public opinion

The American political scientist V. O. Key (1961) once said that
'to speak with precision of public opinion is not unlike coming to
grips with the holy ghost'. The main problem for those seeking a
precise definition is that public opinion manifests itself in many
different ways and is expressed through a variety of political
organisations and institutions. Public opinion can be reflected in
opinion polls, elections and referendums, and in the postbags of

elected representatives and government officials. The media also claim to reflect public opinion, although this is distorted by its own vested interests. In addition, public opinion can be channelled through political organisations such as parties and pressure groups.

Public opinion can be expressed through pressure groups in a number of ways. The actual formation of a group is an expression of public concern, even when the group has a small membership. For example, the creation of groups such as Shelter and the Child Poverty Action Group in the 1960s reflected a wider public concern about the failure of the welfare state to provide for the poor. The size of a group's membership is also taken as a basic indicator of public support, particularly in the case of open membership groups (see Chapter 2). In closed membership groups, size is limited by eligibility, and the percentage of eligible members who join the group is perhaps a better indicator. The rate of growth of group membership is also an important indicator. The rapid growth in the membership of environmental groups in the 1980s, for example, was seen as a reflection of popular backing for action to protect the environment (see Exhibit 8.1). By the same token a declining membership may be seen as evidence of a fall in public support for a group's aims and policies.

Groups can mobilise public support in other ways. Large demonstrations and protest meetings may involve non-members. For example, in the case of the miners' protests against pit closures in 1992, and the anti-poll tax demonstrations during the late 1980s, many participants were not actually members of the pressure groups which organised the events. Another form of non-member participation is voluntary financial donations. The public can demonstrate its support for a group by making donations without actually joining the organisation. Indeed, one notes that many charities do not have members as such, but rely on donations from the public both to finance the services they provide and their lobbying efforts.

As we saw in Chapter 3, some question the representative role of pressure groups, particularly those adopting a New Right perspective. They believe that pressure groups distort the representative process and undermine the public interest. Their arguments are not without foundation. Many pressure groups are not very democratic and appear to be dominated by élites. There is evidence to support the contention that some groups face greater barriers than others when seeking to establish themselves as formal organisations. Moreover, the size of a group's membership is not necessarily correlated with the level of underlying public support, nor with its power and influence. However, despite such imperfections, pressure groups nevertheless provide a useful link between the government and the governed, and an important channel through which the public can participate in political activity. It is also clear that, if anything, they are growing in importance as representative institutions.

Exhibit 8.1 **Membership of environmental groups (UK)**

Group	(Thousands)		
	1971	1981	1991
Civic Trust	–	2	4
Council for the Protection of Rural England	21	29	45
Friends of the Earth	1	18	111
Greenpeace	–	30	408
National Trust	278	1,046	2,152
Ramblers' Association	22	37	87
Royal Society for Nature Conservation	64	143	250
Royal Society for the Protection of Birds	98	441	852
Woodland Trust	–	20	150
World Wide Fund For Nature	12	60	227

Source: Central Statistical Office, *Social Trends*, 24 (1994)

The growth in pressure-group politics
The number of pressure groups appears to have increased during the post-war period, particularly since the 1960s. Marsh (1983) pointed out that half the 184 pressure groups listed in the *Guardian Directory of Pressure Groups* were formed after 1960.

Analysis of a random sample of 445 organisations listed in the *Directory of British Associations* (*DBA*) in 1994 also suggests that a large proportion of today's groups were established in this period. Forty-eight per cent of this sample were formed after 1960. Studies of the poverty and environmental lobbies reveals a similar picture: about half the groups date from the 1960s onwards (Lowe and Goyder, 1983; Whiteley and Winyard, 1987). It should be noted, however, that this apparent upturn in pressure group activity may be part of a longer historical cycle. Further analysis of the *DBA* sample suggests that the Victorian period also saw a significant growth in pressure groups: 16 per cent of the groups in the sample were formed before 1900, the majority of these in the second half of the last century. Indeed, there are strong parallels between the new political movements of today and some of the great nineteenth-century moral campaigns, such as those against drink, slavery and cruelty to animals (Hollis, 1974; Moran, 1985).

The contemporary importance of pressure groups is reflected in the fact that a much larger proportion of people are members of pressure groups than of political parties. In a survey by Parry et al. (1992), 64 per cent of respondents claimed to be members of a voluntary group, 43 per cent were members of a trade union or staff association, while less than 7 per cent claimed to be members of a political party. Some pressure groups have huge memberships. The Royal Society for the Protection of Birds has over 850,000 members, four times the membership of the Labour Party. Other large memberships include the Automobile Association (seven million members), the Consumers' Association (over one million) and the National Trust (over two million). Many members are, however, passive. They do not get involved in the political activities of the group. Even so, it is recognised that being a member of a group is an important factor which can mobilise people on political issues. In the study of public participation by Parry and colleagues about one-third of mobilised political activity (that is, where an individual had become politically active as a result of suggestion from someone else) had been prompted by formal groups. This study also found that those individuals which were well-integrated in groups were in general more likely to participate in political activities.

Why have pressure groups become a more significant channel of public representation? One possible explanation is that their growth has reflected the rising levels of affluence over the post-war period (Cotgrove, 1982; Inglehart, 1977). According to this 'post-affluence' theory, prosperity has drawn attention away from material needs and towards quality of life issues, such as the environment. As a result, more and more people are willing to join pressure groups which promote these issues. Those who join such groups are more likely to be better off financially than those who do not, though this applies to almost all groups, not just those concerned with quality of life issues (Parry et al., 1992). Another factor is the impact of a more highly-educated population which is a feature of post-affluent societies. It is argued that a more articulate and highly-educated public is more likely to indulge in group politics, and again there is much evidence to suggest that this is the case (Parkin, 1968; Parry et al., 1992).

Even though post-affluence theory has some foundation, it cannot fully explain the rise of pressure-group politics. Material conditions continue to be the main concern of many pressure groups, such as business, trade unions and the poverty lobby. Moreover, in the last decade or so we have witnessed increasing poverty and material deprivation in sections of our own community. Yet, though in many respects the conditions of post-affluence have been undermined, groups concerned with quality of life issues have become stronger in terms of public support.

The growth of pressure-group politics may also be explained in terms of changes in the social structure of Britain, in particular the fragmentation of British society resulting from the breakdown of previously rigid class divisions (Moran, 1985). As a result of these changes, it appears that political preferences are not as sharply defined as they once were and people now have a more complex set of interests and values. The two main political parties, which have depended so heavily on class-based support can no longer fully accommodate these more complex preferences. So people join pressure groups – which are more specialised, focusing around specific interests and single issues, thereby catering more effectively for these preferences – and participate less in traditional party politics. There is some evidence to support this explanation. Individuals are less bound by party loyalties, as indicated by the fall in party memberships and increased volatility amongst voters. Even so, party politics is still a very powerful force in spite of the changes in the structure of British society. The parties are very adaptable to new situations and have sought to broaden their appeal to address these new preferences and interests. For example, in recent years all the major parties have responded to public concern about the environment by developing policies and including them in their political programmes.

A third explanation of the rise of groups is based on a perception that ordinary people are more willing today to protest about decisions which affect their lives. Certainly in the last few decades we have seen the rise of groups whose tactics give priority to protest and direct action, such as CND, the animal rights movement and the environmental lobby. We have also seen an apparent growth in NIMBY-ism, with local groups also adopting direct action tactics (see Chapter 9 below). A tendency towards protest was detected by a number of social surveys undertaken in the 1970s (Barnes and Kaase, 1979; A. Marsh, 1977). However, subsequent surveys of the 1980s did not find a significantly greater desire to undertake protest activity among the general public (Heath and Topf, 1987; Parry et al., 1992). These indicate that the percentage of respondents who admit to having been involved in a protest or demonstration lies in the range of 5–6 per cent, about the same level as indicated by the surveys of the 1970s.

The growth of protest may have been overstated, but there is much to suggest that the public is more assertive than in the past, and is more willing to get involved in political activity when faced with an unjust decision (Heath and Topf, 1987). There are also signs that people are increasingly willing to undertake collective action in such circumstances, although this still remains a less popular option than other forms of participation, such as signing petitions and contacting MPs on an individual basis. The British Social Attitudes survey of 1987 gives an indication of this (Heath and Topf, 1987). When asked what they would do if a law was being considered which they believed would be unjust or harmful, only 8 per cent of respondents said they would form an organisation, and 10 per cent said they would raise an issue within an organisation to which they already belonged, while 65 per cent indicated they would sign a petition and 52 per cent said they would contact their MP. Among those who had actually responded to such a proposed law 34 per cent had signed a petition, 11 per cent contacted their MP, while only 5 per cent had raised the issue with an organisation to which they belonged and only 2 per cent had actually formed an organisation to protest about the changes. Another survey undertaken during the mid-1980s did find more evidence of group activity, with over 11 per cent of respondents having at some time supported or worked in an organised group to raise issues (Parry et al., 1992). However, this response was smaller than the percentage of respondents who had signed petitions (63 per cent) or contacted politicians or officials (36 per cent).

Despite the rising profile of protest campaigns over the last couple of decades, there appears to have been no dramatic upsurge in the tendency to undertake protest among the general population as some predicted. While there seems to have been a growth in the general assertiveness of the public, and this has been reflected in an increasing willingness to participate in collective action, it has also fed through into individual actions, such as contacting MPs and officials and signing petitions, which remain the most popular avenues of participation apart from voting. It would appear, therefore, that increased assertiveness is not translated directly or automatically into pressure-group action and cannot fully explain its growth.

These explanations have something to contribute to our understanding. Each identifies significant social, cultural and political trends which partly, at least, explain the growth of pressure-group politics. No single explanation is complete, yet none is irrelevant. Taken together they help us identify a number of valid reasons why pressure groups have become more significant over the last few decades.

Persuading the public

Pressure groups are not merely conduits of opinion. They are active organisations which seek to influence and persuade the public to support their case. In the remainder of this chapter we shall explore the various ways in which groups try to win public support.

There are at least four reasons why pressure groups undertake public campaigns. First, public backing is often needed in order to launch an issue on to the political agenda. Government has its own agenda and is often reluctant to take on new issues. But if groups can generate enough public concern, then the government may be forced to consider issues outside its original agenda. For example, over the last few decades environmental groups have sought to raise public awareness of pollution and other environmental issues, with considerable success. The public has become more concerned about these issues, and the government has had to respond.

Second, public support is valuable as part of a broader campaign to influence government policy. The Campaign for Lead Free Air (CLEAR) – outlined in Exhibit 8.2 – illustrates how successful a public campaign can be, even when faced with a government that does not wish to change its policy and vested interests opposed to change. Groups often need to demonstrate public support for their case when promoting or opposing legislation. This is particularly so where issues cut across party lines or where a free vote is allowed. A good example is the abortion issue where the groups on both sides of the debate not only seek to persuade MPs to support their case, but also make a direct appeal to public opinion in an attempt to demonstrate that their respective causes have widespread support. These tactics are not, of course, confined to unwhipped issues. Groups often try to build public support when seeking to amend government legislation, hoping that this will pressure MPs into a rebellion, or that the government will recognise the strength of feeling on the matter and introduce its own amendment (see Chapter 7).

Exhibit 8.2 **The campaign for Lead Free Air**

The experience of the Campaign for Lead Free Air (CLEAR) demonstrates how a successful public campaign can influence policy, even in circumstances where powerful pressure groups oppose change and where the government is reluctant to alter its policy. CLEAR was established in 1982 against a background of concern about the impact of airborne lead upon children's mental health and educational development. It was believed that lead-based petrol additives were responsible for dangerously high levels of airborne lead. Some countries, notably the USA, had taken steps to deal with the problem by promoting the use of lead-free petrol. The UK government also reviewed the problem. As a compromise between the oil companies who opposed change and the anti-lead groups who wanted a ban on lead additives, it proposed a reduction in the lead content of petrol.

In an attempt to press the government to ban lead additives altogether, CLEAR mounted a public campaign highlighting the dangers of lead pollution from car exhausts. The campaign had a high-profile launch in January 1982. It had widespread support in the media, with a number of newspapers including the *Guardian* and the *Observer* backing the campaign. The campaign was also supported by 200 politicians from all parties, including thirty-five Conservative MPs and all the opposition party leaders. In addition, support was forthcoming from a range of other organisations, such as the trade union movement, the teachers' unions, the BMA, health authorities, the Institute of Environmental Health Officers and a range of environmental pressure groups. CLEAR was also able to demonstrate widespread public support. An opinion poll undertaken by MORI found a majority in favour of a ban. It also found that 77 per cent of those asked believed that lead-free petrol should be introduced even if this led to a rise in petrol prices.

The campaign was boosted by two other developments: first, the leaking of a letter written by the government's own medical adviser, which warned of the dangers of lead in petrol, publicly contradicting the government's official view; secondly, CLEAR's case was strengthened enormously by the support of the Royal Commission on Environmental Pollution for a ban on leaded petrol. In the face of public pressure, the government changed its mind, and backed a move towards lead-free petrol. Later the tax system was used to encourage unleaded petrol (which is taxed at a lower rate than leaded petrol). By 1993 unleaded petrol accounted for just under half the petrol sold in the UK. As a result of this trend, lead emissions from car exhausts fell by 70 per cent between 1980 and 1990.
Source: D. Wilson (1983)

Third, there are situations where groups aim to stimulate public debate when other channels are deadlocked. Even groups which possess extensive political contacts and which are well-regarded in Whitehall sometimes have to go public in order to move things along. A classic case was the campaign by the Chief Fire Officers' Association in 1988 to raise public awareness about the hazards of furniture containing flammable foams. These foams had been implicated in an increasing number of deaths, and the Association had argued for a ban on their use by furniture manufacturers. The government listened to its case, but refused to impose a ban. Frustrated at the lack of progress, the Association called a press conference criticising the existing regulations. This intervention was widely supported by the media, which had given a lot of coverage to the issue in the preceding weeks. The public outcry which ensued placed enormous pressure on the government to act and within a week a ban on combustible foam was announced.

Finally, a campaign can be used to reassure and pacify the public rather than to stimulate opposition or support for a particular view. Groups which pursue this objective are usually on the defensive, perhaps fearing government intervention on the back of public hostility. In some cases groups will attempt to pacify the public in advance of a lobbying campaign to change the law in their favour, as the Homosexual Law Reform Association did successfully in the 1960s. When groups seek to pacify public opinion, they are often launching a pre-emptive strike against the campaigns of their opponents. A good example was the BNFL publicity campaign during the 1980s, which included the promotion of the Sellafield Visitors' Centre. This represented a clear attempt to improve the image of the industry in the minds of the public, while at the same time seeking to counteract bad publicity generated by the anti-nuclear lobby.

There are many different tactics which a group may employ when seeking to influence the public. For analytical purposes these can be divided into two categories: protest (or 'direct action') campaigns and media campaigns. In practice though, the two kinds of approach are often inseparable with protests relying heavily on media coverage to attract public attention.

Protest and direct action

Protest campaigns have a variety of purposes: to express concern about a problem; to act as a rallying point for those with grievances, and to raise public awareness. Some forms of direct action, as we shall see, have even more ambitious aims, such as to render a law unworkable or to cause some form of disruption. However, in this context our main interest is in the publicity value of protest and its impact upon public attitudes.

The most common form of protest is the organisation of marches and demonstrations. If well-organised and peaceful, and if covered sympathetically by the media, these campaigns can be effective in demonstrating to the public and to decision-makers the extent of concern about a particular issue (see Exhibit 8.3). However, such protests, even when they satisfy these criteria, are rarely effective on their own. In almost all successful cases, marches or demonstrations have been used in conjunction with other tactics which have in some way affected the outcome. The poll tax, for example, was not defeated simply by the scale of the demonstrations against it – most of which did not meet the criteria set out above anyway – but by a range of factors: the general unpopularity of the tax; the non-payment campaign; the rising costs of collection and the fears of Tory MPs faced with an election defeat.

Exhibit 8.3 **The anti-roads protesters**

In March 1994 the government announced cuts in its road building programme, the first in over a decade. Although spending on road building was to remain high, at over £2 billion a year, around 30 per cent of the road schemes planned were shelved. One factor behind this decision was undoubtedly the government's own desire to curb public expenditure in line with its broader economic policy. But the cuts were also a political response to public protests about the road building programme.

Although these protests were localised, many attracted national attention. Campaigners against the M3 extension at Twyford Down near Winchester, which cut through two sites of special scientific interest, two ancient monuments and a designated area of outstanding natural beauty, were ultimately unsuccessful in preventing the new road. However, their protests, which involved confrontations with security guards and the police, attracted media attention and made the general public more aware of the consequences of the road programme. Their efforts also stirred others to act. In east London for example protesters against the construction of the M11 link road declared part of the route as an independent republic (Wanstonia). They then occupied houses and trees which were due for demolition and had to be forcibly removed by police. These events received full coverage in the national media and generated further public concern. Again though, as the road was under construction the government was unlikely to back down at this stage.

In other cases, where roads were being planned rather than actually constructed, protesters had more impact on the development in question. For example, in 1993 the government backed down on the controversial plan to build a road through Oxleas wood in south-east London, in the face of strong local protests. The government also delayed its plans to turn the M25 into a fourteen-lane highway by postponing the planning inquiry due in November 1994 for a further year. The Department of Transport had received over 10,000 objections to the scheme, along with representations from a wide range of environmental and conservation organisations such as the National Trust, English Nature and the Council for the Protection of Rural England.

The cases described here were only the tip of the iceberg. As the government announced the cuts in the roads budget it was estimated there were at least 250 local anti-road groups throughout the UK actively fighting new developments. These campaigns, although localised, were co-ordinated by a national body based in London – Alarm UK. The fact that the campaigns have been well-organised at a national level partly explains their success. Local campaigns can easily be isolated, whereas if an issue is seen as having national significance it cannot so easily be dismissed. Moreover, by attracting the attention of the national media, the campaigners can get their point across to a much wider audience.

There are at least three other factors which also contributed to the success of the anti-roads lobby. First of all, it became obvious that the protest groups were widely supported by the public, indicated by the fact that the protesters came from all walks of life. According to the *Economist* (19 February 1994, p.27), members of these protest groups can be divided into three main categories: NIMBY protesters, people who are directly affected by the development in terms of lower house prices, pollution and so on; radical greens, who oppose new roads on ideological or philosophical grounds; and Shire Tories, Conservative voters who are concerned about the damage done by roads to the countryside.

Secondly, there was pressure on the government from its own backbenchers. A number of Tory MPs were worried about public reaction to the road building programme, particularly those whose constituents were adversely affected. These MPs lobbied ministers on an individual basis, and also formed a backbench anti-roads group to issue and to co-ordinate their activities.

Thirdly, the protesters had allies within Whitehall. The Department of Transport's enthusiasm for roads was not shared by other departments. These included the Department of the Environment, concerned about the effects upon pollution; and the Treasury, anxious about the rising cost of the roads programme. These departments argued that the programme should be reviewed. This pressure, exerted 'behind closed doors', coupled with the public pressure on the government to reconsider the roads programme, resulted in the cut-backs announced in March 1994.

Moreover, demonstrations can backfire. A poorly organised or badly attended demonstration reflects adversely on the campaign and can undermine its case. For example, the 'People's Marches for Jobs', organised by the trade unions in 1981 and 1983 were regarded by some as a failure due to poor organisation and lack of purpose (Bagguley, 1991). A further problem is the outbreak of violence, of the kind which which has plagued marches and demonstrations organised by the Anti-Nazi League in recent years, which may deter potential supporters, no matter how noble the cause. Finally, unsympathetic media coverage can lessen the impact of even the most peaceful and well-organised demonstration, a point we shall return to later.

Marches and demonstrations are organised mainly for their publicity value as a show of strength, intensity of feeling and solidarity. Other types of protest, while attracting publicity, can have a more direct impact on the activity or problem which is causing concern. When undertaking these forms of direct action, a group takes matters into its own hands rather than relying on established methods of decision-making to resolve the problem. Such actions are often illegal, such as the activities of radical groups within the animal rights movement, which include bombing campaigns and breaking into laboratories. There are other forms of civil disobedience which, though illegal, are relatively peaceful, such as the mass trespasses undertaken by ramblers to highlight the problems of public access to private land. Even so, as with legal demonstrations, civil disobedience can end in violence.

There are other forms of direct action, which are neither illegal nor likely to involve violence. An example is the consumer boycott, such as that organised against South African produce by anti-apartheid campaigners until the collapse of this regime. However, in some cases, even where such activities are not strictly speaking illegal, there may be an attempt by parties affected by the action to seek a legal judgment on the matter. For example, in the case of the teachers' unions' boycott of pupil testing (see Chapter 6), a Conservative local authority (unsuccessfully) sought an injunction against the teachers' action.

There have been a number of attempts in recent years to limit the scope for protest. The Conservative government's trade union legislation has progressively limited the scope for strike action, a major sanction of the trade union movement which was used heavily in the 1970s to pressure government. The Public Order Act of 1986 gave police greater powers to deal with marches and demonstrations. The Act created new offences, such as disorderly conduct, which made it easier to arrest and remove protesters, and clarified the law relating to riot and violent disorder. It also gave the police extra powers to impose restrictive conditions upon marches, requiring organisers to give advance notice, and enabling the police to apply for a ban on marches in a particular area. The police also have powers to impose restrictions on static demonstrations and may limit the duration of the event and the number of participants involved. A further attempt to control protests and demonstrations formed part of the Criminal Justice and Public Order Act of 1994. This introduced a new offence of aggravated trespass, which enables magistrates to punish protest-ers, such as hunt saboteurs and other demonstrators who cause disruption on private land, much more severely than in the past.

The impact of radical forms of direct action is much more difficult to evaluate than the other forms of protest, such as marches and peaceful demonstrations. Sanctions, boycotts, strikes, mass trespass, disruption and so on, are often much more than publicity stunts. They can cause real problems for the gov-ernment and can produce a result even when public support is lacking – as was the case with many of the trade union strikes of the 1970s and 1980s. However, the impact of these forms of direct action are certainly enhanced when there is public support or widespread sympathy for the grievances raised. The experience of the teachers' boycott and the poll tax non-payment campaign show what can be achieved in these circumstances.

The role of the media

As we have seen, a great deal of protest activity is either media-oriented or has some publicity value. This leads us to consider the role of the mass media in pressure-group politics. There are four main areas which need to be explored. First, the importance and relevance of the media in politics generally. Second, the ways in which pressure groups can actively use the media to gain pub-licity. Third, the adoption of campaigns by the media which have been initiated by pressure groups. Fourth, the circumstances where the media act as a pressure group in its own right, defend-ing and advancing its own interests.

As Seymour-Ure (1991, p.6) points out, 'mass media' is a simple term which grows more elusive once analysed. For our purposes, however, we hope to avoid these conceptual complexi-ties, by focusing on the two main forms of mass media, which are most significant from the point of view of pressure groups: the press (newspapers and large-circulation magazines) and broad-casting (radio and television). The importance of these lies in their ability to present issues raised by groups to a large propor-tion of the general public. Almost every home has a TV set and a radio, while national daily newspapers reach around 60 per cent of the population. Media coverage therefore has enormous potential to raise public awareness. Although the precise impact of the media is open to debate, it is undoubtedly true that its potential has increased in the post-war period, particularly with the rise of television.

Television broadcasting has grown partly at the expense of the press and the radio. As a source of news, TV is by far the most popular, although newspapers continue to be the main source of local news (Seymour-Ure, 1991, p.149). Most pressure groups operating at the national level certainly regard TV coverage as the most important, but they are also aware of the importance of the other forms of mass media, and in particular of the extent to which stories cross-fertilise between different parts of the media, for example newspaper coverage of a particular issue often attracts the interest of broadcasters and vice versa.

Pressure groups appreciate the role of the media in raising public awareness and building public support. One in five respondents to the Study of Parliament Group survey (Rush, 1990a) regarded the media as the most important pressure point when seeking to influence policy. In the survey by Baggott (1992), a lower but nevertheless significant percentage of groups – 13 per cent – regarded the media as the most important target.

Most pressure groups believe that it is essential to maintain good media relations. According to Baggott (1992) four out of five groups claimed that they were in contact with the media at least once a week; half had daily contact with the media (see Exhibit 5.2). It also appears that this relationship is becoming professionalised. Many groups now employ people who have previously worked in the media to handle their public relations efforts. These people not only have experience and knowledge of how the media work, they also possess a wide range of contacts working in the media – often former colleagues – who can be helpful when the group wishes to go public. Most of the larger and wealthier pressure groups (trade unions and professional associations, the big charities, large businesses and trade associations) have a press and public relations unit staffed by specialists, though some

prefer to use public relations firms to handle media matters. It
should be remembered that many of the commercial lobbying
firms, discussed in the previous chapter, also provide public relations services too, and in some cases provide for their clients a
seamless service covering all aspects of the campaigning process.

Managing the media
The growing use of public relations and media specialists by pressure groups reflects the influence which they believe the mass
media have over public opinion and policy decisions. At the very
least, pressure groups are aware that they must be able to attract
favourable media coverage when they need it. There are many
different techniques which groups can adopt in order to attract
attention. A number of campaigns in recent years have used
advertising. Poster or press advertisements get the message across
directly to the public. They also generate further media coverage
for the campaign. Often articles are 'planted' by public affairs
specialists through their extensive range of contacts in the media.

Large-scale publicity campaigns, such as that organised by the
brewers in 1989 against the government's proposed reforms of the
public house system (see Exhibit 7.1), are extremely expensive,
costing millions of pounds, and are affordable only by the wealthiest pressure groups. However, those with modest budgets have
also employed advertising techniques, to good effect. For example, the Officers' Pensions Society managed to bring about a
change in the rules governing pensions for war widows, in a
superbly organised press advertising campaign which cost less
than £250,000, most of which was recouped by public donations
made in response to the advertisements (see Exhibit 8.4).

Exhibit 8.4 **The war widows' campaign for equal pensions**

There had been concern for a number of years about the
unequal treatment of women whose husbands had been
killed while serving in the armed forces. The widows of ser-

vicemen who died before 1973 received about half the pension of those whose husbands were killed after this date. Hence the widow of a soldier fatally wounded in the Falklands conflict would receive over twice the amount received by the widow whose husband had been killed in the Second World War.

In 1989 the Officers' Pensions Society decided to launch a high-profile campaign for equal treatment of war widows. This comprised a £250,000 press advertising campaign, which used real cases to illustrate the disparities. Dame Vera Lynn, a celebrity clearly associated in the public mind with the nostalgia of the Second World War period, spearheaded the campaign. Her presence provided a timely reminder of the sacrifices made by the troops in that conflict, raising public concern about the plight of their widows.

The campaign was very successful. Not only did it win support among the general public, but on the Tory backbenches as well. The Prime Minister was pressed to intervene to correct the anomaly. The government was persuaded, and provided for the equal treatment of war widows at a cost of £110 million a year.

Exhibit 8.5   **The English Collective of Prostitutes' poster campaign**

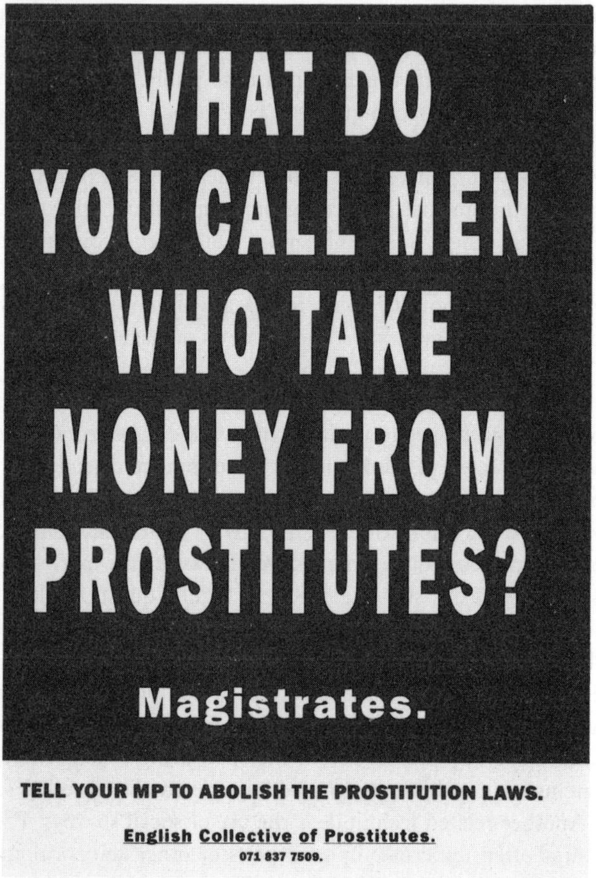

Source: Bartle Bogle Hegarty Ltd. Reproduced by permission

In some cases groups have persuaded other organisations, rather than the general public, to help meet the costs of advertising. An example was the striking poster campaign launched by the English Collective of Prostitutes in 1992 (see Exhibit 8.5). The posters, part of a campaign to abolish the laws regulating prostitution, were designed for free by the advertising agency Bartle Bogle Hegarty and appeared on seventy sites, also provided free by their owners. It was widely regarded as a witty and well-organised campaign which helped raise public awareness.

Another set of techniques can be grouped together under the heading of 'news management'. When an issue is already topical, groups find it relatively easy to get their views across simply by briefing the media. Indeed, groups are often approached by reporters, hungry for information. On other occasions, groups face an uphill struggle. They may wish to draw attention to an issue which is not attracting media attention. It is in these circumstances that groups may adopt news management techniques.

One of the most common methods is where the pressure group publishes a report highlighting an issue. These reports can be compiled by the group itself, or the work can be 'contracted out' to another agency, academics or management consultants. This tends to give the findings greater credibility in the eyes of the media and the public because the agency which has compiled the report is perceived as independent. However, in many cases the independence of such agencies is highly questionable. Those involved are often pressured to steer clear of recommendations which might upset the organisation which has commissioned the report. Even where those involved in compiling the report are independent-minded professionals who have the integrity to stand up to any pressure from the sponsoring organisation, their conclusions can be reinterpreted when journalists are briefed.

Another related technique is the use of social surveys. Pressure groups often undertake opinion polls or other statistical analyses in an effort to back up their case. The results are often attractive to the media since articles can easily be written around them. As with reports, surveys are sometimes undertaken by the groups themselves, but the results often carry greater weight if the work is undertaken by an independent market research or polling agency. Again, some market researchers are more independent than others. There is also a similar problem of interpretation, since survey results can be manipulated by those who have commissioned the research when briefing the media.

There are other ways in which groups can attract the media. As mentioned above, some use protests or demonstrations to attract attention. Others have been more inventive in their efforts to engage the attention of the media. The environmental movement has used a range of publicity stunts in the past, many of which have been highly effective. In 1983 for example, Greenpeace pulled off a remarkable stunt which involved dumping sludge discharged from the nuclear plant at Sellafield outside the headquarters of the Department of the Environment in London. The TV cameras were there to film the careful removal of the waste by men in protective suits only days after the Secretary of State for the Environment had declared that there was no danger from the Sellafield discharge. This stunt was highly effective in attracting the attention of both the media and the public.

Another high-profile media campaign of recent times has been that waged by the environmental group 'Surfers Against Sewage'. The group was formed in 1990 to campaign against the disposal of sewage in bathing waters around the British coast. In an effort to capture media attention, the group's members have surfed in the most disgusting conditions, complete with gas masks, and floated across sewage-ridden water in large brown inflatable dinghies. Their activities have gained much publicity, including coverage by news and television documentaries and have helped fuel the public concern about the health hazards of British bathing waters.

Not all publicity stunts succeed and some fail spectacularly, such as the symbolic burial of 5,000 fur coats organised in 1991 by Lynx, the now-defunct animal welfare group. The coats, which were made from mink, leopard, ocelot and wolf, were declared a potential health hazard by Devon County Council after being buried on a farmer's land. Environmental Health Officers ordered that they be dug up, much to the embarrassment of the group, which received quite a lot of adverse media coverage as a result of this farce.

Active and passive media coverage

Much media coverage is fairly passive, in that particular pressure groups or their campaigns are neither explicitly endorsed nor criticised. Even so, one cannot deny that bias against certain groups exists in the media. Negative attitudes are revealed in three main ways: where the media choose not to report a pressure group campaign; where a campaign is not given the coverage it merits; and by reporting their activities in unsympathetic or even hostile terms. The first two forms of bias are easily deniable by the media, and are difficult to prove conclusively. Explicitly hostile reporting is more easily detectable, and is found more commonly in the press, particularly the tabloid press, than in the broadcast media.

One can point to a number of pressure-group campaigns which have received extremely hostile coverage from the press. Perhaps the most notable example is the Campaign for Nuclear Disarmament, which was heavily criticised by sections of the press, particularly in the 1980s as public support for the campaign grew. Others which have been explicitly criticised by sections of the press include trade union campaigns for workers' rights and campaigns for equal opportunities and racial equality.

The media also openly support certain campaigns. Some are positively endorsed by the media, who play an active role in building public support. There are many examples of this. In the 1960s the *Sunday Times* campaign on behalf of those suffering from the side-effects of the drug Thalidomide was a classic case (H. Evans, 1984). But such campaigns are not the preserve of the broadsheets. For example, the campaign to impose restrictions on potentially dangerous dogs, which culminated in the Dangerous Dogs Act of 1991, was led by tabloid newspapers (notably the *Daily Star* which famously taunted the Home Secretary, who had initially refused to take steps to deal with the problem, with the headline 'You Wet Windbag').

Broadcasters, although burdened more heavily with rules governing impartiality, often feed upon pressure-group campaigns in a way which leads to the mobilisation of public support. News programmes often pick up issues raised by pressure groups, while documentaries, such as ITV's 'World in Action', BBC TV's 'Panorama' and Channel 4's 'Dispatches', address these issues in greater depth.

Drama programmes can reach an even wider audience and the issues which they generate can have a massive impact on public opinion. 'Cathy Come Home', a television play of the 1960s, focused attention on the plight of homeless families and created a huge public outcry. Pressure groups realise the importance of popular drama and some actively seek to influence the content of productions in an effort to advance their cause. Soap operas are often approached by pressure groups with ideas for a particular storyline (Wareham, 1991). For example, in the case of one popular ITV soap opera, where two of the leading characters had recently become pregnant, scriptwriters were subsequently lobbied by a pressure group promoting breastfeeding. Pressure groups are also on the look-out for anything which undermines their campaign or presents it in a bad light. For example, in recent years a number of drama programmes have been heavily criticised by anti-smoking and anti-alcohol groups for portraying excessive smoking and drinking as socially acceptable behaviour.

Finally, consumer programmes, such as BBC TV's 'Watchdog' and (the now-defunct) 'That's Life' have been actively involved in a wide range of successful campaigns in recent years. 'That's Life' was instrumental in promoting changes in the law regarding the sale of tobacco products to children, and spearheaded a successful campaign in the 1980s to make children's playgrounds safer. Among 'Watchdog's' successes was a campaign to prevent electrical appliances from being sold without a plug. This campaign drew attention to incidents where people had been electrocuted as a result of badly-wired plugs on TVs, kettles and other appliances. The government responded in 1992 with new regulations which required suppliers of electrical goods to fit plugs to their products before being sold.

When parts of the media actively support a campaign they are in effect acting as pressure groups in their own right, using their resources and their political influence to lobby for change. In most of the cases mentioned, the media have acted more like a cause group than an interest group, although it should be noted that even where the media appear to be acting on behalf of an outside organisation they are not necessarily motivated by altruism. The endorsement of a campaign (and, for that matter, opposition to it) can have implications for viewing, listening or circulation figures, which in turn may affect 'the bottom line'.

Commercial interests can intrude in other ways. For media which take advertising, there are further considerations. The coverage of particular issues can offend powerful commercial interests, which may use their leverage to influence editorial decisions. For example, the tobacco industry has in the past used the threat of withdrawing advertising from newspapers intending to publish articles about the dangers of smoking (Taylor, 1984). One should also note that media organisations often have other financial interests, whose profitability might be affected by a particular campaign. In these cases editors may face pressure from owners, keen to maintain the overall profitability of their businesses.

There are occasions when media organisations act more overtly as interest groups, openly defending and advancing their self-interests in the policy process. The media are regarded as a powerful interest for a number of reasons. It is a profitable industry and has considerable financial resources. It is well-connected politically having access to senior decision-makers and possessing good parliamentary contacts. Finally, and perhaps most importantly in the era of mass communication, the media have in their own hands the means to manipulate public opinion.

Politicians are well aware of the potential power of the media, and for most of the post-war period have been keen not to offend media organisations. In the Thatcher era, however, some of the more established media groups found themselves unable to influence the direction of policy. This was partly because of the government's approach to policy-making and partly because of the arrival of new media corporations which desired change. The 1980s saw new attempts to regulate press and broadcasting standards, and a Broadcasting Act which was intended to bring greater competition into the industry. Those within the media who opposed these moves found themselves fighting a tough rearguard action. Although they were unable to alter the direction of change, they did manage to dilute some of the government's proposals, thereby slowing the pace of change (see Chapter 6).

Conclusions

When a group goes public it is sometimes seen as an indication of weakness. According to this view, public campaigns are undertaken mainly by groups which lack influence elsewhere. Certainly public campaigns have their limitations. They are usually ineffective in the absence of pressure through other channels, such as Whitehall and Westminster. Public campaigns are often costly, particularly if they involve advertising. Finally, they can be highly unpredictable and, in some cases, counter-productive. Indeed, public campaigns have the potential to produce an adverse response, stimulating more opposition than support. In particular, if they lead to direct criticism of the government, this may actually undermine the kind of close, constructive relationship between the group and the executive, as described in Chapter 5, and the group may lose rather gain influence by pursuing a high profile campaign.

In spite of these pitfalls, public campaigns are increasingly used even by groups which do have close contacts with decision-makers, as a means of reinforcing their position. Moreover, as Alderman (1984, pp.122–3) has pointed out, going public is not necessarily a sign of weakness, but is often a valuable component of a wider campaign to influence policy. According to him such tactics can be as effective as discreet negotiations with ministers and civil servants. The cases we have examined during the course of this chapter support this view, though they also confirm that the outcome also depends on a range of other factors, which include how well the campaign is organised, the attitude of the media and, ultimately, the overall responsiveness of decision-makers to public opinion.

9

Other pressure points: beyond Whitehall and Westminster

British pressure groups have tended to focus their lobbying efforts upon decision-makers at a national level. There are a number of reasons for this. Britain is a centralised state, the key decisions being taken by the central rather than local government. It is therefore rational for groups to concentrate upon influencing the executive, either directly, or indirectly through parliamentary lobbying and public campaigns. In addition, pressure-group organisation itself reflects the national focus of British politics. As British politics is dominated by national institutions, such as the central executive, Parliament, the national media and the political parties, so pressure-group politics is dominated by national organisations, such as the BMA and the NFU.

Furthermore, the emphasis on national politics and decision-making has been reinforced by a belief among pressure groups that Britain has a high degree of independence from other states. Hence there was little value in lobbying institutions beyond national borders in an attempt to put pressure on national decision-making. However, Britain's membership of the European Community (and now of the European Union) has altered this perception significantly. Pressure groups have begun to develop supra-national lobbying strategies which focus on building support among European political institutions. They have also become more active at a local level, despite the continuing focus on national politics and the increasing centralisation of executive power in Britain. In this chapter we shall explore the growth of these alternative pressure points, beginning with the local level.

Local pressure groups

Many organisations are active at the local level. Newton's (1976) study of local politics in Birmingham in the 1970s identified over 4,000 local organisations, a third of which had been politically active in the previous twelve months. According to Stoker (1988, p.107) 'most local authorities operate in the context of a world of active groups'. This is confirmed by Parry et al. (1992) who found that a third of local leaders were faced by 'a lot of groups', while officials encountered pressure groups to an even greater extent. This study also found that groups were a major source of protest at the local level, with one-third of protest activity being inspired by voluntary groups and just under a third by economic groups such as trade unions.

Pressure-group activity at the local level is often portrayed as being undertaken by rather apolitical, inexperienced people who have a poor understanding of the political system. These are 'sporadic interventionists' (Dowse and Hughes, 1977), ordinary people who do not normally get involved in politics, and whose involvement is short-term. The vast majority of people who join local groups do not do so primarily for political reasons. Most of the organisations which are formed at this level are established mainly for other, non-political reasons, such as recreational clubs and societies (see Bishop and Hoggett, 1986) which are formed mainly to provide mutual support in the pursuit of various leisure activities. Even so, local organisations do become involved in politics for a variety of reasons. A foray into the political arena may be necessary to defend the interests of the group's members. For example, a parents' and toddlers' group facing closure as a result of cuts in the council budget may lobby to try to avert this. On the other hand, some groups become involved in local politics to promote action rather than to defend their position: for example, a recreational group for the elderly lobbying for a pedestrian crossing on a busy road.

The focus upon recreational, leisure and amenity groups is, however, a little misleading. Other community groups are more overtly political to begin with, having been formed on the basis of a particular grievance. Action groups, promoting and defending the rights of tenants, pensioners, ethnic groups, women and so on, are explicitly political organisations. In some cases the core members of such groups are seasoned political activists.

Other groups active at the local level also have a more overt political role and are involved regularly and continuously in politics (see Exhibit 9.1 for a typology of groups found at the local level). These include economic groups (such as trade unions and business associations), service providers in the voluntary sector and local branches of national pressure groups.

Exhibit 9.1 **A typology of local groups**

Several different types of group can be found at the local level:

1 Economic or producer groups: these include local branches of trade unions, chambers of trade and commerce and local branches of employers and trade associations.

2 Community groups: representatives of sections of the community, such as the elderly, women, ethnic minorities and tenants. Also include users of particular services such as recreational, leisure and amenity groups.

3 Cause groups: those promoting particular ideas or beliefs. National cause groups lobby local authorities directly. Some, such as CND, Friends of the Earth and the League Against Cruel Sports, have a network of local branches.

4 Voluntary sector groups: representatives of those who provide voluntary services. For example, local charities and local branches of national organisations such as Age Concern, Women's Royal Voluntary Service, MENCAP.

Source: Stoker (1988)

The growth of pressure group activity at local level

Pressure-group activity at the local level has increased in recent decades (Gyford, 1984). Several factors have been behind this. First, local authorities have themselves encouraged participation, creating greater scope for pressure group activity (Elcock, 1986, p.15). Many councils have developed consultative machinery – joint committees, forums, public meetings and so on – in an effort to accommodate the views of outside groups (Gyford, 1991). Changes in the planning process have also given local groups increased scope for participation. For example, in 1978 the Department of Transport altered public inquiry procedures relating to new roads, giving groups more access to information and a greater opportunity to put their case than previously existed.

However, some changes, particularly over the last decade, have reduced the opportunities for local organisations to participate. Central government has discouraged local authorities from going beyond the statutory minimum required in terms of public participation (Gyford, 1991, p.73). It has also resorted to special procedures to by-pass local planning procedures. For example, the creation of development corporations and enterprise zones has enabled developers in some cases to proceed in the face of strong local protests. Yet even where attempts have been made to limit participation – as in the use of the hybrid bill procedure to authorise the Channel Tunnel (Holliday, 1992) – pressure groups have nevertheless been able to make their views known.

A second factor behind the growth of pressure-group politics at the local level has been the changing pattern of service delivery. The administrative decentralisation of some services, such as housing, for example, has made it easier for local groups to approach service providers (Hambleton and Hoggett, 1984). Other changes, initiated mainly by central government, have also attracted certain organisations into local politics. Privatisation, contracting out and the encouragement of the voluntary sector have drawn organisations such as private contractors and voluntary groups into a closer relationship with local decision-makers.

Central government policies have stimulated local pressure in other ways. The 'opting-out' legislation, which enables schools and housing estates to move out of local authority control, has produced a great deal of political activity at grassroots level. The ballots (of parents or tenants) which must be held for opting out to proceed, have resulted in the formation of local groups, either for or against the policy. As a result, many schools and council housing estates have become a battleground for pressure-group politics in recent years. Yet it should be noted that although opting out has encouraged local participation, its underlying purpose is to remove services from local authority control, in the long run reducing the scope for pressure groups at this level.

Similarly, the creation of new quasi-governmental agencies by the Conservative government has to an extent by-passed local decision-making in a number of areas, thereby reducing the potential impact of pressure groups. As Gray (1994, p.68), has noted, this happened largely because of the relative isolation of these new bodies and partly due to their newness. It takes time for groups to develop relationships with these bodies, even if the latter wish to encourage this. Yet even where these bodies wish to isolate themselves they may be forced into a relationship. For, as Gray goes on to note, attempts to erode participation often produce an increasing demand for greater involvement, thereby limiting in practice the extent to which local participation can actually be by-passed.

The third and final explanation for the growth of local pressure group activity lies in the same social, political and cultural trends discussed in Chapter 8, which together explain the rise of pressure-group politics over the last few decades, namely, post-affluence theory; the decline of class politics; and the growing assertiveness of the public. The impact of the third factor appears to have been particularly evident at the local level (Lowe, 1986). A feature of this trend has been the rise of the so-called NIMBY (Not In My Backyard) groups. These groups, which are often highly successful in delaying or blocking new developments are, as the term suggests, localised. However, the decisions that they oppose are not always made at a local level. Indeed, many NIMBY campaigns have been established in response to decisions initiated by national government or multinational companies.

Not In My Backyard (NIMBY) groups

NIMBY groups are not an entirely new phenomenon, though their activities have become more prominent in recent years, partly in view of their media-oriented tactics. Looking at cases over the last decade, it seems that the decisions most likely to inspire NIMBY action include transport developments (such as the Channel Tunnel, the associated rail link and new roads – see Exhibit 8.3), industrial developments (especially those which have health and safety implications) and housing developments in rural areas. Not all NIMBY groups are opposed to new developments, however. Some are established to campaign against an existing development. An example of this is Mothers and Children Against Toxic Waste (MACATW), a group located at New Inn in Wales, which has campaigned vigorously to prevent a local chemical processing plant from burning toxic waste.

NIMBYs are often criticised for undermining socially desirable developments on the basis of self-interest. Indeed, it should be noted that the cost of NIMBY campaigns, in terms of damage to the economy, disruption, postponement and delay has been estimated as high as £1.5 billion a year (*Sunday Times*, 8 January 1989, p.A10). It is true that NIMBY groups act primarily on the basis of self-interested motives. They wish to protect lifestyles, homes, children, health and so on. But these are legitimate reasons for protest and one cannot blame people for wishing to oppose developments which affect their personal well-being. Even where a development is socially and economically necessary, it is unfair that some people should bear the burden for the rest of society. Even where compensation schemes exist they are generally inadequate. Moreover, NIMBY campaigns are often useful in generating wider public concern about potential threats to the environment in which people live. Indeed, many attract outside support from those who have no self-interest in the issue, as in the case of the opposition to the roads programme, for example (see Exhibit 8.3 above).

Some NIMBY groups have achieved considerable success in recent years, although it is much easier to delay a development, or win concessions, than to stop it entirely. Delay can, however, be an effective weapon in a longer-term effort to change government policy. Anti-nuclear, road and rail protesters, for example, have all at some time forced government to rethink its policies by using delaying tactics. Moreover, outright victory is possible, as the case of the anti-nuclear waste groups (shown in Exhibit 9.2) illustrates.

Exhibit 9.2 **The local campaigns against nuclear waste**

In October 1983 the Secretary of State for the Environment announced that two sites had been chosen for the disposal of radioactive nuclear waste. Elstow (Bedfordshire) was selected for the disposal of low-level waste and Billingham (Teesside) for 'long-lived' intermediate waste. Although normal planning procedures were suspended, local protests were strong enough to force the government to change its mind. In Billingham a local group calling itself BAND (Billingham Against Nuclear Dumping), working in conjunction with the local authorities, successfully campaigned for the abandonment of the 'long-lived' intermediate waste project. A major factor here was the withdrawal of support for the project by the owners of the proposed site, ICI, though this in turn was partly due to local pressure on the company.

The government had also decided to expand the list of possible sites for low-level nuclear waste. Fulbeck in Lincolnshire, South Killingholm in Humberside and Bradwell in Essex joined Elstow on the unenviable shortlist. Each locality formed its own protest group to oppose the government's plans (for example, LAND – Lincolnshire Against Nuclear Dumping). Together the groups also formed an umbrella group called Britain Opposed to Nuclear Dumping (BOND). This show of solidarity enabled the threatened communities to present a united front and to focus their efforts upon changing government policy. Without this solidarity, the communities might have ended up attacking each other's case in an attempt to avoid being chosen, thus reducing the pressure on the government to back down on its policy.

The groups worked alongside the main local authorities involved, who were also opposed to the plans. Three of the county councils formed a coalition and made representations to government and to Parliament opposing the policy. The councils also played a major role in developing the technical case against the proposals by employing their own experts and by undertaking fact-finding missions to other countries to see how they handled the problem. The campaign was further boosted by other reports, including one from the House of Commons' Environment Committee which was highly critical of the government's policy.

The campaign was successful in mobilising public opinion, both locally and nationally, against the policy of nuclear waste disposal. The media took a close interest in the issue, particularly in the aftermath of public concern surrounding nuclear energy which followed the Chernobyl disaster. The media's attention was also attracted by direct action organised by the groups. These tactics, which included a blockade of the proposed sites, making it difficult for them to be properly surveyed, also hampered the implementation of the government's plans.

Politicians of all parties came together to oppose the policy. One Tory MP, Michael Brown, whose constituency included South Killingholm, threatened to resign if the government went ahead with its plans. Another, Sir John Wakeham, was the chief whip at the time and although he could not publicly disagree with government policy, his ministerial colleagues will have certainly appreciated the strength of local feeling among his constituents on this matter. Although only four parliamentary seats were likely to be affected by a protest vote, it was perhaps the proximity to the general election that proved in the end to be the decisive factor. A matter of weeks before the poll, in May 1987, the government announced that it was abandoning its plans for the disposal of low-level waste.

Source: Blowers (1990)

The influence of local pressure groups

It is difficult to generalise about the influence of pressure groups at the local level. Some observers are rather pessimistic about the ability of groups to influence local decisions. Brier and Hill (1982), for example, describe three cautionary case studies in which local campaigners – a tenants' association, a dog lovers' society and a residents' association – proved largely ineffective. What was common to all three cases was that those involved were mostly inexperienced in politics. Brier and Hill conclude (p.205) that 'for the groups studied, political involvement appeared neither satisfying nor particularly educative as an experience'. Similarly, Dowse and Hughes (1977) in their study of 'sporadic interventionists' also found that members of the two groups they studied (a motorway protest group and a waterskiing club whose activities had been restricted by the local council) were disappointed with the impact of their hard-fought campaigns and became disillusioned with the political process more generally. In similar vein Dearlove (1973), in a study of local decision-making in Kensington and Chelsea, observed how councillors were reluctant to respond to so-called 'unhelpful' groups which made new demands or claims which conflicted with councillors' own views as to the proper scope of council business. As a result these groups were relatively ineffective.

Others are more optimistic, believing that even where campaigns fail to achieve their objectives, participation can be an educative experience. They argue that individuals who become involved in politics, perhaps at a local level, acquire knowledge and experience which may be useful in future (Barber, 1984; Pateman, 1970). Recent research has pointed out that the educative effect of participating in voluntary groups is small but nevertheless positive (Parry et al., 1992, p.291).

In addition, pressure groups can be effective. Decision-makers at the local level regard pressure groups as increasingly influential. Almost a third of political leaders who responded to the survey by Parry et al. believed that organised groups exerted influence over local issues. Of all the actors at this level (officers, parties, the local population) only councillors were rated as having more influence than pressure groups (Parry et al., 1992 p.393). One can also find many cases where local groups have been influential in winning concessions, delaying the implementation of policies indefinitely or even reversing decisions (see Exhibits 9.2 and 9.3). Nevertheless, it does appear that some groups, for a variety of reasons, have a greater chance of success than others. Let us now examine the reasons why this is the case.

Exhibit 9.3 **Saffron Boot House Action Group**

This case illustrates that local groups can be effective and influential. But it also demonstrates that such campaigns can often last a number of years and that those involved require considerable organisational and political resources, as well as a great deal of determination in order to succeed.

The Saffron Lane council estate in Leicester was built in the late 1920s. In the early stages of the building programme, there was a shortage of bricks which meant that the builder (Henry Boot Construction Company) had no alternative but to build the houses using reinforced clinker-concrete columns. Over fifty years later it was discovered that these houses, about a 1,000 in total, had developed unforeseen structural defects of a serious nature. Although Leicester City Council did not believe the houses to be unsafe for human habitation, it was clear that they would have to be demolished and the residents re-housed. Following discussions with the Department of the Environment, the City Council produced a ten-year plan to demolish the so-called 'Boot' houses and rebuild them.

By 1989, 500 of the homes had been rebuilt. However, the remaining phases of the rebuilding programme collapsed largely because of a change in central government policy which affected the financing of the scheme. The tenants in the remaining houses were furious and formed the Saffron Boot House Action Group (SBHAG) to campaign for the continuation of the rebuilding programme. A number of options were put forward to resolve the problem. For example, private developers proposed a redevelopment which included the building of private homes on the estate. The tenants rejected this idea, largely because the new houses would be much more densely packed in order to leave space for the private development. Meanwhile the City Council, though sympathising with the plight of the tenants, could only afford to rebuild twelve houses a year. At this rate, with 500 Boot houses still remaining, the programme would not be completed until well into the next century.

This was obviously unacceptable to the tenants. SBHAG, along with the local councillors representing the ward and the local MP (all Labour) continued to press both the Labour-run City Council and the Department of the Environment for the reinstatement of the programme. Eventually, in 1993, a compromise was reached, and one that was acceptable to the majority of tenants. The houses would be replaced by a development consisting of one-third housing association homes and two-thirds council properties. Given central government's hostility to council house building, this represented a significant victory for the tenants. Indeed, the government has refused to give such concessions to other, less well-organised tenants who have faced similar problems.

What factors lay behind the group's success? First of all the group was extremely well-organised and enjoyed the support of a stable and close-knit local community. The group met regularly, kept its supporters fully informed about developments, and was efficiently administered. It was helped in all these respects by full-time community workers who acted in an advisory and administrative role. Second, the group worked closely with elected representatives, in particular the councillors representing the ward, who were extremely active in their support for the tenants' case. Third, the local media gave the issue a great deal of coverage, enabling the tenants to generate wider public support for their plight. The fact that the City Council was sympathetic to the plight of the tenants was undoubtedly important. Councillors from all the main parties were supportive, but members of the ruling Labour group were especially so. The tenants' campaign also attracted the support of officers. Notably, the City Council's housing department made representations on the issue to the Department of the Environment in an effort to resolve the situation. Finally, the group was able to put its views to key decision-makers at the Department, on a number of occasions. On one occasion, members of the group 'ambushed' the housing minister while he was attending a housing conference and secured an opportunity to put their case. Meanwhile, the case had also been put to civil servants in the Department of the Environment who wanted to see the issue resolved, and this is likely to have been reflected in their advice to ministers.

Which groups are the most influential and why?

The factors which enhance the influence of local groups are broadly the same as those which operate at a national level. Groups need to be coherent, well-organised and adequately resourced. They need to demonstrate that they have support from the local community. They have to be able to mobilise support among elected representatives as well as developing constructive relationships with permanent officials. In order to be successful groups must be strong in all these areas.

The political environment within which local groups operate is also a very important factor. This has been analysed by Wilson and Stoker (1991) who have assessed the impact of some of the changes in the environment of local government in recent years upon two kinds of group: business and non-business groups.

Wilson and Stoker agree that many of the policy changes of the 1980s, such as competitive tendering, for example, have increased the level of business/local authority interaction. They also believe that business groups are likely to exert increasing influence over local decision-making in the future. But they do not see these organisations dominating local politics. Indeed, they note that business groups have a number of limitations which prevent them achieving a dominant position, including the lack of co-ordination between business organisations at the local level. Their view is supported by Parry at al. (1992, p.390), who found that political leaders did not necessarily perceive the best-resourced groups, such as business, as being more effective than others. Indeed, this research found non-business groups such as civic and residents' associations as being among the most effective organisations at local level. Wilson and Stoker also agree that non-business groups can exert considerable influence. But the extent of this influence is determined to some extent once again by the political environment, in particular by the ways in which local authorities direct and control their local pressure-group universe.

Three models are identified by Wilson and Stoker. First, the *arms-length management strategy* – where councils seek to establish an independent body to act as a buffer between themselves and local groups. Secondly, *sponsorship* – where councils actively support local groups, with grants for example. Third, there is *encapsulation*, where local authorities promote representative forums in order to incorporate pressure groups into the decision-making process. Wilson and Stoker conclude that local authorities will continue to seek to mould and shape their pressure-group environment. Yet they also appreciate that the pressure-group world at a local level has a life of its own and can elude attempts to control or manage it.

The patterns of interaction between pressure groups and local decision-makers varies considerably between different localities (Stoker, 1988). This adds to the usual problems one faces when seeking to generalise about the activities of pressure groups and their influence (see Chapter 2). These problems are further compounded by the fact that 'work on local pressure groups has been conspicuous by its absence' (Wilson and Stoker, 1991, p.21). The lack of research in this field means that our knowledge of local pressure-group activity is still fairly limited; it is certainly an area where more research is required.

Pressure groups at the European level

For the remainder of this chapter we shall consider another arena where pressure-group activity has increased in recent years: decision-making at the European level. It has been estimated that interest representations at this level increased tenfold in the 1970s and 1980s, while the period 1985–90 alone saw a fourfold increase in pressure-group activity (Andersen and Eliassen, 1991). Meanwhile the number of European-wide groups – federations of national groups (also known as Euro-groups – see below) – grew from 300 in 1970, to 439 in 1980, to over 800 in 1990 (Butt Philip, 1991). Lobbying at the European level, however, is not confined exclusively to Euro-groups. National pressure groups have also become more closely involved with decision-making at the European level in recent years. In a survey of over 100 British groups undertaken in 1992, two-thirds reported increased contact with the European Community institutions over the previous decade, while 12 per cent of groups had established an office in Brussels for the purpose of lobbying (Baggott, 1992).

There is a strong belief among commentators that as well as increasing in volume, lobbying has improved in a qualitative sense. Lobbying at the European level has certainly become more sophisticated and professionalised in recent years (Greenwood and Jordan, 1993; Mazey and Richardson, 1992). A feature of this has been the explosion in the number of professional lobbyists located in Brussels. The European Commission (1992) has identified 3,000 lobbyists, a three-fold increase on the figure a couple of years previously. The Commission also estimates that there are around 10,000 individuals who are employed by lobbyists at the European level.

It is also clear that when lobbying European institutions British pressure groups have been subjected to a kind of learning process, rather as Sargent (1987) noted in the specific case of business groups. Initially, pressure groups have faced unfamiliar structures of decision-making and as a result have been less successful than they might otherwise have been. By continuing to lobby at this level, groups have acquired valuable experience and knowledge of the decision-making process in Europe which has often proved useful in subsequent campaigns.

Why the expansion in lobbying?

There are three related reasons why British pressure groups have expanded their lobbying efforts in Europe. First, European institutions are increasingly perceived by groups as having much more influence over domestic policy decisions than was previously the case. Some groups, such as the farming lobby, have been affected by European Community decisions for many years, and compared with most other groups became involved in lobbying at this level at an early stage. As the powers of the European Community extended, other groups, too, became aware of the need to focus their attention here. The Single European Act (SEA) of 1987 was a key development, extending the powers of the Community in areas such as environmental policy and technology, while creating the drive towards an single (or internal) market which required the imposition of Community-wide standards and regulations governing a whole range of trades and industries. The result was that 'in some sectors the bulk of new regulatory activity now takes place not in Whitehall but in Brussels' (Miller, 1990, p.59). The SEA also altered the balance of power between European institutions and national governments by extending qualified majority voting in the Council of Ministers, a move which was designed to undermine the ability of individual member governments to block new laws and regulations. The Maastricht Treaty (1992), which created the European Union, has extended further the competences of European institutions into areas such as public health and consumer protection and has further altered decision-making processes, as we shall see in a moment.

Second, pressure groups began to see European institutions as more accessible and receptive to their views. Again both the SEA and the Maastricht Treaty contributed greatly to this. The extension of the Community's competences created a demand, particularly from the European Commission, for the kind of information and expertise that groups were able to provide. As a result it became much more open and accessible to groups which could provide such assistance. At the same time, alterations made to the decision-making process created a greater incentive to lobby both the Commission and the European Parliament. The greater use of qualified majority voting, already mentioned, meant that groups could no longer rely on a veto by their national government and were therefore obliged to minimise the risk of defeat by seeking to influence proposals at a much earlier stage in the process. As a result, attention was focused increasingly on the Commission in view of its role as the main initiator of legislation (Kohler-Koch, 1994). The SEA also raised the profile of the European Parliament by giving it the power to propose amendments to legislation relating to the single market. The Maastricht Treaty has strengthened these powers and extended them to other areas, such as environmental policy for example.

Third, groups which lacked influence at home began to take Europe seriously as a means of challenging the British government's policies (see Exhibit 9.4). The results they achieved encouraged them to devote more resources to lobbying at a European level. Among these groups were those which had been wholly or partly excluded from the decision-making process in Britain during the 1980s – the trade unions and local authorities, for example – and others unhappy with the policies of the British government – such as groups representing the poor, the environmental lobby, women's organisations and equal opportunity groups. Their hopes were raised, not only by the extension of the Community's competence and by the changes mentioned above which undermined Britain's veto, but also by the willingness of European institutions – particularly the Commission and the Court of Justice – to challenge the policies of the British government (see Exhibit 9.5).

Exhibit 9.4 **The importance of lobbying at the European level**

The following cases illustrate that important decisions are made at the European level and that groups have a clear incentive to lobby Community institutions.

- During the latter part of the 1980s, Friends of the Earth along with other environmental groups lobbied the European Commission over Britain's exemptions from a Water Quality Directive governing the nitrate content of water. The Commission subsequently put pressure on Britain in an attempt to secure compliance. In 1988 the British government, fearing a challenge in the European Court, agreed that it would in future seek to abide by the standards set out in the directive.

- The company which manufactures 'tetrapak' cartons for milk and orange juice, was worried about a new European Community directive on packaging waste. The company had talks with the European Commission in an attempt to persuade them that their product was not harmful to the environment. The Commission accepted these arguments and the directive was subsequently amended in response to the company's representations.

- The trade unions, which have had a poor relationship with the British government over the last fifteen years, increased their lobbying efforts at the European level during the 1980s. They were encouraged by a number of initiatives which appeared to undermine key policies of the British government. For example, legislation arising from the European Community's Social Charter of 1989 (opposed by the British government) has forced Britain into amending some of its own laws on worker protection, such as the rules on entitlement to maternity pay for example. Britain opted out of the Social Chapter of the Maastricht

Treaty, in principle exempting it from the Community's social legislation. In practice, however, the refusal to sign the protocol will not prevent other member states from seeking to persuade Britain to adopt minimum standards in this field. Britain is therefore unlikely to be entirely insulated from the development of European-wide social policies, and the incentive for groups such as the trade unions to lobby in Europe therefore remains.

- In 1992, the European Parliament rejected proposals from the Commission to ban high performance motorcycles. This was brought about by a vigorous lobbying campaign by motorcycling associations at national and European level which managed to secure the support of enough MEPs (262 out of 518) to vote against the measure.

- Organisations promoting equal opportunities have been encouraged by a series of European Court judgements. In 1982 for example, Britain amended its laws on equal pay following a decision from the Court. In 1986, another judgement led the British government to alter social security rules in order to enable women as well as men to claim an allowance when caring for sick or disabled relatives. Britain has also been forced to introduce common retirement ages for men and women in response to a further decision. These judgements have given pressure groups an incentive to support test cases which have implications for domestic law.

European lobbying strategies

As we have seen, many British pressure groups now realise the value of lobbying at the European level. They have also begun to appreciate the complex nature of lobbying at this level. Groups face a variety of options when seeking to influence policy, and in this section we examine these options by looking at the role played by each of the main Community institutions in the policy process.

Efforts to influence European Community decisions can be divided into two main categories: a national strategy, and what could be called a 'Euro-strategy'. A national strategy is where groups choose to target their own governments in an attempt to secure favourable decisions through the Council of Ministers. Although the Council of Ministers is not open to direct lobbying by groups, there are many opportunities for influencing the policy of member governments. Groups can put their case to ministers and civil servants through the normal channels (see Chapter 5) in the hope that their arguments will prevail when matters are being discussed in the Council. In addition, the most powerful lobbies are able to make contact with members of the Committee of Permanent Representatives (COREPER), which consists of civil servants drawn from the member states. The COREPER officials

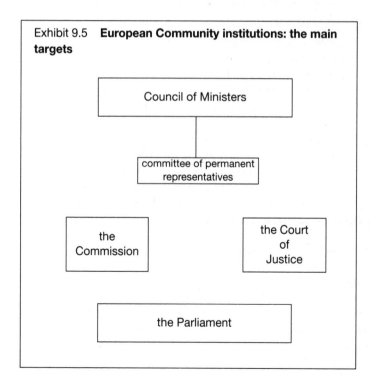

Exhibit 9.5   **European Community institutions: the main targets**

have a key role in the 'behind the scenes' negotiations which take place between states in an effort to secure decisions by the Council of Ministers.

The national strategy

The national strategy has been credited with a number of advantages (Greenwood et al., 1992, pp.22-3). It is often argued that the relationships which exist between pressure groups and national governments are stable, well-developed and reliable channels of representation. In addition, it is believed that most pressure groups carry more weight with their own government than with European institutions and that the impact of lobbying is therefore maximised by focusing on national government institutions. A further reason for concentrating on the national level is that the responsibility for implementing European Community policies falls upon the member states. By focusing on national government, groups may be able to exert considerable influence over policy implementation, so having some bearing on the actual impact of the policy at the domestic level.

Nevertheless, others have suggested that the importance of the national strategy has been overstated. In recent years, according to some observers, British pressure groups have become much more confident and familiar with lobbying European institutions (Greenwood et al., 1992, p.23). Furthermore, the extension of competences and changes to the decision-making process means that a strategy which is based solely on persuading national government is a high risk one. In an effort to reach a compromise, it is possible that governments may 'sell out' particular interests to which they have earlier given a commitment. It is therefore increasingly the case, as Mazey and Richardson (1992, p.103) point out, that 'a wise group will not rely on its ministry but will develop its own Brussels contacts'.

Euro-groups

One can identify several strategies of representation at the European level, or 'Euro-strategies'. The orthodox strategy (Averyt, 1977) involves the representation of interests through European pressure groups (Euro-groups) which focus their lobbying efforts mainly on the Commission. There are a large number of Euro-groups, representing a wide range of interests. Examples include the Union of Industrial and Employers' Confederation of Europe (UNICE), the European Trade Union Confederation (ETUC), the Committee of Agricultural Organisations in the European Community (COPA) and the European Bureau of Consumers' Unions (BEUC). There are also pan-European cause groups such as the European Environmental Bureau (EEB) and the Euro-group for Animal Welfare. There is considerable disagreement surrounding the effectiveness of these organisations, and some have been found to be rather weak and fragmented (Grant, 1989a; Sargent, 1987). But some are effective. Indeed the European Commission has in the past encouraged the formation of these organisations and has been particularly receptive to representations made through these channels (Butt Philip, 1991; Greenwood et al., 1992).

According to one survey, around three-quarters of British pressure groups are in some way connected to Euro-groups (Baggott, 1992). They are certainly important vehicles of representation, though British groups are not entirely reliant on them. Increasingly, occasions arise where British groups act independently, either alone or in conjunction with Euro-group lobbying, making direct contact with the Commission and other institutions such as the European Parliament. In the past it was exceptional for national groups to be represented directly in Brussels (Kohler-Koch, 1994).

The European Commission

Let us now focus upon the Commission and the way in which it interacts with both national pressure groups and Euro-groups. According to one of the leading authorities on the European Community, the Commission is the main target for most interests (Nugent, 1994, p.259). This is because of its central role in relation to all stages of policy-making from formulation through to implementation. Mazey and Richardson (1993) also identify the Commission as the number one target for pressure, followed (in order of priority) by the Council of Ministers, the European Parliament and the European Court.

The European Commission is surprisingly small – fewer than 4,000 officials are directly involved in policy-making. This, coupled with the extension of competences, has created a dependence upon outside organisations that can provide expertise and information. As a result the Commission is fairly accessible to such groups. Information flows between groups and the Commission are also facilitated by a complex system of advisory committees, numbering over 1,000, upon which groups are represented (Mazey and Richardson, 1992).

Relationships between the Commission and outside groups are shaped by another feature of the Brussels bureaucracy – its fragmentation (Nugent, 1994). The Commission is divided into twenty-three directorates, each of which has its own particular brief. There is considerable rivalry between the directorates and co-ordination tends to be poor. This loose structure provides a range of access points to pressure groups, although they may find that some directorates are more open to some groups than to others (Mazey and Richardson, 1992). For example, as Grant (1993, p.187) notes the directorate DGIII (Internal Market and Industrial Affairs) is often seen as being particularly receptive to the problems of business, while DGXI (Environment, Nuclear Safety and Civil Protection) is perceived as causing the greatest difficulties for these groups. However, Grant warns that it is dangerous to generalise about the predispositions of the directorates, pointing out that relationships with outside organisations can be shaped by highly specific factors, such as the personalities of those being lobbied, for example. Some officials, it appears, are simply more willing to listen to the views of outside organisations than others.

While it makes sense for groups to cultivate relationships with those directorates that are friendly and receptive to their views, the fragmented and uncoordinated nature of the policy process in the European Community means that groups cannot rely solely on good contacts with one or two directorates which share their perspective. Ideally, groups need to be in touch with all directorates whose activities might potentially encroach upon their interests. At the very least groups need to maintain a basic presence in all these areas. This involves gathering intelligence about the directorates' position, their activities and the personalities working in them, so as to be as fully informed as possible about future policy developments.

The European Parliament

Though regarded in the past as a fairly weak and ineffective institution, the European Parliament is today a much more important target for those who wish to influence Community legislation. The rising profile of the Parliament can be traced back to 1979 when MEPs became directly elected rather than nominated by member states. In the UK (Northern Ireland excepted), a first-past-the-post/single member system is adopted for these elections. Although turn-out has remained low and the constituencies are too large to have a distinct local identity, direct election at least established an important link enabling locally based groups to focus upon particular MEPs.

As mentioned earlier, changes in the decision-making process have enhanced Parliament's role. Before the Single European Act of 1987, Parliament had the right to be consulted on a range of legislative matters. The SEA, however, gave MEPs the opportunity to propose amendments to legislation relating to the single market, under the co-operation procedure. Where Parliament produced an absolute majority of MEPs against the Council of Ministers' position, the Council of Ministers could only overrule the Parliament by a unanimous vote. Parliament could also table specific amendments to legislation. If the Commission supported the amendment in question then the Council could adopt the amendment by majority vote. A unanimous vote would be required where the Council wished to adopt an amendment proposed by the Parliament, but rejected by the Commission. The available evidence seems to suggest that these procedures have enabled Parliament to exert some influence over single market laws. Between 1987 and 1992, of 1,724 amendments it proposed to legislation concerning the single market, 1,052 were accepted by the Commission and 719 by the Council of Ministers (Mazey and Richardson, 1992, p.96).

The Maastricht Treaty extended the powers of the Parliament, giving it new powers of co-decision on issues relating to environmental policy, research and development, European transport systems and the single market. This means that where the Council of Ministers cannot agree with the Parliament's position, the differences are then referred to a conciliation committee (composed of representatives from both the Council and the Parliament) which seeks to produce a compromise solution. If the problems cannot be resolved at this stage, the Parliament can still veto the legislation by mustering an absolute majority of MEPs against the measure.

These changes make the Parliament an even more attractive focus for pressure-group campaigns. But it still remains a lower order target for those groups which have good contacts with the Commission. And it is still a relatively weak body. As Nugent (1994, p.208) has noted 'notwithstanding all its efforts and the increased influence it has achieved, the European Parliament is still commonly regarded as being a rather special sort of advisory body rather than a proper parliament'. Even so, it is not without influence, and groups will increasingly find MEPs useful allies when attempting to persuade the more powerful Community institutions to think again.

The European Court of Justice

As the supreme court, the Court of Justice plays a decisive role in the interpretation of European law. Cases can also be brought before British courts, who are expected to give European law precedence over domestic law when there is a conflict between the two. The European Court is not lobbied in the conventional sense. Individuals and organisations, who wish to mount a challenge to a particular domestic law, may seek to bring cases before the Court. Cases can also be brought by the Commission and by member states.

One can find a number of examples in recent years where judgements by the European Court, or by British courts interpreting European law, have directly challenged the policy of the British government. This has happened on a range of social and economic issues such as rights for part-time workers, retirement ages for men and women and contracting-out of public services. In all these cases decisions by the courts have led the British government, with great reluctance, to alter domestic laws.

Although the primacy of European law has given pressure groups added incentive to support test cases that could lead to changes in the law, the growing use of legal processes to fight government policy decisions is in fact part of a broader trend. In recent decades there has been a growth of judicial activism at the domestic level too. This has created greater opportunities for organisations and individuals to put pressure on government through the courts under British law. For example, in 1992, in a case brought by the miners' unions, the High Court found that the government had not followed established procedures in announcing its pit closure programme. Even when such cases are lost (as in the Law Society's challenge to the government's new Legal Aid regulations in 1993), or, as in the case of the miners, the government finds other means of implementing its policy, court decisions can still provide a great deal of welcome publicity for a campaign. The European Court and European legislation have therefore opened up further opportunities for groups to take legal action as a means of applying pressure, rather than creating an entirely new tactic (Harlow and Rawlings, 1992).

Effectiveness of lobbying at the European level

As Greenwood et al. (1992 p.246) have observed 'nobody can really claim that political integration has made the nation state obsolete'. Important policy decisions will continue to be made at national level, particularly regarding implementation, and pressure-group activity will continue to reflect this. Moreover, as we have seen, many groups adopt a national strategy – which involves persuading one's own government to pursue a particular course of action – when seeking to influence policy at the European level.

However, as the European Community's powers extend, it is obviously important that groups understand these supra-national decision-making processes. They need to adopt a much broader strategy which enables them to influence European institutions such as the Commission and the Parliament, when necessary. The most successful groups in future will be those which have good political contacts at both the national and at the European level.

Lobbying at the European level has its costs, however. As Butt Philip (1991, p.xi) has noted 'lobbying the community is thus a multi-level, multi-dimensional activity which requires skill, time and often substantial resources for success to be achieved.' Hence it should come as no surprise to learn that the wealthy producer interests tend to be most influential at this level (Mazey and Richardson, 1992). The superiority of these groups is also enhanced by their greater experience of dealing with European institutions, compared with other lobbies. However, this advantage is offset to some extent by the relative openness of lobbying at this level – for example, it is possible for groups such as those representing environmentalists and consumers to obtain access to senior policy-makers – and by the ever-changing decision-making process in Europe, which means that past experience will not necessarily be a good guide to future strategy.

Conclusions

The rise of lobbying at both the local and European levels is too important to be ignored. Although most pressure groups will continue to focus mainly on the national level, this chapter has shown that they cannot rely entirely on good contacts with these decision-makers. In recent years, as we have seen, campaigns mounted beyond Westminster and Whitehall have enjoyed some success. Moreover, it seems that, increasingly, decisions relate to all three levels: European, national and local. The government's road building programme, for example, though a national policy, has involved local authorities in those areas affected and the European Commission – which in fact challenged the British government's failure to make adequate environmental assessments of certain schemes. As the European Community's competences are extended, and as locally based campaigns continue to increase, groups will find that, in order to be successful, they will have to adopt lobbying strategies that are both more flexible and more comprehensive and which aim to build support among decision-makers not only at national level, but at the local and the European levels too.

10

Conclusion

This chapter has three purposes: first, to comment upon the recent trends in pressure-group politics that have been identified throughout the book; second, to assess the contribution of groups to 'good government'. Third, to explore a number of possible reforms which might improve this contribution.

Recent trends in pressure-group politics

Despite the difficulties of drawing out general conclusions about pressure group politics (see pp.27–8), it has been possible to identify a number of recent trends. These are summarised below.

The political environment

Many groups have found the political environment inhospitable since the election of the Conservative government in 1979. The Thatcher government appears to have been heavily influenced by the New Right perspective on groups, discussed in Chapter 3. Some groups, which normally expected to be consulted prior to legislation, were ven fewer opportunities to comment on proposals at an early stage. An important factor here was the government's substantial parliamentary majority, which enabled it to get measures through, largely unscathed. However, many formal aspects of the consultation process were retained, and government was often forced for practical reasons to consult groups at the parliamentary stage and during the implementation of its policies.

Following Thatcher's departure, the political environment for most groups seemed to improve. This was largely because this was a pre-election period, although the Major government appeared initially at least to be less confrontational in its approach. After the 1992 election, the government was in a much weaker position because of its small majority. Nevertheless, it adopted a fairly authoritarian approach and ignored the views of groups in a range of policy areas. Its record on prior consultation was not significantly better than that of its predecessor. Yet it was less able than the Thatcher government to force measures through. As a result groups were able to make life much more uncomfortable for the government and some (such as the teachers for example) were able to win significant concessions.

The changing political environment has not affected all groups equally, as we saw in Chapter 6. Some have clearly benefited from the long period of Conservative government. These include business organisations, right-wing ideological groups and conservative moral groups. Others appear to have less access and influence, such as the trade unions, local authorities and some public sector professions, such as teachers and doctors. However, as we noted there are considerable variations within these categories. In addition, we observed that a large proportion of groups appear to have experienced neither an increase nor a decrease in their political access or influence in this period (see p.123).

Political culture
The underlying political culture has continued to favour the growth of pressure-group politics. The continued decline of class politics, the growing importance of single issues, particularly quality of life issues, and the growing assertiveness of the public have all been reflected in increased participation in pressure groups. This trend also reflects to some extent dissatisfaction with other representative institutions, such as the political parties. In addition, the expansion of education, particularly higher education, and the continued growth of the mass media may also have encouraged participation by creating more awareness both of current issues and of the role of groups in the policy process.

Group membership has certainly grown, particularly among those concerned with quality of life issues, such as the environmental lobby. Indeed, the combined membership of the main environmental groups more than doubled in the 1980s to over five million people. Participation in local groups also seems to have increased quite significantly in recent years, as reflected in the rise of NIMBY groups. In contrast, some groups have experienced a decline in membership partly as a result of changes in the social structure, notably the trade unions. But, on balance, participation in pressure groups is increasing.

Strategy and tactics
Pressure groups have adjusted their strategies and tactics to take account of changes in the political environment and trends in political culture. They have also had to respond to changes in the decision-making process, resulting partly from these developments. While the executive remains the most effective channel for lobbying, groups are more aware of the need to establish good contacts with other pressure points, such as Parliament and the media. Indeed, even those groups which have traditionally enjoyed close and constructive links with the executive know they cannot rely entirely on these relationships. In recent years they have therefore made greater efforts to strengthen other political contacts in order to facilitate parliamentary lobbying and public campaigning when the need arises.

This development has been further stimulated by the attitude of government towards certain interest groups, which were previously regarded as insiders. These have been forced to build support in Parliament and among the public in an effort to modify policies which they oppose. The long period of Conservative domination has also led groups to focus on particular channels as a means of modifying government policies, such as the Conservative backbenches and the House of Lords.

Meanwhile, the impact of Europe on domestic policies has also encouraged groups to develop broader political strategies. Rather than relying on good contacts with the British executive, groups have forged links with European institutions. Such moves are not confined to those which are excluded or ignored by the British government. Increasingly, groups across the board are developing strategies which are much more comprehensive than in the past. They are also having to be extremely flexible in distributing lobbying resources among the various options, in a way which maximises their influence over policy.

Finally, in this context one cannot avoid noticing that pressure-group campaigns are becoming professionalised. This has happened in a number of ways. First, groups now directly employ specialists to a far greater extent. These include people who have made a career out of lobbying or who have relevant professional experience – such as journalists, former MPs or ex-civil servants and so on. Secondly, there has been a rise in organisations that specialise in lobbying and in return for a fee provide services for those wishing to influence political opinion. In this way the practice of lobbying is therefore not only becoming professionalised, but is increasingly commercialised as well.

Good government?

There are many views about the role of pressure groups in a democracy and their contribution to what could be called 'good government'. Which is the most accurate? Perhaps the best approach is to look at the contribution of groups with respect to three specific features of 'good government': democracy, efficiency and accountability.

Democracy

Do pressure groups enhance or undermine democracy? As we saw in Chapter 4, the quality of democracy in pressure groups is variable. Many groups have a passive membership, dominated by an élite with little scope for participation. Only the larger interest groups tend have formal systems of participation, such as electoral mechanisms, and even here turn-out is low. The lack of formal democratic mechanisms does not mean, however, that group leaders are unresponsive to rank-and-file members. There are other ways in which leaders and members can communicate (see p.69). Moreover, other mechanisms, such the threat of resignation or the existence of a rival group, can limit the leadership's freedom to act autonomously.

Groups are also criticised for undermining the public interest, as interpreted and expressed by democratically elected politicians. According to this view, pressure groups represent intense and partial views. If they are allowed to dominate, decisions will benefit special interests at the expense of those who are poorly organised or not organised at all. The latter are assumed to be in the majority, and groups are therefore seen as undemocratic. This has been identified as a particular problem at local level where groups are often dominated by the articulate middle class.

Defenders of pressure-group politics disagree with this analysis (see for example, D. Wilson, 1984). They argue that groups enhance the democratic process, by organising opinion and communicating it to decision-makers who are themselves often distant from the people. Moreover, they reject the idea that democratically elected politicians are always the best judges of the public interest. Representative democracy is itself flawed. Elections are infrequent. Electoral systems do not reflect public preferences in depth or detail. Minorities are under-represented in systems which emphasise majority rule. Pressure groups can help address these shortcomings by reflecting public preferences more continuously and in greater detail. They also organise minorities and enable their views to be heard.

Representative democracy and pressure-group democracy should be seen as complementary, rather than in conflict with each other. Both can contribute to a society, where leaders respond to public preferences without riding roughshod over minorities. The two systems need to be balanced and integrated, to ensure that the contribution of both is enhanced. We look at ways in which this might be achieved in the final section of this chapter.

Efficiency
Another criticism of groups is that they impede efficiency (see p.51). It is believed that they do this by preventing economic

and social change which benefits society in general, or by impeding the emergence of coherent policies which could solve particular problems. Trade unions and professional bodies are often accused of standing in the way of such progress, as are NIMBY groups which, as we saw earlier (see p.198) can incur economic costs by blocking certain developments, such as new roads for example.

But groups can also contribute towards greater efficiency. They have knowledge, expertise and information about the policy environment which can help government to develop more effective policies. In addition, their co-operation can enable policies to be implemented efficiently. If government takes groups into its confidence, consults them and obtains their assistance, this does not necessarily weaken the government's position. Indeed, as Graham and Tytler (1993, p.147) observe in the context of education policies, 'partnerships and consultation do not lessen government power to govern, they can enhance its effectiveness'. The Conservative government's education policies have been inefficient in several respects. In particular, the failure to consult the teaching profession, and other interested parties such as the local authorities, led to unworkable schemes which had to be modified later for practical reasons.

In the future governments may well adopt a more constructive approach than that practised in Britain. According to Drucker (1993), society is increasingly dominated by organisations. This will continue because knowledge, which he sees as the key resource in post-capitalist society, is largely controlled by organisations. At the same time, government has become powerless to govern in the sense that it has a limited capacity to make decisions and enforce them. Drucker is critical of what he sees as the dominance of special interests. But rather than try to ignore this 'society of organisations', by forcing measures through without their support, he seems to accept that the best approach is to share power with groups and to harness them in the pursuit of economic and social objectives.

Accountability

Finer's book *Anonymous Empire* (1958), which did much to stimulate academic interest in pressure-group politics, criticised the faceless, voiceless and unidentifiable nature of lobbies. They have since been attacked on many occasions for their lack of openness and accountability. In some cases, accountability between members and leaders is poor. In their defence, groups argue that their leaders are accountable to their members in a variety of ways, even where electoral mechanisms are non-existent (see above). Pressure groups, as private organisations, can also be very secretive about their dealings with decision-makers and opinion formers, although the relationships between groups and decision-makers have been more heavily scrutinised as a result of the growing interest among academics and the media in the period since Finer wrote.

Added to this, groups often publicise not only their own activities, but those of other groups as well, in an attempt to raise public awareness of their campaigns and to promote criticism of their opponents' tactics. This has raised the profile of groups and forces them to account in public for their actions. According to Des Wilson (1984, p.23) groups also play a role in improving the public accountability of decision-makers. He believes that pressure groups undertake a valuable surveillance function. This involves scrutinising government policy, monitoring its activities and keeping the public informed. On top of this, pressure groups can force government to justify its policies in public, again strengthening accountability.

Reforming pressure-group politics

The pressure-group world certainly has the potential to contribute to democratic, efficient and accountable government; yet it can also undermine it. Is it possible to enhance the positive contribution of pressure groups while reducing the negative effects? There are a number of possible approaches which might be considered as a means of achieving this, and these will now be discussed briefly.

Regulating the internal affairs of groups

One approach is to reform pressure groups in order to make them more open, democratic and accountable. This already happens in some areas. The trade unions, for example, are heavily regulated. Their internal decision-making processes have been altered by the Conservatives' trade union and employment legislation. As a result they are now more democratic, more open and more accountable to their members. Similarly, pressure groups that are also registered charities are regulated by law. Charity law sets out certain requirements regarding the accountability of groups possessing charitable status, and places certain restrictions on their activities, particularly with respect to lobbying and campaigning. Moreover, government often seeks to regulate the activities of groups in a variety of informal ways: by conferring a certain status upon them (for example, insider groups which must play by the rules of the game), or by manipulating them through the allocation of financial resources.

It is possible that the legal framework within which groups operate could be altered so as to make them more responsive and accountable to their rank-and-file members. For example, groups which have a membership above a certain size could be compelled to hold ballots for the election of leaders and the endorsement of the policies of the organisation. Groups, again of a certain scale, could also be required to fulfil minimum standards of openness. This could take the form of an annual report, containing published accounts showing the source and uses of funds and summarising the group's activities over the year. In fact, most groups already provide this information on request, but to make it a requirement would be one way of ensuring that basic information about pressure groups is available within the public domain.

There are problems with this kind of approach, however. First, it could be argued that such regulation places too heavy a financial burden on groups, many of which are not generously resourced to begin with. Secondly, regulation of this kind could be seen as placing too great a burden on the state. Even a basic regime would cost money and additional resources would be needed to ensure that these requirements were being complied with. Third, it could be seen as an infringement of liberty and privacy. Groups are supposed to be autonomous, private organisations in charge of their own affairs. State regulation might be seen as the thin end of the wedge, leading ultimately to state control of groups, which would be undesirable. Finally, it would be difficult to devise a system which encapsulated all groups. Businesses (which do not have members as such) and small campaigning bodies (which do not have a mass membership) would be exempt from the kind of scheme described above.

Perhaps a gradual, piecemeal approach would be preferable to a blanket system of regulation. Charity law could be strengthened to improve the public accountability of pressure groups which are registered charities (although charities are not supposed to engage in political activity, they are allowed to inform the public and decision-makers). Trade union law could be extended to professional bodies and trade associations, while companies could be required to establish consultative processes which enable workers or the local community to have a say. Other mass member groups, not covered by any of these regimes, could have their own system which applied to those above a certain scale (measured either by the number of members or size of income) requiring them to give more information about their activities and giving their members a greater role in decision-making.

Relationships with decision-makers

Another approach focuses on the relationship between pressure groups and decision-makers. There are a number of possible ways in which these relationships can be improved. First of all, groups can be given clearer rights to be consulted about legislation. One notes here the recommendations of the Hansard Society Commission on the Legislative Process (1993) which include the publication of clear guidelines on consultation by the government. Secondly, attempts could be made to open up the consultation process to greater scrutiny. In this context the Hansard Society Commission recommended that secrecy at the consultation stage be minimised. One possibility is the publication of documents which list those consulted, the points they have raised and the government's response. Third, pressure groups might be allowed to present their case regarding legislation more openly in Parliament. This could be done, as discussed in Chapter 7, by a greater use of the special standing committee procedure or by allowing groups to give evidence prior to a bill being considered in depth.

Such changes would give pressure groups more opportunity to put their case and more time to raise public concern about the issues in question. However, one could also propose a number of reforms which would seek to clarify, regulate and open to public scrutiny relationships between groups and decision-makers. These include further restrictions on external interests of MPs and their links with pressure groups. It would not be a good idea, for reasons outlined in Chapter 7, to seek to prevent MPs from having any outside interests. But there now seems to be much more public support for specific restrictions preventing MPs from receiving money in return for lobbying. At the same time there is support for greater disclosure by MPs of their interests and for a tougher regulatory regime to ensure that rules are being upheld and transgressors punished. In addition, new restrictions on the employment of ex-ministers, as recommended by the Nolan Committee, have been widely welcomed.

Final remarks

Pressure groups are not perfect institutions. It has been fashionable in recent years, certainly among ministers, to disparage them as vested interests whose sole aim is to subvert the democratic process and undermine the public interest. However, it must be remembered that pressure groups represent legitimate preferences and interests in society. Moreover, they are not entirely self-interested. Interest groups do raise matters of concern to the wider public, while cause groups provide an important channel for people with common preferences and shared values regarding society as a whole.

Modern democracy cannot function properly without pressure groups. As a means of representation they are as legitimate as the ballot box. Of course, there is no guarantee that pressure groups will be democratic, accountable or efficient. But there is no guarantee that political parties or politicians will satisfy these criteria either. Of course, government must have direction and leadership, and must strive to put the public interest above sectional claims. But this is no reason for excluding groups. Pressure groups can speak on behalf of the public. They can represent the whole range of opinions. Together they can mediate between the government and the governed, and can contribute to the effective running of the state. Moreover, their expertise is valuable to policy-makers. They can assist with implementation and play a useful role in reviewing the impact of policies. It is in the interests of good government to work with pressure groups rather than against them.

Bibliography

Adeney, M. and Lloyd, J. (1987), *The Miners' Strike 1984–5. Loss Without Limit* (London: Routledge and Kegan Paul).

Age Concern (1990), *Annual Report* (London: Age Concern).

Alderman, G. (1984), *Pressure Groups and Government in Great Britian* (London: Longman).

Allen, G. (1994), *Reinventing the Commons*. Thomas Paine Memorial Lecture, Thetford, 30 January.

Andersen, P. P. and Eliassen, K. A. (1991) 'European Community lobbying', *European Journal of Political Research*, September, 20(2), pp.173–87.

Ashley, J. (1994), *Acts of Defiance* (Harmondsworth: Penguin).

Averyt, W. (1977), *Agro Politics in the European Community: Interest Groups and the Common Agricultural Policy* (New York: Praeger).

Baggott, R. (1987), 'Health v wealth: the politics of smoking in Norway and the UK', *Strathclyde Papers on Government and Politics*, 57.

(1988), 'Pressure groups in Britain: change and decline?' *Talking Politics*, Autumn, 1(1), pp.25–30.

(1992), 'The measurement of change in pressure group politics', *Talking Politics*, Autumn, 5(1), pp.18–22.

(1994), *Pressure Groups: A Question of Interest?* (Sheffield: PAVIC Publications).

Bagguley, P. (1991), *From Protest to Acquiescence* (London: Macmillan).

Baldwin, M. (1990), 'The House of Lords' in M. Rush (ed.), *Parliament and Pressure Politics* (Oxford: Clarendon), pp.152–78.

Ball, A. and Millard, F. A. (1986), *Pressure Politics in Industrial Societies:*

A Comparative Introduction (Basingstoke: Macmillan).

Barber, B. (1984), *Strong Democracy: Participatory Politics for a New Age* (Berkeley, CA: University of California Press).

Barker, A. (ed.) (1992), *Quangos in Britain* (Basingstoke: Macmillan).

Barnes, A. and Kaase, M. (1979), *Political Action – Mass Participation in Five Western Democracies* (Beverly Hills: Sage).

Beer, S. (1956), 'Pressure groups and parties in Britain', *American Political Science Review*, 50(1), pp.1–23.

(1982), *Britain Against Itself* (London: Faber and Faber).

Benewick, R. (1973), 'Politics without ideology: the perimeters of pluralism' in R. Benewick, *Knowledge and Belief in Politics: The Problem of Ideology* (London: Allen and Unwin).

Bentley, A. F. (1967), *The Process of Government* (ed. P. Odegard) (Cambridge, MA: Belknap).

Benyon, J. (1985), 'Going through the motions – the political agenda, the 1981 riots and the Scarman inquiry' *Parliamentary Affairs*, October, 38(4), pp.409–22.

Berry, S. (1992), 'The rise of the professional lobbyist: a cause for concern?', *Political Quarterly*, July–September, 64(3), pp.344–51.

Birch, A. H. (1984), 'Overload, ungovernability and delegitimation: the theories and the British case', *British Journal of Political Science*, April, 14(2), pp.135–60.

Birkinshaw, P., Harden, I., and Lewis, N. (1990), *Government by Moonlight: The Hybrid Parts of the State* (London: Unwin Hyman).

Bishop, J. and Hoggett, P. (1986), *Organising Around Enthusiasms: Mutual Aid in Leisure* (London: Comedia).

Black, D. (1987), *Recollections and Reflections* (London: British Medical Journal).

Blowers, A. (1990), 'Public interest and local authorities: the case of radioactive waste', *Town and County Planning*, February, pp.57–8.

Bown, F. (1990), 'The defeat of the Shops Bill, 1986' in M. Rush, (ed.), *Parliament and Pressure Politics* (Oxford: Clarendon) pp.213–33.

Brand, J. (1989), 'Faction as its own reward: groups in the British Parliament 1945–1986', *Parliamentary Affairs*, April, 42(2), pp.148–64.

Brand, J. L. (1965), *Doctors and the State: The British Medical Profession and Government Action on Public Health: 1870–1912* (Baltimore, MD: Johns Hopkins University Press).

Brier, A. and Hill, T. (1982), 'Participation in local politics: three cautionary case studies' in L. Robins, (ed.), *Topics in British Politics* (London: The Politics Association).

British Medical Journal (1994), 12 March, p.732.

Brittan, S. (1975), 'The economic contradictions of democracy', *British Journal of Political Science*, April, 5(2), pp.129–60.

(1988), *A Restatement of Economic Liberalism* (Basingstoke: Macmillan).

Brown, C. (1989), 'Pluralism: a lost perspective', *Talking Politics*, Spring, 1(3), pp.95–100.

Bull, M. (1992), 'The corporatist ideal type and political exchange', *Political Studies*, June, 40(2), pp.255–72.

Burch, M. (1989), 'The energy committee' in G. Drewry, (ed.), *The New Select Committees: A Study of the 1979 Reforms* (Oxford: Clarendon).

Butt Philip, A. (1991), *Directory of Pressure Groups in the European Community* (Harlow: Longman).

Byrne, P. (1988), *The Campaign for Nuclear Disarmament* (Beckenham: Croom Helm).

Cabinet Office (1992), *Questions of Procedure for Ministers* (London: Cabinet Office).

Castles, F. (1967), *Pressure Groups and Political Culture* (London: Routledge and Kegan Paul).

Cawson, A. (1982), *Corporatism and Welfare* (London: Heinemann).

(1985), *Organised Interests and the State: Studies in Meso-Corporatism* (Beverly Hills, CA: Sage).

Central Statistical Office (1994), *Social Trends*, 24 (London: HMSO).

Charlesworth, A., Collins, N. and Bradley, I. (1990), 'Agricultural partners under pressure' *Politics* 10(1), pp.3–8.

Clarke, T. and Clements, L. (eds) (1977), *Trade Unions Under Capitalism* (London: Fontana).

Cotgrove, S. (1982), *Catastrophe or Cornucopia: The Environment, Politics and the Future* (New York: John Wiley).

Cox, A. (1988), 'The Old and New Testaments of corporatism', *Political Studies*, June, 36 (2), pp.309–15.

Dahl, R. (1961), *Who Governs?* (New Haven, CN: Yale University Press).

(1982), *Dilemmas of Pluralist Democracy* (London: Yale University Press).

Davies, A. and Williams, J. (1991), *What Next? Agencies, Departments and the Civil Service* (London: Institute for Public Policy Research).

Davies, M. (1985), *The Politics of Pressure: The Art of Lobbying* (London: BBC).

Dearlove, J. (1973), *The Politics of Policy in Local Government* (London: Cambridge University Press).

Defence Select Committee (1988), *Business Appointments*, 2nd Report 1987/8 (HC 392) (London: HMSO).

Directory of British Associations (1994), ed. S.P.A. and T.J.W. Henderson (Beckenham: CBD Research).

Dowse, R. E. and Hughes, J. A. (1977), 'Sporadic interventionists', *Political Studies*, March, 25(1), pp.84–92.

Drewry, G. (ed.) (1989), *The New Select Committees*, 2nd edition (Oxford: Clarendon).

Drucker, P. F. (1993), *Post-Capitalist Society* (Oxford: Butterworth, Heinemann).

Dubs, A. (1989), *Lobbying: An Insider's Guide* (London: Pluto).

Dunleavy, P. (1988), 'Group identities and individual influence. Reconstructing the theory of interest groups' *British Journal of Political Science*, January, 18 (1), pp.21–50.

Dunleavy, P. and Leary, B. O. (1987), *Theories of the State* (Basingstoke: Macmillan).

Durham, M. (1989), 'The Thatcher government and the moral right', *Parliamentary Affairs*, January, 42(1), pp.58–71.

Eckstein, H. H. (1960), *Pressure Group Politics: The Case of the BMA* (Stanford: Stanford University Press).

Elcock, H. (1986), *Local Government. Politicians, Professionals and the Public in Local Authorities*, 2nd edition (London: Methuen).

European Commission (1992), *An Open and Structured Dialogue Between the Commission and Special Interest Groups*, SEC (92) 2272 (Brussels: Commission of European Communities).

Evans, H. (1984), *Good Times, Bad Times* (London: Coronet).

Evans, R. (1983), 'Competing charities' *The Times* 5 October, p.2.

Finer, S. E. (1958), *Anonymous Empire*, 1st edition (London: Pall Mall). (1966), *Anonymous Empire*, 2nd edition (London: Pall Mall).

Fogarty, M. (1990), 'Efficiency and democracy in large voluntary organisations', *Policy Studies*, Autumn, 11(3), pp.42–8.

Fulton Committee (1968), *The Civil Service; Vol I: The Report of the*

Committee, Cmnd 3638 (London: HMSO).

Galbraith, J. K. (1974), *The New Industrial State* (Harmondsworth: Pelican).

Gamble, A. (1988), *The Free Economy and the Strong State. The Politics of Thatcherism* (London: Macmillan).

Gamson, W. (1975), *The Strategy of Social Protest* (Homewood, IL: Dorsey).

Garner, R. (1991), 'The animal lobby', *Political Quarterly*, April–June 62(2), pp.285–91.

Gilmour, I. (1983), *Britain Can Work* (Oxford: Martin Robertson).

(1993), *Dancing With Dogma* (London: Pocket Books).

Graham, D. and Tytler, D. (1993), *A Lesson For Us All* (London: Routledge and Kegan Paul).

Gramsci, A. (1971), *Selection from Prison Notebooks* (ed. Q. Hoare and G. Nowell-Smith) (London: Lawrence and Wishart).

Grant, W. (ed.) (1985), *The Political Economy of Corporatism* (London: Macmillan).

Grant, W. (1989a), *Pressure Groups, Politics and Democracy in Britain* (Hemel Hampstead: Philip Allan).

(1989b), 'Pressure groups: new trends in their finance', *Contemporary Record*, November, pp.2–5.

(1993), *Business and Politics in Britain*, 2nd edition (Basingstoke: Macmillan).

Grant, W. and Marsh, D. (1977), *The CBI* (London: Hodder & Stoughton).

Grant, W. and Sargent, J. (1987), *Business and Politics in Britain*, 1st edition (Basingstoke: Macmillan).

Grantham, C. (1989), 'Parliament and political consultants', *Parliamentary Affairs*, October, 42(4), pp.503–18.

Grantham, C. and Seymour-Uure, C. (1990), 'Political consultants' in M. Rush, (ed.), *Parliament and Pressure Politics* (Oxford: Clarendon), pp.45–84.

Gray, A. and Jenkins, W. I. (1985), *Administrative Politics in British Government* (Brighton: Wheatsheaf).

Gray, C. (1994), *Government Beyond the Centre* (Basingstoke: Macmillan).

Green, D. G. (1987), *The New Right: The Counter Revolution in Political, Economic and Social Thought* (Brighton: Wheatsheaf).

Greenwood, J. and Jordan, A. G. (1993), 'The UK: A changing kaleido-scope' in M. C. P. M. van Schendelen (ed.), *National Public and Private EC Lobbying* (Aldershot: Dartmouth), pp.65–87.

Greenwood, J., Grote, J. R. and Ronit, K. (1992), *Organised Interests and the European Community* (London: Sage).

Grey-Turner, E. and Sutherland, F. M. (1982), *The History of the BMA: Part 2 (1932–81)* (London: BMA).

Gyford, J. (1984), *Local Politics in Britain*, 2nd edition (London: Croom Helm).

(1991), *Citizens, Consumers and Councils: Local Government and the Public* (Basingstoke: Macmillan).

Habermas, J. (1976), *Legitimation Crisis* (London: Heinemann).

(1981), 'New social movements', *Telos*, Fall, 49, pp.33–7.

Hambleton, R. and Hoggett, P. (1984), *The Politics of Decentralisation* (Bristol: School of Applied Urban Studies).

Hamer, D. A. (1977), *The Politics of Electoral Pressure* (Brighton: Harvester).

Hansard Society (1993), *Making the Law*, The Report of the Hansard Society Commission on the Legislative Process (London: Hansard Society).

Harlow, C. and Rawlings, R. (1992), *Pressure Through Law* (London: Routledge).

Heath, A. and Topf, R. (1987), 'Political culture' in R. Jowell, S. Witherspoon and L. Brook, *British Social Attitudes: The 1987 Report* (Aldershot: Gower).

Hennessy, P. (1986), *The Great and the Good: An Inquiry into the British Establishment*, Report No. 654 (London: Policy Studies Institute).

Hindell, K. and Simms, M. (1971), *Abortion Law Reformed* (London: Peter Owen).

Hirschman, A. O. (1970), *Exit, Voice and Loyalty* (Cambridge, MA: Harvard University Press).

Hogwood, B. (1987), *From Crisis to Complacency: Shaping Public Policy in Britain* (Oxford: Oxford University Press).

Holbeche, B. (1986), 'Policy and influence: MAFF and the NFU', *Public Policy and Administration*, 1(3), pp.40–7.

Holliday, I. (1992), 'The politics of the Channel Tunnel', *Parliamentary Affairs*, April, 54(2), pp.188–204.

Hollingsworth, M. (1991), *MPs for Hire: The Secret World of Political Lobbying* (London: Bloomsbury).

Hollis, P. (ed.) (1974), *Pressure from Without in Early Victorian England* (London: Edward Arnold).

Honigsbaum, F. (1979), *The Division in British Medicine* (London: Kogan Page).

(1990), *Health, Happiness and Security: The Creation of the NHS* (London: Routledge, Chapman and Hall).

House of Commons (1990), *Parliamentary Lobbying*, Minutes of Evidence of the Select Committee on Members' Interests 1987–9 (London: HMSO).

(1994), *Register of Members' Interests* (London: HMSO).

Inglehart, R. (1977), *The Silent Revolution: Changing Values and Political Styles among Western Publics* (Princeton, N. J.: Princeton University Press).

Johnstone, D. (1984), *The Middle of Whitehall* (Bath: School of Humanities and Social Science).

Jones, J. B. (1990), 'Party committees and all-party groups' in M. Rush (ed.), *Parliament and Pressure Politics* (Oxford: Clarendon), pp.117–36.

Jones, P. R. (1981), *Doctors and the BMA* (Aldershot: Gower).

Jones, P. R. and Cullis, J. G. (1990), 'The charity as firm: implications for public policy', *Policy and Politics*, 18(4), pp.289–99.

Jordan, A. G. (1977), 'Grey Papers', *Political Quarterly*, January–March, 46(1), pp.30–43.

(1989), 'Insider lobbying: the British version', *Political Studies*, March, 37(1), pp.107–13.

(1990), 'The pluralism of pluralism: an anti-theory', *Political Studies*, 38(2), pp.286–301.

Jordan, A. G. and Richardson, J. J. (1987a), *Government and Pressure Groups in Britain* (Oxford: Clarendon).

(1987b), *British Politics and the Policy Process* (London: Allen & Unwin).

Judge, D. (1990), 'Parliament and interest representation' in M. Rush (ed.), *Parliament and Pressure Politics* (Oxford: Clarendon), pp.18–44.

(1992), 'The effectiveness of the post-1979 select committee system: the verdict of the procedure committee', *Political Quarterly*, January–March, 63(1), pp.91–100.

Kavanagh, D. (1990), *Thatcherism and British Politics* (Oxford: Oxford University Press).

Key, V. O. (1961), *Public Opinion and American Democracy* (New York: Knopf).

Kimber, R. and Richardson, J. J. (eds.) (1974), *Pressure Groups in Britain* (London: Dent).

King, D. S. (1987), *The New Right: Politics, Markets and Citizenship* (London: Macmillan).

King, R. (1985), *The Organisation, Struture and Political Function of Selected Chambers of Commerce* (London: ESRC).

Kohler-Koch, B. (1994), 'Changing patterns of interest intermediation in the European Union' *Government and Opposition*, Spring, 29(2), pp.166–80.

Laclau, E. and Mouffe, C. (1987), 'Post-Marxism without apologies', *New Left Review*, November/December, 166, pp.79–106.

Latham, E. (1965), *The Group Basis of Politics* (New York: Octagon).

Law Society (1992), *Reform of the Legislative Process* (London: Law Society).

Lijphart, A. and Crepaz, M. (1991), 'Corporatism and consensus democracy in eighteen countries: conceptual and empirical linkages', *British Journal of Political Science*, 21(2), pp.235–56.

Lindblom, C. (1977), *Politics and Markets* (New York: Basic Books).

Lowe, P. and Goyder, J. (1983), *Environmental Groups in Politics* (London: Allen and Unwin).

Lowe, S. (1986), *Urban Social Movements* (London: Macmillan).

Mackenzie, W. J. M. (1955), 'Pressure groups in British government' *British Journal of Sociology*, June, 6(2), pp.133–48.

Marsh, A. (1977), *Protest and Political Consciousness* (London: Sage).

Marsh, D. (ed.) (1983), *Pressure Politics: Interest Groups in Britain* (London: Junction).

Marsh, D. and Chambers, J. (1981), *Abortion Politics* (London: Junction).

Marsh, D. and Read, M. (1988), *Private Members' Bills* (Cambridge: Cambridge University Press).

Marsh, D. and Rhodes, R. (eds), (1992a), *Policy Networks and British Government* (Oxford: Clarendon).

(1992b), *Implementing Thatcherite Policies: Audit of an Era* (Buckingham: Open University Press).

May, T. and Nugent, N. (1982), 'Insiders, outsiders and thresholders', Paper Presented to Political Studies Association Annual Conference, University of Kent.

Mazey, S. P. and Richardson, J. J. (1992), 'British pressure groups in the European Community: the challenge of Brussels', *Parliamentary Affairs*, January, 45(1), pp.92–107.

(1993), 'Pressure groups and the European Community', *Politics Review*, September, 3(1), pp.20–4.

McKenzie, R. T. (1958), 'Parties, pressure groups and the British political process', *Political Quarterly*, January–March, 27(1), pp.5–16.

Miliband, R. (1992), *Capitalist Democracy in Britain* (Oxford: Oxford University Press).

Miller, C. (1990), *Lobbying Government: Understanding and Influencing the Corridors of Power* (Oxford: Basil Blackwell).

Mitchell, N. J. (1987), 'Changing pressure group politics: the case of the TUC 1976–84', *British Journal of Political Science*, October, 17(4), pp.509–17.

Moon, J. L., and Richardson, J. J. (1984), 'Policy making with a difference? The technical and vocational education initiative', *Public Administration*, Spring, 62(1), pp.22–33.

Moran, M. (1981), 'Finance capital and pressure group politics', *British Journal of Political Science*, October, 11(4), pp.381–404.

(1985), 'The changing world of British pressure groups', *Teaching Politics*, 14(3), pp.378–85.

Nettl, J. P. (1990), 'Consensus or elite domination: the case of business', *Political Studies*, 13(1), pp.22–44.

Newton, K. (1976), *Second City Politics* (Oxford: Oxford University Press).

Norton, P. (1984), *The British Polity* (London: Longman).

(1990), 'Public legislation' in M. Rush, (ed.), *Parliament and Pressure Politics* (Oxford: Clarendon).

Nugent, N. (1994), *The Government and Politics of the European Union*, 3rd edition (Basingstoke: Macmillan).

O'Connor, J. (1973), *The Fiscal Crisis of the State* (New York: St Martin's Press).

Offe, C. (1984), *The Contradictions of the Welfare State* (London: Hutchinson University Library).

(1985), 'New social movements: challenging the boundaries of institutional politics', *Social Research*, Winter, 52(4), pp.817–68.

Oliver, M. (1990), *The Politics of Disablement* (London: Macmillan).

Olson, M. (1965), *The Logic of Collective Action* (Cambridge, MA: Harvard University Press).

(1982), *The Rise and Decline of Nations* (New York: Yale University Press).

Pahl, R. and Winkler, J. (1974), 'The coming corporatism' *New Society*, 10 October.

Parkin, F. (1968), *Middle Class Radicalism* (Manchester: Manchester University Press).

Parry, G., Moyser, G. and Day, N. (1992), *Political Participation and Democracy in Britain* (Cambridge: Cambridge University Press).

Pateman, C. (1970), *Participation and Democratic Theory* (Cambridge: Cambridge University Press).

Perkin, H. (1989), *The Rise of Professional Society* (London: Routledge and Kegan Paul).

Pirie, M. (1988), *Micropolitics: The Creation of Successful Policy* (Aldershot: Wildwood House).

Potter, A. (1961), *Organised Groups in British National Politics* (London: Faber).

Poulantzas, N. (1975), *Classes in Contemporary Capitalism* (London: New Left Books).

Pross, P. (1986), *Group Politics and Public Policy* (Oxford: Oxford University Press).

Public Policy Consultants (1988), *The Government Report* (London: PPC).

Pym, F. (1984), *The Politics of Consent* (London: Sphere).

Read, M., Marsh, D. and Richards, D. (1994), 'Why did they do it?' Voting on homosexuality and capital punishment in the House of Commons', *Parliamentary Affairs*, July, 54(3), pp.374–86.

Regan, P. (1988), 'The 1986 Shops Bill', *Parliamentary Affairs*, April, 41(2), pp.218–35.

Richards, P. J. (1972), *The Backbenchers* (London: Faber).

Richardson, J. J. (1990), 'Government and groups in Britain: changing styles', *Strathclyde Papers on Government and Politics*, No. 69 (Glasgow: University of Strathclyde).

Richardson, J. J. and Jordan, A. G. (1979), *Governing Under Pressure*

(Oxford: Martin Robertson).

Richardson, J. J., Maloney, W. A. and Rudig, W. L. (1992), 'The dynamics of policy change', *Public Administration*, Summer, 70(2), pp.157–75.

Roberts, G. (1971), *A Dictionary of Political Analysis* (London: Longman).

Rose, R. (1984), *Do Parties Make a Difference?* 2nd edition (London: Macmillan).

RSPCA (1989), *Annual Report* (Horsham: RSPCA).

Rush, M. (ed.) (1990a), *Parliament and Pressure Politics* (Oxford: Clarendon).

(1990b), 'Lobbying Parliament', *Parliamentary Affairs*, April, 43(2) pp.141–8.

(1990c), 'Select committees', in M. Rush, (ed.), *Parliament and Pressure Politics* (Oxford: Clarendon).

Ryan, M. (1978), *The Acceptable Pressure Group: A Case Study of the Howard League for Penal Reform and Radical Alternatives to Prison* (Farnborough: Saxon House).

(1983), *The Politics of Penal Reform* (London: Longman).

Sargent, J. (1987), 'The organisation of business interests for European Community representation in W. Grant and J. Sargent, *Business and Politics in Britain*, 1st edition (Basingstoke: Macmillan).

Schattschneider, E. E. (1960), *The Semi-Sovereign People* (New York: Prentice-Hall).

Schmitter, P. and Lehmbruch, G. (eds) (1979), *Trends Towards Corporatist Intermediation* (Beverly Hills CA: Sage).

Self, P. and Storing, H. J. (1962), *The State and the Farmer* (London: Allen and Unwin).

Seymour-Ure, C. (1991), *The British Press and Broadcasting Since 1945* (Oxford: Basil Blackwell).

Silkin, A. (1973), 'Green Papers and changing methods of consultation in British government', *Public Administration*, 51(4), pp.427–48.

Smith, M. J. (1990), 'Pluralism, reformed pluralism and neo-pluralism: the role of pressure groups in policy-making', *Political Studies*, 38(2), pp.302–22.

(1991), 'From policy community to issue network: salmonella in eggs and the new politics of food', *Public Administration*, Summer, 69(2), pp.235–55.

(1993), *Pressure, Power and Policy* (Brighton: Harvester Wheatsheaf).

Stewart, J. D. (1958), *British Pressure Groups* (Oxford: Clarendon).

Stoker, G. (1988), *The Politics of Local Government* (London: Macmillan).

Streeck, W. and Schmitter, P. C. (eds) (1985), *Private Interest Government: Beyond Market and State* (London: Sage).

Taylor, P. (1984), *Smoke Ring: The Politics of Tobacco* (London: Bodley Head).

Tebbit, N. (1988), *Upwardly Mobile* (London: Weidenfeld and Nicolson).

Thomas, R. H. (1983), *The Politics of Hunting* (Aldershot: Gower).

Treasury and Civil Service Select Committee (1984), *Acceptance of Outside Appointments By Crown Servants*, 8th Report, 1983/4 (HC 302), (London: HMSO).

(1991), *The Acceptance of Outside Appointments by Crown Servants*, 4th Report 1990/1 (HC 269), (London: HMSO).

Truman, D. B. (1951), *The Governmental Process* (New York: Knopf).

Wareham, M. (1991), 'Likely stories', *Independent*, 17 October, p.15.

Webster, C. (1988), *Health Service Since the War. Volume I Problems of Health Care in the NHS before 1957* (London: HMSO).

Welfare, D. (1992), 'An anachronism with relevance: the revival of the House of Lords in the 1980s and its defence of local government' *Parliamentary Affairs*, April, 54(2), pp.205–19.

Whitehead, P. (1985), *The Writing on the Wall* (London: Joseph).

Whiteley, P. F., and Winyard. S. J. (1987), *Pressure for the Poor* (London: Methuen).

Williamson, P. J. (1989), *Corporatism in Perspective* (London: Sage).

Wilson, D. (1983), *The Lead Scandal* (London: Heinemann).

(1984), *Pressure: The A to Z of Campaigning in Britain* (London: Heinemann).

Wilson, D. and Stoker, G. (1991), 'The lost world of British local pressure groups', *Public Policy and Administration*, Summer, 6(2), pp.20–35.

Wilson, G. K. (1990), *Interest Groups* (Oxford: Basil Blackwell).

Wilson, H. H. (1961), *Pressure Groups: The Campaign for Commercial Television* (London: Secker and Warburg).

Young, H. (1991), *One of Us* (Basingstoke: Macmillan).

Index